Balance of Payments Issues in Central and Eastern European Countries' Run-Up to Euro Area Accession

STUDIEN ZU INTERNATIONALEN WIRTSCHAFTSBEZIEHUNGEN

Herausgegeben von Prof. Dr. Michael Frenkel

Band 9

PETER LANG

Frankfurt am Main · Berlin · Bern · Bruxelles · New York · Oxford · Wien

Katja Funke

Balance of Payments Issues in Central and Eastern European Countries' Run-Up to Euro Area Accession

PETER LANG
Internationaler Verlag der Wissenschaften

Bibliographic Information published by the Deutsche Nationalbibliothek
The Deutsche Nationalbibliothek lists this publication in the Deutsche Nationalbibliografie; detailed bibliographic data is available in the internet at <http://www.d-nb.de>.

Zugl.: Vallendar, Wiss. Hochsch. für Unternehmensführung, Diss., 2006

ISSN 1618-503X
ISBN 978-3-631-55694-8
US-ISBN 0-8204-8723-6

www.peterlang.de

Danksagung

Viele Menschen haben zum Gelingen dieser Arbeit beigetragen, und ich möchte mich an dieser Stelle bei ihnen bedanken.

Ganz herzlich bedanken möchte ich mich insbesondere bei ...

... Herrn Prof. Dr. Michael Frenkel für die Übernahme und Betreuung meiner thematischen Fragestellung und die vielfältige Unterstützung.

... Herrn Prof. Dr. Jürgen Weigand für die Übernahme des Korreferats.

... den Kolleginnen und Kollegen am Lehrstuhl und Christiane Nickel für viele kreativen Diskussionen und fachliche Hinweise.

... meinen Eltern für die interessierte Begleitung meines Ausbildungsweg und der ganzen Familie für die herzliche Aufmunterung besonders in schwierigen Zeiten.

... Boris für sein Verständnis und die immerwährende Unterstützung in guten und schlechten Zeiten—ohne ihn wäre diese Arbeit nicht möglich gewesen.

Table of Content

Figures

Tables

Abbreviations

ADF	Augmented Dickey-Fuller
ARDL model	Autoregressive distributed lag model
BIS	Bank of International Settlements
BOP	Balance of payments
BPS	Balance of Payments Statistics
CA	Current account
CEECs	Central and eastern European countries
CPI	Consumer price index
DF	Dickey-Fuller
EBRD	European Bank for Reconstruction and Development
EC	European Community
ECB	European Central Bank
EFTA	European Free Trade Association
EMU	European Monetary Union
ERM II	Exchange Rate Mechanism II
EU	European Union
EU-12	Group of twelve EU countries that are part of the Euro area as of 2001
EU-15	Group of fifteen EU member states before EU enlargement in 2004
EU-25	Group of twenty-five EU member states after EU enlargement in 2004
FDI	Foreign direct investment
G-6	Group of six (France, Germany, Italy, Japan, UK, and United States)
GDP	Gross domestic product
GNI	Gross national income
IIP	International investment position

IIR	Institutional Investor Rating
IMF	International Monetary Fund
log	logarithm
MG estimator	Mean group estimator
M&A	Mergers and acquisitions
NPV	Net present value
OECD	Organisation for Economic Co-operation and Development
OLS	Ordinary least square
PMG estimator	Pooled mean group estimator
PV	Present value
SDDS	Special data dissemination standard
UK	United Kingdom
ULC	Unit labor costs
UN	United Nations
UNCTAD	United Nations Conference on Trade and Development
USA	United States of America
USD	U.S. dollar
WEO	World Economic Outlook
WTO	World Trade Organization

ed(s).	editor(s)
e.g.	exempli gratia
etc.	et cetera
i.e.	id est
o/w	of which

1 Issues in central and eastern European countries

1.1 Issues in central and eastern European countries—Why should one care?

On 1 May 2004 eight central and eastern European countries (CEECs) together with Cyprus and Malta entered the European Union (EU).[1] For the CEECs, this achievement was a milestone in the countries' efforts toward political and economic reforms and toward full membership in the European Monetary Union (EMU).[2] Over the past fifteen years these countries have transformed from communist states to Western-oriented democracies and from centrally planned economies to market economies.

While the economic progress made by the CEECs during the first fifteen years after the break-down of the planed-economy system is remarkable, the transformation process is not yet completed. The remaining difference between the economic development of the CEECs and the euro area concerns mainly three areas: (i) per capita income level, (ii) economic growth, and (iii) the structure of the economy. Regarding the first area, in 2003 the CEECs reached an average per capita income of about half of that earned in the euro area.[3] The CEECs' economies grew, however, more than twice as fast as the euro area. In 2004 the annual change in real GDP amounted to an average of 4.5 percent in the CEECs compared to 2.1 percent for the euro area. With respect to economic structure the CEECs compared to the euro area rely to a relatively larger extent on the primary (4 percent of gross value added in 2003) and secondary sectors (31 percent of

---

1 Malta and Cyprus are not considered in this study since they have no communist history and did not have to go through a process of political and economic transition. The paths of their economic development and their current situation are, therefore, hardly comparable to those of the CEECs.

2 Upon EU accession, new EU member states also entered Stage 3 of the EMU. They have the status of EU member state with a derogation (see glossary on page 42) (Article 122 of the Treaty Establishing the European Community, European Community (2002), hereafter referred to as the Treaty). They are obliged to adopt the acquis (see glossary on page 42) and are, therefore, bound by Article 4 of the Treaty. The new EU member states are, thus, members of the EMU, though they are not fully participating in Stage 3; i.e., they do not participate in the euro area. Since the new EU member states did not negotiate an opt-out similar to those of Denmark or of the United Kingdom (UK), they are required to join the euro area as soon as they meet the entry criteria as laid down in the Maastricht treaty (see glossary on page 42).

3 Average per capita income is an unweighted average of the CEECs' per capita income in 2003, calculated from gross domestic product (GDP) on a purchasing power parity basis.

gross value added in 2003) while the euro area economic structure is characterized by a relatively larger tertiary sector (71 percent of gross value added in 2003).

Though there is no preset timetable for the CEECs to adopt the euro, currently all eight CEECs plan to have entered the euro area by 2010. Estonia, Lithuania, and Slovenia already joined the Exchange Rate Mechanism II (ERM II) in June 2004 and might, therefore, adopt the single currency by early 2007. Latvia and Slovakia entered the exchange rate mechanism in May 2004 and November 2005, respectively. The remaining three countries are expected to make an effort to join ERM II within the next one to two years.

For any country, adopting the euro means giving up its own monetary policy as well as the exchange rate as a means of adjustment to asymmetric economic shocks. If such shocks occur within a currency union and if no other mechanism, e.g., flexible prices and wage flexibility, exists to ensure an efficient reaction to such an event, the necessary adjustment might imply high economic costs; this might have a negative impact on economic growth and thus on welfare.[4] It is therefore in the interest of the CEECs to ensure that the level of economic convergence with the euro area is reached before adopting the single currency so that asymmetric shocks are unlikely to occur or that the countries can cope with such shocks even without the possibility to adjust the exchange rate vis-à-vis the rest of the euro area.

For the euro area countries the enlargement of the euro area means that the monetary policy will have to take into account the economic developments of a larger and economically more diverse geographic region. Furthermore, the external balance and thus the stability of the currency of the euro area will depend on the developments in all euro area countries and external imbalances in the new EU member states would affect the euro and thus also the current euro area countries. It is, therefore, in the interest of the EU-12 to ensure that the CEECs enter the euro area only if they do not impose the threat of economic instability to the currency union.

Since both the new EU member states and the current euro area countries can expect to benefit from an enlargement of the euro area only if the level of economic convergence of the acceding countries toward the euro area is reasonably high, the EU closely monitors the convergence process and the

---

4 The analysis of costs and benefits of a currency union and the prerequisites for a beneficial outcome of a currency union are subjects of the wide body of literature on optimal currency areas. See for example Mundell (1961), McKinnin (1963), Kenen (1969), Tower and Willett (1970), and Krugman (1990).

progress made in this process. A new EU member state enters the euro area once it fulfills the convergence criteria that are specified and quantified in the Treaty establishing the European Community (hereafter referred to as the Treaty).

In the context of euro area enlargement various questions are of interest, firstly concerning the CEECs' actual economic convergence and secondly regarding the economic linkages between the economic variables that are monitored in order to asses economic convergence. This study presents three analyses that concentrate on selected aspects of these questions.

The study comprises five chapters and is structured as follows. The first chapter gives an introduction into the subject and an overview of major historical and economic developments and also looks at the current economic situation and the degree of convergence reached by the CEECs.

Chapters two through four present the three analyses that build the main body of this text. The second chapter takes a closer look at the sustainability of the CEECs' external balances. Looking at the factors that determine the structure and, thus, the sustainability of external financing, the third chapter provides an empirical analysis of the driving forces behind foreign direct investment (FDI) flows from industrialized countries to transition economies and emerging markets. The fourth chapter analyzes in more detail the interrelation between two of the major economic factors that are taken into account when monitoring economic convergence, namely public finance and the external balance. Chapter five summarizes the findings of the different studies and discusses the implications of the findings for the CEECs and their way to full EMU membership. Furthermore, the chapter provides an outlook and some concluding remarks.

1.2 Historical developments from communist regime to EU membership

While the transition period began for all CEECs around the same time, the way in which the countries started the process and in which they went through the early years of transformation differed from country to country.[5] The process of political and economic transformation of former communist countries was preceded by the downturn of the Soviet Union. In the early 1980s the Soviet Union started to face serious political and economic problems that led to a loss of power for the

5 The recent political developments in the CEECs as outlined in this section are described in Burglund and Aarebrot (1997) and Webb (2002). The political history of Central and Eastern Europe before the decline of the communist block and at the beginning of the transition process are outlined in more detail in Niedernhauser (2003).

communist party as well as a decline in the international importance of the Soviet Union. As a reaction to these developments, after taking office in March 1985, Mikhail Gorbachev implemented a number of reforms, known as the programs of *glasnost* (political openness) and *perestroika* (economic reconstruction). Internally, Gorbachev relaxed the censorship and the political repression and took first steps toward a democratization of the political system. With respect to the Soviet Union's external relations, Gorbachev also pursued a new way in the Soviet Union's foreign policies. The idea behind this was that the world had become interdependent and that there were universal interests and values that should prevail over class interests and the old East-West divide. Gorbachev's policy reflected the belief that all countries had the right to decide for themselves the nature of their political and economic systems. In the late 1980s, this change in the Soviet policies encouraged the peoples of the CEECs to move one after the other out of the Soviet camp and turn toward the West. The reforms also led to a reawakening of the nationalist movements in the republics constituting the Soviet Union. The Baltic countries, i.e., Estonia, Latvia, and Lithuania, called for greater independence and as a consequence regained full sovereignty in 1991.

Among the communist countries, Hungary was the first to open up toward the West. From the beginning of the 1980s on, Hungary looked for Western trading partners and for Western assistance in the restructuring of the economic system. However, under the communist regime the economy continued to decline and the foreign debt reached a level that the country was no longer able to repay. As a consequence in 1989 the communist regime was replaced by a multiparty parliamentary democracy. During the 1990s the state-owned enterprises were privatized and the Hungarian economy moved from a command economy producing goods mainly for the Soviet market toward a market economy with strong economic ties to the West and especially to the EU.

In Poland, the shortage in food and housing in 1980 resulted in first strikes that led to the foundation of an illegal labor union (Solidarity). The economic situation in Poland did not improve and Solidarity remained popular even after it was banned in the early 1980s. In 1989 due to increasing pressure from the population, Solidarity was relegalized and participated in the negotiations on substantial political reforms. In 1990 a Solidarity-led government took power and adopted a radical reform program. As part of the reform program, the privatization of the state-controlled industry began in the early 1990s. The enduring economic difficulties, e.g., growing unemployment and corruption, caused widespread discontent and political instability. Over the past fourteen years Poland has faced continuous change in the country's leadership.

Slovenia in mid-1990 declared its independence after electing the first noncommunist government in the beginning of the same year. Before gaining sovereignty Slovenia was a republic of the communist Yugoslavia, which distanced itself from the Soviet Union's rule. Since the beginning of the 2000s, the pace of the privatization of the economy accelerated. At the same time the introduced structural reforms increased the attractiveness of the country's economy for foreign investors. Due to its historically close ties to Western Europe, Slovenia quickly integrated into the European economic area. Compared to the other CEECs a relatively higher portion of the country's trade takes places with the EU-15 and a relatively lower portion remains for transactions with other new EU member states and other countries of the former communist bloc.

The Czech Republic and the Slovak Republic from 1918 through January 1993 were part of Czechoslovakia. The Czechoslovakian communist regime collapsed in late 1989 when the communist party leadership resigned after massive antigovernment demonstrations. Economic reforms started in the 1990s after the shift in the political regime. The reforms affected especially the Slovak part of the economy that was dominated by subsidized state-owned heavy industry. The economic problems, e.g., an inefficient and obsolete industry base, rising inflation, and high unemployment, together with reemerging nationalist movements resulted in the separation of the Slovak from the Czech part of the country. The Slovak Republic thus gained independence in the beginning of 1993.

The political situation in the Slovak Republic between 1994 and 1998 was dominated by a continuous stalemate between the government and the president that caused a standstill for reforms and hindered the country's efforts in gaining credibility with the international community and joining the Western bloc. In 1999, a new pro-European government took over and implemented effective reforms to the tax and the social welfare system. From that point forward, the Slovak economy was able to attract urgently needed FDI and the country experienced a notable surge in economic growth.

After the collapse of the communist regime, the Czech Republic's formerly state-owned companies were quickly privatized. As a consequence, the economy in the early 1990s experienced high growth before problems prevailed in the process of transformation from a state-run to a private economy. An economic slowdown occurred in 1997 after many of the large industrial conglomerates refrained from restructuring and looked for government aid instead. The problem was partly solved when most of the state-owned banks were privatized at the end of the 1990s. Since then the economy has been recovering from recession and prospering exports to the EU as well as high FDI inflows supported growth especially in the beginning of the 2000s.

The Baltic countries (Estonia, Latvia, and Lithuania) declared their independence in the beginning of the 1990s and Moscow recognized the sovereignty of the three states in 1991. During the 1990s, all three countries privatized the majority of their state-run companies. Within the process of transformation the countries profited from their moderate fiscal policies. All three countries actively sought FDI inflows within the privatization process. In 1993, the three countries signed a free-trade agreement. Between 1993 and 2005, the three former Soviet republics have moved from Eastern-oriented command economies to modern market economies with strong ties to the West.

The diversity in the CEECs' political situation at the beginning of the transformation process and the differences in the pace of convergence and in the path taken through the past fifteen years also reflect upon the economic development over the transition period as well as the current economic situation. The next section provides an overview of the economic developments during the transition process and of the degree of economic convergence reached.

1.3 Economic convergence from command economies to EMU accession

1.3.1 EMU accession and convergence criteria

According to the decision of the European Council (1993) in Copenhagen, before being admitted to join the Union, candidate countries are required to fulfill the economic and political conditions known as the *Copenhagen criteria*. These criteria require a prospective member to be a stable democracy respecting human rights, the rule of law, and the protection of minorities; to have a functioning market economy; and to adopt the common rules, standards, and policies that make up the body of EU law.

The rules laid down in the legal framework of the EU reflect the importance assigned to economic convergence in the context of EU accession. Article 4 of the Treaty states that "the activities of the Member States and the Community shall entail compliance with the following guiding principles: stable prices, sound public finances and monetary conditions, and a sustainable balance of payments." Furthermore, the concrete criteria (so called convergence criteria or Maastricht criteria) are laid down in Article 121 of the Treaty. With respect to the economic prerequisites, the article measures

> a high degree of sustainable convergence by reference to the fulfillment of each Member State of the following criteria: the achievement of a high degree of price stability; ... the sustainability of the government financial position; ... the observation of the normal fluctuation margins provided by the exchange rate mechanism (ERM I) of the European Monetary System

(EMS)6, for at least two years, without devaluating against the currency of any other Member State7, [and] the durability of convergence achieved by the Member States and of its participation in the exchange rate mechanism of the European Monetary System being reflected in the long-term interest rate levels.

With respect to the external balance, Article 121 states also that "the situation and development of the balance of payments and current account" should be taken into account when assessing the progress made with respect to economic convergence.

Looking at some of the major economic indicators, i.e., per capita income, growth, and inflation, reveals that over the past decade there has been notable progress in the processes of convergence between the CEECs and the EU-15. The CEECs, however, have not yet reached the level of living standard and economic stability of the EU-15.

The initial level of and the change in the CEECs' per capita income relative to the EU-15 per capita income from 1997 through 2004 shows the sizable difference in wealth of the two country groups and at the same time underlines the remarkable economic development experienced by the central and eastern European transition economies and especially the Baltic countries. Recording in 1997 a per capita income of less than 40 percent of the level seen in the EU-15 countries, Estonia, Latvia, and Lithuania over a seven-year period managed to narrow this gap by about 10 percent (see Table 1). Despite their positive economic performance, the CEECs still record a significantly lower per capita GDP than the EU-15. Apart from Slovenia, Hungary, and the Czech Republic, the CEECs' per capita income level is only half of that reached in the old EU member states.

Economic prosperity during 1990s differed across the CEECs and, while all countries went through a recession at the beginning of the transition, growth resumed more quickly in the central European countries, recording positive growth rates since 1991 than in the Baltic countries (see Figure 1). This observation reflects the divergent initial conditions from which the countries started into transition, the difference in the timing, and the diverse approaches taken with respect to reforms. The Baltic countries started from the lowest per capita income level and the initial output collapse was substantially larger in the

---

6 According to the European Council Resolution on the new exchange-rate mechanism, "the Council has decided to establish an exchange-rate mechanism (ERM II) to replace the existing European monetary system (EMS) at the beginning of the third stage of economic and monetary union (EMU)" on January 1, 1999. See European Council (1997).

7 The euro serves as the reference currency of ERM II. See European Council (1997).

three countries than in the other CEECs.[8] After emerging from their transition recession around 1995 their economies started to grow at a remarkable pace.[9] Real GDP growth in the three countries surpassed that of most of the other transition economies, and over the period 1997-2004 the Baltic economies grew by more than half of their initial level; i.e., cumulative growth for Estonia, Latvia, and Lithuania amounted to about 65 percent, 69 percent, and 59 percent, respectively (see Table 2). If the three countries had not experienced a slowdown in 1999 following the Russian crisis, they would all have had what is called sustainable growth acceleration with eight or more years of growth in excess of 3.5 percent.[10]

Table 1: Relative per capita GDP in purchasing power standards (EU-15 = 100)

	1997	1998	1999	2000	2001	2002	2003	2004	Average 1997-2004
EU-25	90.7	90.8	90.9	91.1	91.2	91.3	91.6 1)	91.8 1)	91.2
EU-15	100.0	100.0	100.0	100.0	100.0	100.0	100.0	100.0	100.0
Czech Republic	62.8 2)	60.6 2)	59.5	58.6	59.7	61.3	62.5	64.3	61.1
Estonia	36.6 2)	37.8 2)	37.2	39.3	40.4	42.3	44.0	45.7	40.4
Hungary	45.6 2)	46.7 2)	47.5	48.3	51.0	53.1	54.5	55.9	50.3
Latvia	29.6 2)	30.5 2)	31.0	32.1	33.7	35.3	37.2	39.7	33.6
Lithuania	33.5 2)	35.3 2)	34.1	34.8	36.7	38.4	41.6	43.9	37.3
Poland	39.8 2)	40.7 2)	41.3	41.8	41.4	41.4	41.8	42.9 1)	41.4
Slovak Republic	42.6 2)	43.1 2)	42.7	43.3	44.1	46.6	47.5	47.8	44.7
Slovenia	64.3 2)	65.0 2)	66.9	66.1	67.5	68.2	69.8	71.4	67.4

1) Forecast,
2) Estimates
Source: Eurostat (2005) and own calculations.

8 The magnitude of the initial output collapse in the Baltic countries might have been caused by the relatively stronger economic linkage that the Baltic countries had with Russia compared to the other CEECs.

9 For a detailed analysis of the economic development in the Baltic countries see World Bank (2005c).

10 See Hausman, Pritchett, and Rodrik (2004) for a definition of sustainable growth acceleration.

Figure 1: Real GDP development in the Baltic countries and the CEEC-5 [1)]

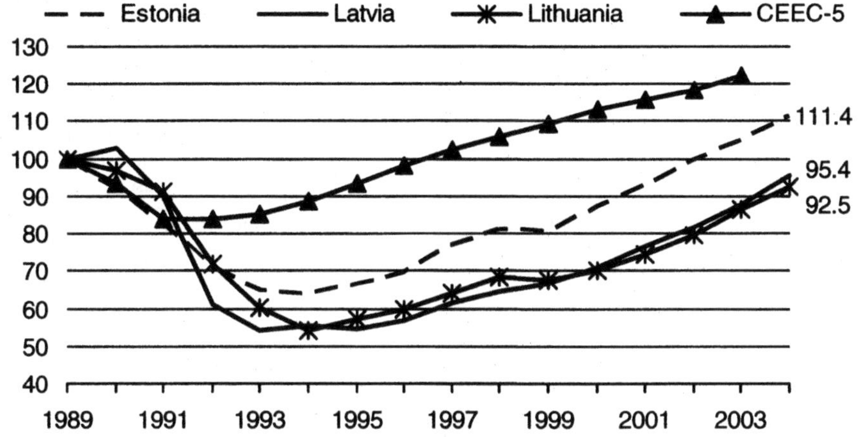

1) CEEC-5 refers to the CEECs excluding the Baltic countries, i.e., the Czech Republic, Hungary, Poland, the Slovak Republic, and Slovenia.
Source: World Bank (2005c).

Table 2: Annual percentage change in real GDP

	1997	1998	1999	2000	2001	2002	2003	2004	Cumulative growth 1997-2004
EU-25	2.7	3.0	3.0	3.9	1.9	1.2	1.2	2.4	21.0
EU-15	2.6	2.9	3.0	3.9	1.9	1.1	1.1	2.3	20.4
EU-12	2.6	2.9	2.9	3.8	1.9	0.9	0.7	2.1	19.2
Czech Republic	-0.7	-1.1	1.2	3.9	2.6	1.5	3.2	4.4	15.9
Estonia	11.1	4.4	0.3	7.9	6.5	7.2	6.7	7.8	64.8
Hungary	4.6	4.9	4.2	6.0	4.3	3.8	3.4	4.6	41.9
Latvia	8.3	4.7	3.3	6.9	8.0	6.4	7.2	9.8	69.4
Lithuania	7.0	7.3	-1.7	3.9	7.2	6.8	10.5	7.0	58.7
Poland	7.1	5.0	4.5	4.2	1.1	1.4	3.8	5.3	37.2
Slovak Republic	4.6	4.2	1.5	2.0	3.8	4.6	4.5	5.5	35.1
Slovenia	4.8	3.9	5.4	4.1	2.7	3.5	2.7	4.2	35.9

Source: Eurostat (2005) and own calculations.

Table 3: Fulfillment of convergence criteria

	Price stability	Government budgetary position	Exchange rates [1)]	Long-term interest rate convergence
Measure for convergence criterion	Average inflation rate over past year must not exceed reference value, which was calculated to be 2.4 percent	Country must not be subject of a Council decision under Article 104(6) on the existence of an excessive deficit	Normal fluctuation margins of the ERM II must be observed for at least two years	Average long-term nominal interest rate over past year must not exceed reference value, which was calculated to be 6.4 percent
Czech Republic	yes	no	no	Yes
Estonia	yes	yes	no	n.a. [2)]
Hungary	no	no	no	No
Latvia	no	yes	no	Yes
Lithuania	yes	yes	no	Yes
Poland	no	no	no	No
Slovak Republic	no	no	no	Yes
Slovenia	no	yes	no	Yes

1) The exchange rate criterion requires the observance of the normal fluctuation margins of ERM II for at least two years without severe tensions. Since none of the CEECs has participated in ERM II for two years, they cannot fulfill this criterion even if the euro-exchange rate has been stable over the past several years.

2) Due to the absence of a harmonized benchmark long-term government bond or comparable security, the European Commission identified an interest rate indicator based on bank lending rates. The indicator in the year to August 2004 was on average 4.6 percent. The European Commission concluded there were no reasons to conclude Estonia would not fulfill the long-term interest criterion.

Source: European Commission (2004).

The catching-up was less pronounced in those CEECs that started the convergence process from a higher level of relative per capita income. The Czech Republic in 1997 recorded the second highest level of per capita GDP among the CEECs. Over the seven years through 2004 the country's gap of relative per capita income with respect to the EU-15 narrowed only by about two percentage points (see Table 1). Compared to the Baltic countries the Czech Republic realized only a moderate accumulated real GDP growth of about 16 percent between 1997 and 2004. Hungary, Poland, the Slovak Republic, and Slovenia showed a better economic performance than the Czech Republic and recorded an accumulated real growth of more than 35 percent over the same period.

Despite the overall favorable economic development in the CEECs, a closer look at the single countries reveals weaknesses regarding the sustainability of the convergence process. A formalized assessment of the degree of economic convergence between the CEECs and the EU-12 is done by the European Commission, which publishes the results of the assessment in an official document, the Convergence Report. The assessment is done at least every two years and the most recent Convergence Report was published by the European Commission in October 2004. Since the first new EU member state only joined ERM II in May 2004, at the time of the latest assessment none of the CEECs fulfilled the exchange rate criterion, which requires a participation in ERM II for at least two years.[11] While Hungary and Poland did not meet any of the requirements, the Slovak Republic managed to achieve a long-term interest rate below the critical level and the other five CEECs fulfill at least two of the remaining three Maastricht criteria (see Table 3 and Figure 2). Estonia and Latvia comply with all convergence measures but the exchange rate criterion.

Half of the countries, i.e., the Czech Republic, Hungary, Poland, and the Slovak Republic, in 2004 were subject to an excessive deficit procedure, which is a consequence of a budget deficit above the 3 percent of GDP threshold level. This indicates that the countries might be threatened by an unsustainable situation with respect to their public finances. While the gross government debt in all of the CEECs is relatively low (see Figure 2 and Table A 1-3), the countries that did not meet the public finance criteria face high—and in the case of Poland even increasing—public deficits (see Figure 2 and Table A 1-2). The public finance situation is one of the criteria that have been assessed to be a critical issue for the further convergence between the CEECs and the euro area.[12]

11 Nominal euro-exchange rates were, however, relatively stable over the past four years and annual percentage changes in the nominal exchange rate—with the exception of the euro-exchange rate of the Lithuanian Litas and the Polish Zloty in 2003—were below 10 percent (see Table A 1-4).

12 See assessments of the convergence programs by the European Commission (2005a-2005h).

Figure 2: Performance of the CEECs with respect to the convergence criteria [1)]

(a) Change in CPI

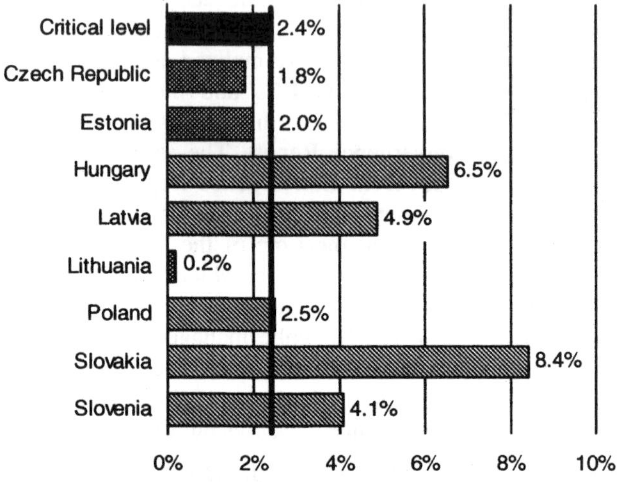

(b) Long-term interest rate

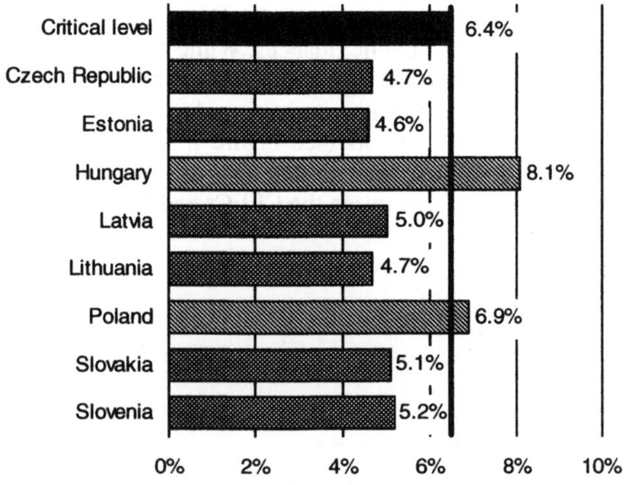

Figure 2: Performance of the CEECs with respect to the convergence criteria [1) (concluded)

(c) Public deficit as percentage of GDP

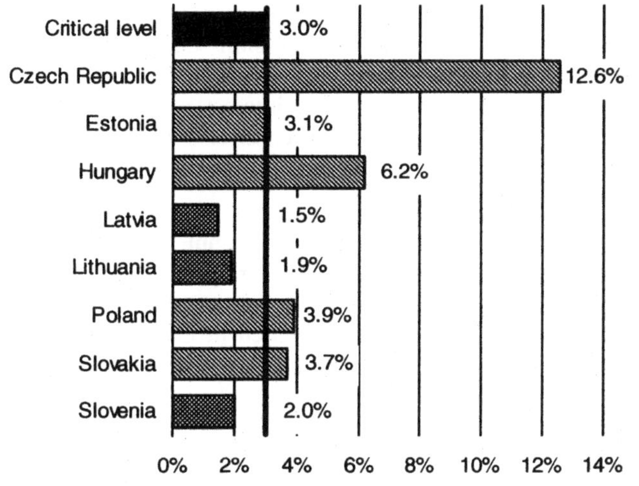

(d) Public debt as percentage of GDP

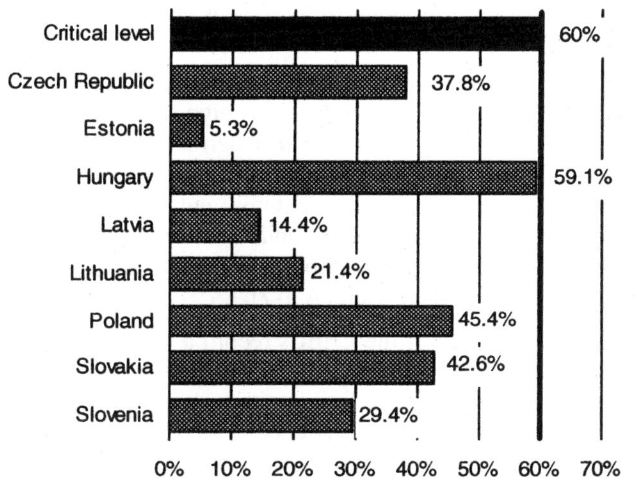

1) The exchange rate criterion is not taken into account since none of the CEECs had been taking part in ERM II for the required minimum period of two years.

Source: European Commission (2004).

The observed level of the convergence indicators and their recent developments suggest that the CEECs might find it less difficult to fulfill the inflation criterion or to meet the long-term interest rate requirement than to achieve a public finance situation that allows them to comply with the Maastricht criteria with their envisaged accession schedule. Since the late 1990s, inflation rates showed a tendency to decrease in all CEECs. Furthermore, according to the Convergence Report long-term interest rates in all CEECs but Hungary and Poland met the convergence criteria.[13] The government budgetary position evolved, however, with a less uniform trend across countries.

For many transition countries, external sector imbalances are a serious threat to sustainable economic development. Besides the specified quantitative convergence criteria, the Treaty also requires the new EU member states to have a sustainable balance of payments before adopting the euro. This can become a critical aspect for the CEECs, which in many cases run sizable current account deficits in the context of their catching-up process (see Table A 1-6). Such deficits might be economically sound to the extent that they reflect an effective allocation of resources by economic agents that may bring future benefits. In this respect strong investment growth that is not fully matched by domestic savings due to consumers' adjustment to improved long-term income expectations can be the economic reason behind net external financing. The sustainability of the external financing is, however, a major concern if the current account deficit persists and if it cannot be covered by long-term capital inflows.

In addition to large current account deficits, the stock of external debt for some of the CEECs is relatively high and could be an indicator for the development of an unsustainable external position (see Figure 3). The World Bank assesses the level of external indebtedness of non-high income countries. Two of the CEECs, namely Estonia and Latvia, are classified to be severely indebted to foreign debtors and another four countries, namely Hungary, Lithuania, Poland, and the Slovak Republic, belong to the group of moderately indebted countries (see Table A 1-7).

While most of the CEECs record a relatively low level of public debt and made notable progress with respect to price stability, the public balance and the external balance show a less positive development. If the deterioration of the public deficit and/or the current account continues these could pose a threat to the sustainability of the economic development in the CEECs and the convergence between the CEECs and the other EU countries. As a consequence, the CEECs'

13 Tables A 1-1 through A 1-5 in the chapter's appendix show the evolution of the convergence criteria since 1997.

compliance with the convergence criteria and thus accession to the monetary union might be postponed beyond the timeframe envisaged by the CEECs themselves. Due to political considerations the CEECs might, however, be admitted to the currency union without showing the required economic convergence. In this case entering the euro area might come at high economic costs for both the CEECs and the current euro area countries.

Figure 3: Indicators for the external balance in the CEECs

(a) Current account deficit (2004) as percentage of GDP

(b) External debt (end of 2004) as percentage of GDP

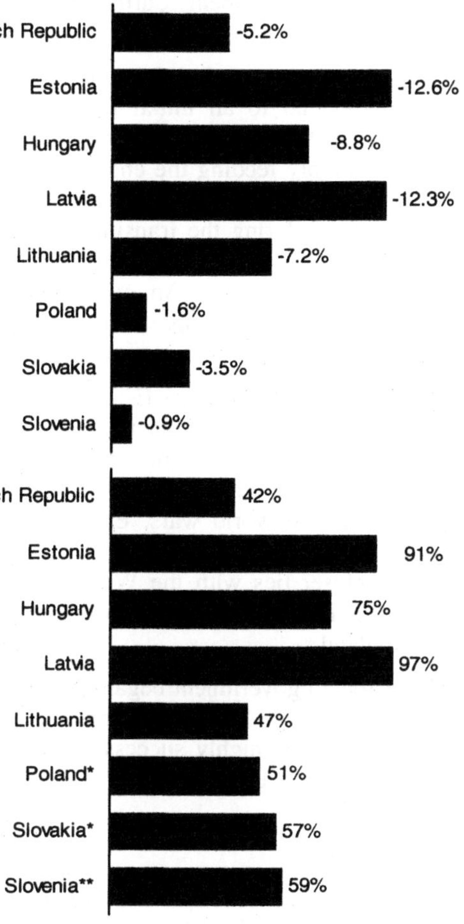

* Based on latest available data: 2003.

** Data taken from International Monetary Fund (IMF, 2005f).

Source: IMF (2005c), European Central Bank (ECB, 2005a), and own calculations.

The assessment of the convergence criteria provides a snapshot of the current economic status. This status is the outcome of past economic developments that have to be taken into account in order to understand the present status of the economy. The next subsection, therefore, provides a brief overview of the economic development in each of the CEECs since the beginning of the transition process and in recent years.[14]

1.3.2 Economic development during the transition process in individual countries

Transformation involved so much fundamental change for each of the CEECs that its start inevitably led to an initial fall of output and GDP in all countries. However, part of the former higher output level of the centrally planned economies was simply feeding the enormous waste that went on throughout the command economy. The pattern of recovery and economic development after the initial recession and during the transition process differed across countries and depended on the policy measures taken, the rigidity of their implementation, and the speed of their realization. An overview of the economic development in individual countries gives an impression of the major evolutions that underlie the different paths taken by the different countries.[15]

Among the Baltic countries Estonia, started into the transition process with an advantage over Latvia and Lithuania. Estonia had the highest per capita income among these countries, a better infrastructure, and the highest education level. Furthermore, basic institutions were well developed from its days of independence between the two world wars. Estonia served as a key gateway for trade between the former Soviet Union and the West, which allowed the country to develop much closer ties with the West than the other Baltic economies. This contact was facilitated by the traditional links with the Nordic countries, particularly Finland.

The Estonian government began the economic reform process earlier than the other Baltic countries. The government's stabilization strategy that followed price liberalization was highly successful. After experiencing in 1999 its worst year economically since the country's independence, largely because of the

---

14 The description of the recent economic development and the current economic situation of the CEECs is not intended to be comprehensive but to describe the broad economic developments and to point out the major internal and external imbalances. This should provide an appropriate background for the analysis presented in the second part of this study.

15 For a detailed assessment of the economic developments during the transition process, see European Bank of Reconstruction and Development (EBRD, 1995-2004).

impact of the August 1998 Russian financial crisis, the country recovered quickly. The privatization has been largely completed and the state-owned privatization agency was dissolved in autumn 2001.

Over recent years real GDP growth was strong despite the economic slowdown in the country's main trading partners. Inflation, largely driven by external factors and increasing domestic demand, has been slow and consumer prices in 2004 increased by 3 percent. Estonia is the only CEEC with a public budget surplus (1.8 percent of GDP in 2004) and the country's government debt is remarkably low (less than 5 percent of GDP at the end of 2004). Nevertheless, the European Commission (2005b) and the IMF (2004b) pointed out that a loosening of fiscal policies might add to the prevailing external imbalance. The currency board arrangement has allowed the country to maintain a constant nominal euro-exchange rate since then.

A threat to the sustainability of economic development in Estonia could be the external sector.[16] The current account deficit increased continuously from 5.3 percent of GDP in 1999 to over 15 percent of GDP in 2004. According to the European Commission (2005b, p.2) the "high current account deficit will continue to be the major macro-economic imbalance in Estonia over the foreseeable future, largely reflecting the strong investment needs of the economy in catching up toward EU-average income levels." Though a large portion of the deficit is caused by factor income, largely reinvested earnings of foreign investors that reenter the balance of payments as foreign direct investment, the development is at least partly driven by growing demand for imports. The financing of the current account deficit is another critical aspect. In Estonia net long-term capital inflows, i.e., net foreign direct investment, in 2004 covered less than one third of the current account deficit.

After Latvia regained its independence in 1991, the economy went into a sharp recession as economic links with the former Soviet Union were lost and real GDP fell by almost 50 percent. The government introduced a comprehensive reform program including enhanced fiscal discipline, curtailing subsidies to enterprises, and important steps toward the creation of a competitive and open economic environment. These measures allowed the country to realize the highest average real growth of all CEECs in the late 1990s and the early 2000s. Latvia has completed the privatization of small- and medium-sized enterprises as well as some larger companies including those in gas, shipping, and banking. Due to sluggish processes, some large state-owned enterprises have yet to be privatized.

---

16 See IMF (2004b).

The privatization of state-owned enterprises attracted significant foreign direct investment.

In 2004, the Latvian economy grew at a real rate of 8.5 percent. The country was the fastest growing economy among the CEECs. This development has been driven by domestic investment and private demand as well as increasing demand for Latvia's exports in both the traditional markets of the former Soviet Union and the new markets of the EU. A sound trade policy contributed to this development. After several years of moderate inflation of between 2 percent and 3 percent, the consumer price index (CPI) in 2004 increased by 6.2 percent. While the public sector's financial situation does not give rise to major concern—the government ran a small deficit of 0.8 percent of GDP in 2004 and public debt in the same year stood at 14.4 percent of GDP—overheating could become a problem for the Latvian economy. To counterbalance this threat the IMF (2004d) and the European Commission (2005d) encouraged a further tightening of fiscal policies.

The Latvian current account deficit reached 12.4 percent of GDP in 2004, which was the second highest among the CEECs after Estonia and FDI covered only one third of the deficit. As in the case of Estonia, the current account deficit might be reasonable in the context of intertemporal optimization and consumption smoothing but the financing and the risk inherent in the short-term character of supporting capital inflow need to be monitored.

Like the other two Baltic countries, Lithuania has experienced a remarkable economic expansion since the late 1990s. After the domestic banking crisis in the mid-1990s, the market infrastructure was strengthened and the economy restructured. Though the Russian financial crisis affected the economy negatively, countermeasures by the government resulted in a rapid recovery. Through the transition process prices have been liberalized and trade has been reoriented from the former Soviet Union to the EU. The positive development was supported by FDI inflows from EU member states and the Nordic countries in particular. Privatization is nearly complete and almost all factors of production are privately owned. The State Property Fund, which privatizes state-owned assets and administrates privatization transactions, has to privatize only a few more companies in the energy, chemicals, and telecommunications sector.

The external imbalances and the fiscal deficit are the major risks for the future development of the Lithuanian economy. Despite the slow growth in the EU the country's economy continuous to grow at a high rate; i.e., real GDP increased by 6.7 percent in 2004, which was the second highest growth rate among the CEECs. The growth was mainly driven by vigorous private consumption and investment growth. At the same time the country recorded an inflation rate of 1.1 percent, which was the lowest among the CEECs. The public deficit increased over recent years from 1.5 percent of GDP in 2002 to 2.5 percent of GDP in 2004. The current account deficit widened over the same period from 5.2 percent of GDP to 8.3 percent of GDP and FDI inflows in 2004 covered only half of the deficit. Against this background the IMF (2005e) and the European Commission (2005e) recommend a tighter fiscal policy in order to prevent a further deterioration of the current account.

After the break-up of Czechoslovakia in 1993, the Czech Republic was perceived as the most successful transition economy among the CEECs until 1996. The country achieved economic transformation with minimum unemployment and no hyperinflation. A speculative attack on the Czech koruna in May 1997—partly driven by the market's perception of an unsustainable current account deficit (7.4 percent of GDP in 1996)—interrupted the smooth economic development. The authorities were forced to replace the fixed exchange rate system, maintained since 1991, by a regime with a wider fluctuation band. Furthermore, a strict austerity program that included tight fiscal and monetary policies was introduced. Growth, which resumed in 1999-2000, was supported by considerable FDI inflows. The privatization process in the Czech Republic is largely completed, although a few companies in the energy sector have yet to be turned into private corporations.

In recent years, the Czech Republic has experienced moderate economic growth (3.9 percent real GDP growth in 2004) and low inflation (2.6 percent in 2004). Growth was led by rising exports and related investment. The country ran a sizable public deficit of 11.7 percent in 2003 and 3 percent in 2004. Furthermore, the current account deficit since 2000 continuously ranged between 5 percent of GDP and 6 percent of GDP. Over two thirds of the 2004 current account deficit (5.2 percent of GDP) was covered by FDI inflows. This reflects the large stock of FDI and its high profitability. Dividends and reinvested earnings accounted for nearly two thirds of the current account deficit. In the case of the Czech Republic, international observers such as the IMF and the European institutions see the maintenance of fiscal stability as the main challenge for the sustainable development of the country's economy.[17]

Among the central European countries, Hungary began its transition with some substantial advantages including higher living standards and a more pragmatic economic policy that was initiated during the communist period.

---

17 See IMF (2004a) and European Commission (2005a).

Furthermore, structural reforms and stabilization measures were implemented soon after the change of regime. By the mid-1990s, however, macroeconomic performance deteriorated, with the reemergence of unsustainable current account and fiscal deficits. As a response to these developments the country launched a second round of deep and far-reaching reforms that included the restructuring of enterprise, the banking system, and the public sectors. A strong fiscal-stabilization package (1995-1998) and the maintenance of sound macroeconomic policies helped to complete the structural reforms and was followed by robust economic performance, with average real GDP growth of 4.4 percent from 1997 through 2001. Output growth was driven mainly by private consumption. Since 2000, the focus of economic policy shifted from structural reforms to improving living standards and upgrading public infrastructure. Wages, pensions, and public sector investments have increased. As a consequence the government managed to decrease the sizable public deficit only gradually. The privatization of Hungary's state-owned assets is largely complete.

Over recent years, growth continued at a slightly moderated level. Despite a restrictive monetary policy and some fiscal tightening in 2003 the positive development continued as investments and exports picked up. Inflation decreased from over 18 percent in 1997 to 4.7 percent in 2004, which is still a sizable annual increase in the price level.

Though the Hungarian government managed to reduce the imbalance in the public household over the past two years from a peak level of 8.5 percent of GDP in 2002 to 4.5 percent of GDP in 2004, the public deficit remains sizable. Furthermore, the country faces the highest burden of public debt (57.6 percent of GDP) among the CEECs. The current account deficit widened continuously from 2.1 percent of GDP in 1997 and stabilized in 2003-2004 at about 9 percent of GDP. This level seems to be unsustainable and significantly higher than what would be required to stabilize external debt.[18] Less than half of the deficit was covered by FDI inflows. Hungary will need to tighten its fiscal policy to ensure sustainability of public finances and to support the correction of external imbalances.

Poland began its transition to a market economy in 1990 under exceptionally difficult macroeconomic conditions, which included high inflation and a high level of external debt. The country has undergone a successful economic transformation since then. The government took huge risks by liberalizing prices, making the zloty convertible, fixing the exchange rate, and

18 See IMF (2004c) and European Commission (2005c).

lowering import barriers despite an enterprise sector that was considered in large part value subtracting, rather than value adding. The country successfully mastered the effects of the Russia crisis.

After a slowdown in growth in the early 2000s, the government adopted a policy program to restore fiscal equilibrium and rebalance macroeconomic policies. This came in response to concerns about the negative impact of macroeconomic policy that followed a tight monetary policy compensating for expansionary fiscal policy. As a consequence inflation continued to fall and came down from 10.1 percent in 2000 to 0.7 percent in 2003. In 2004 inflation increased slightly to 3.6 percent. Economic growth picked up from 2003 on and amounted to 5.3 percent in 2004. Despite the relative positive economic development, unemployment in Poland increased in recent years from about 10 percent in the late 1990s to about 19 percent in 2004 (see Table A 1-8). The external balance decreased in the recent past when the current account deficit improved from 7.5 percent of GDP in 1999 to 1.5 percent of GDP in 2004. According to international organizations and European institutions, Poland will have to implement further structural reforms especially in support of continued economic growth and to allow a reduction of unemployment.[19] The government will have to follow a conservative fiscal policy to support a positive economic development.

In the Slovak Republic, after an initial decline in output as a result of postindependence external shocks, the country's economic performance improved but due to a lack of structural reforms economic growth became increasingly unsustainable. After 1998, the government implemented decisive reform measures that resulted in substantial structural changes and included the privatization of the main banks and utilities, the improvement of fiscal transparency and control, the introduction of a second pillar in the pension system, and a strengthening of the legislative framework. While the privatization process is largely completed, some companies in the energy and the telecommunications sector are still publicly owned and will have to be privatized.

Despite a difficult external environment, economic growth recovered and inflation declined. The Slovakian economy over the past three years grew by between 4.5 percent and 5.5 percent per year. This is faster than any of the other four central European economies. Inflation slowed down from almost 9 percent in the beginning of the 2000s to about 3.6 percent in 2004. These developments came along with a substantial improvement in the fiscal and the external balances.

19 See European Commission (2005f) and IMF (2004e).

As a result of a fiscal-moderation package implemented in 2003 the fiscal deficit narrowed from about 6 percent of GDP in the beginning of the 2000s to 3.3 percent of GDP in 2004. Due to better export performance the current account deficit narrowed from 8.4 percent of GDP in 2001 to 3.4 percent of GDP in 2004. A surge in FDI inflows, partly due to the 1999 government program to support the influx of foreign direct investment, supported the positive development.

Despite the positive recent development the unemployment rate in the Slovak Republic persists to be high at about 18 percent. Further structural reforms together with continued fiscal tightening are the major measures suggested by the European institutions[20] and the IMF (2005g) in support of a continued positive economic development and a reduction of unemployment.

Slovenia's initial level of relative prosperity was a key factor for the country's approach to reform, which has differed substantially from other CEECs. The government follows a gradualist and consensual approach to change and frequently postpones key structural reforms. The slow pace of reform and reluctance toward foreign participation in key areas has contributed to a relatively low incidence of FDI. While the country has been able to attract more FDI since 2002, FDI inflows to Slovenia in recent years are relatively small compared with the other CEECs, especially the Czech Republic and the Slovak Republic. Privatization has proceeded more slowly than in most other CEECs, with enterprises in key sectors, i.e., finance, insurance, energy, telecommunications, and the steel industry, remaining under state ownership.

Over recent years the Slovene economy has, nevertheless, achieved solid growth while avoiding the major macroeconomic imbalances that characterized most other transition economies in the region. Tight fiscal and monetary policies have contributed to remarkable stability, allowing the economy to enjoy both external and internal equilibrium with balanced fiscal budgets and open foreign trade. The government decreased the fiscal deficit from about 3 percent of GDP in the early 2000s to about 2 percent of GDP in 2003 and 2004, and the public debt stabilized at a level slightly below 30 percent of GDP. Since 1996, Slovenia has enjoyed single-digit inflation and recorded a price increase of 3.6 percent in 2004.[21] The European Commission (2005h) encourages the Slovenian government to further tighten fiscal policies to maintain the long-term sustainability of public finances.

---

20 See European Commission (2005g).

21 The IMF (2005f) considers inflation pressure one of the major risks to future economic development and to compliance with the convergence criteria.

While the extent of the current account deficits of the CEECs might be in line with the optimal economic path regarding investment and consumption smoothing, the short-term financing of the sizable deficit and the related relatively high rollover requirements of short-term debt and risks of shifts in capital market sentiments might be a reason for concern. Besides imbalances in the external sector, some CEECs face large and in some cases even increasing fiscal imbalances. In the case of most of the CEECs, the European institutions as well as international organizations like the IMF explicitly recommend tackling fiscal imbalances and external imbalances by tightening fiscal policies. In addressing some of the major issues for the future economic development of the CEECs related to the external balance and fiscal policies, the next three chapters take a closer look at the countries' external balance, the driving factors behind prevailing imbalances, and the impact of fiscal policies on the current account. The first chapter assesses the sustainability of the CEECs' external financial position, i.e., the current account and external debt. The second chapter analyzes factors that allow a country to attract long-term financial flows, i.e., FDI, in order to guarantee a solid financing of the current account deficit. Finally, the last chapter studies the impact of changes in fiscal policies on the external balance, more precisely the trade account.

1.4 Contribution of the study

The study adds to existing research on different balance of payments (BOP) issues related to the CEECs' transformation process, EU membership, and euro area accession. The analyses presented in chapters two through four focus on specific aspects of the BOP that are of importance for the progress of economic convergence between the CEECs and the euro area and, thus, for the CEECs' way into the currency union. In this context, the following topics are identified as being important and as lacking coverage.

External sustainability is one of the criteria taken into account in the process of the CEECs' euro area admission. The sustainability of the CEECs' external balance is determined by the structure and the magnitude of real and financial flows recorded in the balance of payments and the structure and level of external liabilities. The existing literature on external sustainability of the CEECs focuses on current account sustainability and pays little attention to external debt issues. To generate a more comprehensive view of the CEECs' external situation we assess the development of the countries' current account balance, the structure of financial flows, and the level and structure of external liabilities. In our assessment we focus on external debt issues. We illustrate the interrelation of the current account and external liabilities and present different concepts for the assessment of external sustainability. Since the discussion of external sustainability so far focused on emerging economies, the methods and indicators—initially tailor-made to the characteristics of emerging market economies—are adjusted to reflect the specific situation of the CEECs before applying them to the eight new member states.

The structure of external liabilities has a major impact on the sustainability of foreign financing. Long-term capital flows are especially important for countries that need external funds to finance long-term investments that are required to support the catching up process, as is the case in the transition economies. FDI is the most important source for long-term external financing for the CEECs. It is, therefore, important to identify the factors that determine the supply of FDI inflows and to define policy measures that would make a country an attractive location for foreign investors. We analyze the driving factors for FDI flows from developed countries to transition economies and other emerging markets. Our empirical analysis offers some innovative aspects: We use bilateral FDI data for a panel of six industrialized countries and over twenty emerging economies to estimate a gravity model. This allows us to differentiate between the impact of host and home country characteristics on FDI flows from industrialized countries to emerging economies. Furthermore, we differentiate between three emerging market regions, namely Asia, Latin America, and the CEECs. This allows us to compare the impact of host country characteristics on FDI flows across host country regions.

Some of the CEECs face both external imbalances and excessive public deficits. To become eligible for euro area accession the CEECs have to tackle both imbalances. Especially with respect to public deficits, EU institutions recommend an expenditure-based consolidation strategy. Among economists, a brought consensus exists that fiscal policy has an impact on the external balance. However, with respect to the direction of this impact the empirical literature provides inconsistent results. This might be due to the application of reduced-form models that do not differentiate between the effects that fiscal policy might have on the different parts of the BOP, e.g., the trade account, income and transfers, and the financial account. Fiscal measures can, however, be expected to impact the subaccounts in different ways. Therefore, we argue that the interaction between fiscal policy measures and the external equilibrium needs to be addressed by analyzing these linkages for the different parts of the BOP separately. We address this issue by investigating the impact of fiscal policy on one important part of the BOP, namely the trade balance through the estimation of structural trade equations. While former empirical studies have analyzed the impact of different demand components, namely consumption, investment, and exports on trade flows, a differentiation between public and private demand has not been taken into account. We add to the existing literature in this area by making this further differentiation when estimating import equations.

Appendix to Chapter 1

Glossary

Acquis Communautaire ~ Community acquis

The Community acquis is the body of common rights and obligations that binds all the member states together within the European Union. It comprises not only community law in the strict sense, but also all acts adopted under the second and third pillars[22] of the European Union and the common objectives laid down in the treaties. Applicant countries have to accept the Community acquis before they can join the European Union. Derogations from the acquis are granted only in exceptional circumstances and are limited in scope. To integrate into the European Union, applicant countries will have to transpose the acquis into their national legislation and implement it from the moment of their accession.

Derogation and opt-out

According to EU law, new EU member states have an obligation to work towards eventually adopting the euro. In EU jargon it is said that they have a derogation. While the accession treaties do not entail a predetermined time path for the adoption of the euro, the new member states are expected to adopt the single currency as soon as they fulfill the convergence criteria laid down in the Maastricht treaty.

The legal framework of EU membership for the new member countries differs from the situation of the United Kingdom and Denmark, who have a so-called opt-out option. The opt-out option allows the two countries to decide not to participate in the European monetary union even if they fulfilled the convergence criteria. In this case the United Kingdom and Denmark can adopt the euro but they are not expected to do so.

The Treaty or the Maastricht treaty

The Treaty on the European Union was signed in Maastricht on 7 February 1992 and entered into force on 1 November 1993. The Maastricht treaty changed the name of the European Economic Community to simply 'the European Community.' As Article A of the Treaty states, "By this Treaty, the High Contracting Parties establish among themselves a European Union."

---

22 The first pillar is the community dimension, which comprises the arrangements set out in the European Community, European Coal and Steel Community, and European Atomic Energy Community treaties. The second pillar covers common foreign and security policy, which comes under Title V of the Treaty. Police and judicial cooperation in criminal matters, which comes under Title VI of the EU Treaty, builds the third pillar of the EU.

Economic convergence criteria

Table A 1-1: Annual change in the consumer price index

	1997	1998	1999	2000	2001	2002	2003	2004
EU-25	2.6 [1)]	2.1 [1)]	1.6 [1)]	2.4	2.5	2.1	1.9	2.1
EU-15	1.7 [1)]	1.3	1.2	1.9	2.2	2.1	2.0	2.0
EU-12	1.7 [1)]	1.2	1.1	2.1	2.4	2.3	2.1	2.1
Czech Republic	8.0	9.7	1.8	3.9	4.5	1.4	-0.1	2.6
Estonia	9.3	8.8	3.1	3.9	5.6	3.6	1.4	3.0
Hungary	18.5	14.2	10.0	10.0	9.1	5.2	4.7	6.8
Latvia	8.1	4.3	2.1	2.6	2.5	2.0	2.9	6.2
Lithuania	8.8	5.0	0.7	0.9	1.3	0.4	-1.1	1.1
Poland	15.0 [1)]	11.8 [1)]	7.2 [1)]	10.1	5.3	1.9	0.7	3.6
Slovak Republic	6.0	6.7	10.4	12.2	7.2	3.5	8.5	7.4
Slovenia	8.3	7.9	6.1	8.9	8.6	7.5	5.7	3.6

1) Estimates
Source: Eurostat (2005).

Table A 1-2: Balance of consolidated general government sector as a percentage of GDP

	1997	1998	1999	2000	2001	2002	2003	2004	Average 1997-2004
EU-25	n.a.	-1.7	-0.8	0.8	-1.2	-2.3	-2.9	-2.6	-1.5
EU-15	-2.4	-1.6	-0.7	1.0	-1.1	-2.2	-2.8	-2.6	-1.6
EU-12	-2.6	-2.2	-1.3	0.1	-1.7	-2.4	-2.8	-2.7	-2.0
Czech Republic	-2.5	-5.0	-3.6	-3.7	-5.9	-6.8	-11.7	-3.0	-5.3
Estonia	1.9	-0.3	-3.7	-0.6	0.3	1.4	3.1	1.8	0.5
Hungary	-6.8	-8.0	-5.6	-3.0	-3.7	-8.5	-6.2	-4.5	-5.8
Latvia	n.a.	-0.6	-4.9	-2.8	-2.1	-2.7	-1.5	-0.8	-2.2
Lithuania	-1.1	-3.0	-5.6	-2.5	-2.0	-1.5	-1.9	-2.5	-2.5
Poland	-4.0	-2.1	-1.4	-0.7	-3.9	-3.6	-4.5	-4.8	-3.1
Slovak Republic	-5.5	-4.7	-6.4	-12.3	-6.0	-5.7	-3.7	-3.3	-6.0
Slovenia	n.a.	-2.2	-2.1	-3.5	-2.8	-2.4	-2.0	-1.9	-2.4

Source: Eurostat (2005) and own calculations.

Table A 1-3: Consolidated gross general government debt as percentage of GDP

	1997	1998	1999	2000	2001	2002	2003	2004	Average 1997-2004
EU-25	n.a.	67.5	66.7	62.9	62.2	61.7	63.3	63.8	64.0
EU-15	71.0	68.9	67.9	64.1	63.3	62.7	64.3	64.7	65.9
EU-12	74.9	74.2	72.7	70.4	69.6	69.5	70.8	71.3	71.7
Czech Republic	12.2	12.9	13.4	18.2	27.2	30.7	38.3	37.4	23.8
Estonia	6.4	5.6	6.0	4.7	4.4	5.3	5.3	4.9	5.3
Hungary	64.2	61.9	61.2	55.4	52.2	55.5	56.9	57.6	58.1
Latvia	n.a.	9.8	12.6	12.9	14.9	14.1	14.4	14.4	13.3
Lithuania	15.2	16.5	23.0	23.8	22.9	22.4	21.4	19.7	20.6
Poland	44.0	39.1	40.3	36.8	36.7	41.2	45.4	43.6	40.9
Slovak Republic	33.1	34.0	47.2	49.9	48.7	43.3	42.6	43.6	42.8
Slovenia	n.a.	23.6	24.9	27.4	28.1	29.5	29.4	29.4	27.5

Source: Eurostat (2005) and own calculations.

Table A 1-4: Annual percentage change in nominal exchange rate (national currency per euro) [1)]

	1997	1998	1999	2000	2001	2002	2003	2004
Czech koruna	4.3	0.3	2.3	-3.5	-4.3	-9.6	3.4	0.1
Estonian kroon	2.9	0.2	-0.6	0.0	0.0	0.0	0.0	0.0
Hungarian forint	9.2	13.7	5.1	2.9	-1.3	-5.3	4.4	-0.8
Latvian lats	-5.7	0.1	-5.2	-10.6	0.2	3.7	10.3	3.8
Lithuanian litas	-10.7	-1.1	-4.9	-13.3	-3.1	-3.4	-0.2	0.0
New Polish zloty	8.6	5.4	7.9	-5.2	-8.4	5.0	14.1	2.9
Slovak koruna	-2.1	3.7	11.6	-3.4	1.6	-1.4	-2.8	-3.5
Slovenian tolar	5.4	2.7	4.6	6.2	5.5	3.7	3.5	2.2

1) A positive (negative) number indicates a nominal depreciation (appreciation) of the national currency.

Source: Eurostat (2005) and own calculations.

Table A 1-5: Long-term interest rate [1)]

	2001	2002	2003	2004
EU-12	5.13	4.99	4.18	4.15
Czech Republic	6.31	4.88	4.12	4.75
Estonia	10.15	8.42	5.25	4.39
Hungary	7.95	7.09	6.82	8.19
Latvia	7.57	5.41	4.90	4.86
Lithuania	8.15	6.06	5.32	4.50
Poland	10.68	7.36	5.78	6.90
Slovak Republic	n.a.	8.72	6.40	4.69
Slovenia	8.04	6.94	4.99	5.03

1) Annual average of monthly harmonized long-term interest rates for convergence assessment purposes.

Source: ECB (2005b).

Table A 1-6: Balance of the current account as percentage of GDP

	1997	1998	1999	2000	2001	2002	2003	2004	Average 1997-2004
EU-25	n.a.	n.a.	n.a.	n.a.	-0.8	0.1	0.0	n.a.	0.1
EU-15	0.9	0.3	-0.2	-0.9	-0.3	0.5	0.4	n.a.	0.0
EU-12	n.a.	n.a.	-0.3	-1.0	-0.2	0.8	0.3	0.4 [1)]	-4.8
Czech Republic	-6.4	-2.1	-2.5	-4.9	-5.4	-5.6	-6.3	-5.2	-4.8
Estonia	-11.5	-8.6	-4.4	-5.5	-5.6	-10.2	-13.2	-15.2	-9.3
Hungary	-2.1	-4.9	-5.1	-8.7	-6.2	-7.1	-8.7	-8.8	-6.5
Latvia	-5.7	-9.7	-9.0	-4.6	-7.7	-6.7	-8.3	-12.3	-8.0
Lithuania	-10.0	-11.7	-11.1	-5.9	-4.7	-5.2	-6.9	-7.2	-7.8
Poland	-3.7	-4.1	-7.6	-6.0	-2.9	-2.6	-2.2	-1.6	-3.8
Slovak Republic	-9.2	-9.6	-5.7	-3.5	-8.4	-8.0	-0.8	-3.5	-6.1
Slovenia	0.3	-0.6	-3.3	-2.8	0.2	1.4	-0.4	-0.9	-0.8

1) Data from Eurostat available through 2003 only. 2004 data taken from the ECB (2005a).

Source: Eurostat (2005), ECB (2005a), and own calculations.

Table A 1-7: CEECs in World Bank country classification

	Classification by income as of 2005 [1)]	Year of graduation to current income group	Classification by indebtedness [2)]
Czech Republic	Upper middle income	1994	Less indebted
Estonia	Upper middle income	1997	Severely indebted
Hungary	Upper middle income	-	Moderately indebted
Latvia	Upper middle income	2001	Severely indebted
Lithuania	Upper middle income	2001	Moderately indebted
Poland	Upper middle income	1996	Moderately indebted
Slovak Republic	Upper middle income	1996	Moderately indebted
Slovenia	High income	1997	Debt not classified

1) Upper middle income country: 2004 gross national income (GNI) per capita of between USD 3,256 and USD 10,065. High income country: 2004 GNI per capita of USD 10,066 and more.
2) Severely indebted means either present value of debt service to GNI exceeds 80 percent or present value of debt service to exports exceeds 220 percent. Moderately indebted means either of the two key ratios exceeds 60 percent of, but does not reach, the critical levels. Severely indebted means three of four key ratios (averaged over 2001-2003) are above critical levels: debt to GNI (50 percent), debt to exports (275 percent), debt service to exports (30 percent), and interest to exports (20 percent). Moderately indebted means three of the four key ratios exceed 60 percent of, but do not reach, the critical levels. All other classified low-income and middle-income economies are listed as less indebted.

Source: World Bank (2005e).

Table A 1-8: Total unemployment rate

	1997	1998	1999	2000	2001	2002	2003	2004
EU-25	n.a.	9.5	9.1	8.6	8.4	8.7	9.0	9.0
EU-15	9.8	9.3	8.5	7.6	7.2	7.6	8.0	8.1
EU-12	10.6	10.1	9.2	8.2	7.9	8.3	8.7	8.9
Czech Republic	n.a.	6.4	8.6	8.7	8.0	7.3	7.8	8.3
Estonia	9.6	9.2	11.3	12.5	11.8	9.5	10.2	9.2
Hungary	9.0	8.4	6.9	6.3	5.6	5.6	5.8	5.9
Latvia	n.a.	14.3	14.0	13.7	12.9	12.6	10.4	9.8
Lithuania	n.a.	13.2	13.7	16.4	16.4	13.5	12.7	10.8
Poland	10.9	10.2	13.4	16.4	18.5	19.8	19.2	18.8
Slovak Republic	n.a.	n.a.	16.7	18.7	19.4	18.7	17.5	18.0
Slovenia	6.9	7.4	7.2	6.6	5.8	6.1	6.5	6.0

Source: Eurostat (2005).

2 Sustainability of the CEECs' external financing

2.1 Introduction

2.1.1 The role of external sustainability for the CEECs

Sizable and persistent current account deficits, experienced by most of the CEECs since the beginning of the transition process, increasingly cause concerns regarding the sustainability of the countries' external balances.[23] Relatively large current account deficits might be seen as a natural phenomenon of the catching-up process and therefore as a consequence of high investment and intertemporal consumption smoothing[24], but the persistently high level of capital inflows needed to finance these deficits in the CEECs caused a substantial increase in the level of external liabilities[25], especially external debt. Moreover, recent experiences in emerging markets have shown that large current account imbalances and a high level of external debt can trigger financial crises, e.g., balance of payment or debt crises. External imbalances in the CEECs and the question whether recent current account deficits as well as the level of external debt are sustainable are becoming a key policy issue for the new EU member countries. This is especially the case given their willingness to adopt the euro within only a few years after having joined the EU and given the requirements regarding external balances associated with euro area accession.

There is a substantial divergence in the external balance between the EU-15 and the CEECs. From 1995 through 2004, the EU-15 experienced on average a current account surplus of 2 percent of GDP.[26] Over the same period, the CEECs recorded on average a current account deficit of 5.5 percent of GDP. The capital inflows associated with these deficits caused the stock of external debt in most CEECs to more than double between 1997 and 2003. As a result of this develop-

23 The notion of external balance refers to both the current account balance and the stock of external debt.

24 The economic reasoning behind the external financing of economic growth is based on the argument of intertemporal consumption smoothing. Assuming that the CEECs' per capita income converges toward the EU-15 level, it is rational for consumers to smoothen their lifetime consumption by consuming up front in anticipation of a future income increase.

25 External liabilities include debt liabilities, domestic equity held by foreign investors, and liabilities underlying financial derivatives. External debt is the amount of outstanding contractual liabilities of residents of a country to non-residents to repay principal and / or interest. An exact definition of external liabilities and external debt will be given in subsection 2.2.1.

26 The euro area between 1999 and 2004 recorded a current account surplus of 0.2 percent of GDP.

ment—according to the World Bank's assessment[27]—Hungary, Lithuania, Poland, and the Slovak Republic are moderately indebted while Estonia and Latvia are severely indebted.

While a broad consensus exists that the sustainability of the CEECs' external balance might be at risk,[28] there is no unanimous way to assess the sustainability of the current account deficit or the stock of external debt. Academic research as well as technical assessment by international organizations—especially after the series of financial crises in Latin America, Southeast Asia, and Europe—concentrated on finding those factors that cause financial crises and on determining the key economic variables that could serve as early warning indicators for an upcoming crisis. Despite these efforts, which concentrated on finding a systematic method to assess a country's external sustainability, no comprehensive single approach has been found that adequately addresses the issue of analyzing external imbalances.

In this chapter, we provide a comprehensive overview of the definition of external debt sustainability, the economic reasoning behind such a definition, and recent developments in the approaches applied to assess external sustainability. To our knowledge, the sustainability of the CEECs' external debt has not been adequately analyzed. We, therefore, apply the assessment methods presented elsewhere to the CEECs and provide an indicative evaluation of the sustainability of the CEECs' stock of external debt. However, the sustainability of the CEECs' current account position has been the subject of various recent publications. We thus draw on this literature wherever appropriate. While we do not undertake an empirical analysis of the CEECs' current account sustainability, our overall assessment of the CEECs' external balance reflects the results from the respective recent empirical literature. We do not intend to develop a comprehensive model for the assessment of the sustainability of the external balance. We rather reconsider existing approaches to external debt sustainability, discuss their suitability for the situation of the CEECs, and modify them where necessary or possible to make them applicable to the CEECs. Finally, we apply the most appropriate concept to assess the CEECs' external debt situation.

The remainder of this chapter is structured as follows. Subsection 2.1.2 provides an overview of the development of the CEECs' external balances. With respect to international flows we take a closer look at the evolution of current account deficits and at the structure of the financial account. Regarding the stock of external liabilities, we consider the development of the external debt burden. In

27 See World Bank (2005a).

28 See for example European Forecasting Group (2004) and IMF (2000b).

order to reveal the potential impact of a financial crisis, subsection 2.1.3 reviews the recent history of financial crises and their impact on economic development. Furthermore, potential effects of a financial crisis in the CEECs on the euro area—especially after the CEECs adopt the euro—are addressed. Sections 2.2 and 2.3 focus on the determination of the external debt burden and the assessment of external debt sustainability. In section 2.2 we describe the linkages between the current account and external debt, discuss issues regarding the valuation of external debt, and define external sustainability. Concepts used to assess a country's external balance and an application of these concepts to the CEECs are covered in section 2.3. More specifically, subsection 2.3.1 provides a discussion of the most common approaches to assess the sustainability of a country's external debt. In subsection 2.3.2 we apply selected concepts to the CEECs. Section 2.4 concludes with a broader look at the overall sustainability of the CEECs' external balance including current account deficits and external debt burdens.

2.1.2 Recent developments in the CEECs' external balances

In this subsection we take a closer look at recent developments in the CEECs' external position. We start with the BOP by looking at the development of the real and financial flows recorded in the current account and the financial account. The prevailing current account balances will also be compared to equilibrium levels. Subsequently, we turn from a flow to a stock perspective and describe the evolution of the countries' external debt.

In the second half of the 1990s and the early 2000s, most central and eastern European new EU member states, with the exception of Slovenia, have been running high deficits in their current account balances (see Figure 4). Slovenia, however, over the past ten years, reported a broadly balanced current account position. Positive trends with respect to the current account balance occurred in Poland and the Slovak Republic. Both countries recorded a significant decline in their deficit in recent years. In Poland, the current account deficit declined from 6.0 percent of GDP in 2000 to 1.6 percent of GDP in 2004. Prior to this recent improvement, a strong increase in investment, which was not matched by national savings, caused the rapid deterioration of Poland's current accounts at the end of the 1990s. The Slovak Republic recorded current account deficits of above 8 percent of GDP in 2001 and 2002, which declined to 3.5 percent of GDP in 2004. The Slovak current account deficit widened considerably in the late 1990s. This was mainly caused by both an increase in investment, which slowed down in the early 2000s, and by a smooth decline in total savings.

The Check Republic's current account deficit, in the early 2000s, remained stable at a level of around 5 to 6 percent of GDP. After decreasing to 2.1 percent in 1998, the current account deficit increased again gradually to about 5.5 percent of GDP until 2001 and remained at this level in the early 2000s.

Figure 4: Current account balance as percentage of GDP (1995-2004)

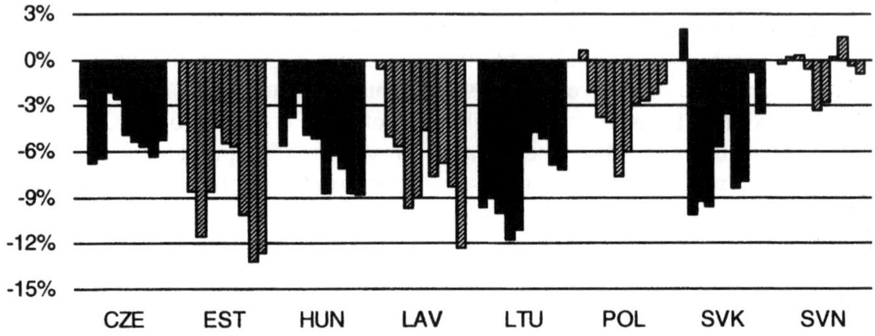

Source: IMF (2005a) and ECB (2005a).

Current account deficits in the remaining CEECs, namely Estonia, Hungary, Latvia, and Lithuania, increased over the past four to five years. The deterioration of the current account was especially pronounced in Estonia and Latvia. Estonia's current account deficit widened from 5.5 percent of GDP in 2000 to 12.6 percent of GDP in 2004. This was mainly the consequence of strong domestic demand and the economic slowdown of Estonia's main trading partners. Latvia's current account deficit almost tripled over the same period, increasing from 4.6 percent of GDP in 2000 to 12.3 percent of GDP in 2004. A surge in investment caused this rapid and persistent widening of the deficit in Latvia and, given the strength of domestic demand, the deficit is not expected to shrink in the near future. Hungary's current account deficit was fairly stable at high levels averaging almost 8 percent of GDP between 2000 and 2004. This was the result of a trade deficit and an income deficit, the latter being mostly related to profit repatriation from FDI (see Figure 5). Due to a sustained decrease in savings Lithuania's current account deteriorated substantially between 1994 and 1999. The deficit narrowed in the early 2000s due to an increase in savings, which were mainly driven by public sector savings, and a dip in the investment ratio. After a short period of improvement between 2000 and 2002 the Lithuanian current account deficit widened again to reach 7.2 percent of GDP in 2004, which is, however, still the lowest deficit among the Baltic countries.

Figure 5: Current account balance and subaccounts balances as percentage of GDP (2004)

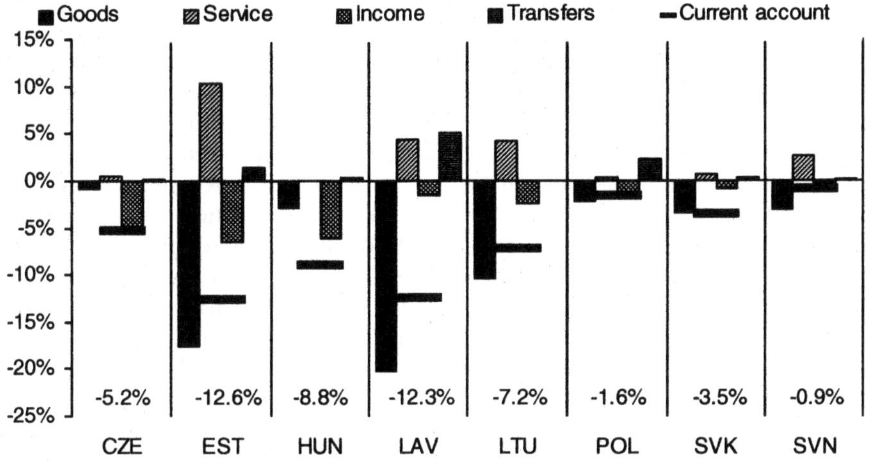

Source: IMF (2005a), ECB (2005a), and own calculations.

Table 4: Current account deficits and equilibrium current accounts

	Actual current account balance (in percent of GDP)		Equilibrium current account estimates (current account balance in percent of GDP)	
	2004	Average 2001-2004	Bussière, Müller, and Fratzscher	Doisy and Hervé
Czech Republic	-5.2	-5.6	-4.5 – -4.8	-4.5 – -4.7
Estonia	-12.6	-10.4	-5.8 – -9.5	
Hungary	-8.8	-7.7	-3.5 – 6.1	-3.4 – -4.7
Latvia	-12.3	-8.8	-8.5 – -9.7	
Lithuania	-7.2	-6.0	-5.5 – -6.0	
Poland	-1.6	-2.3	-2.4 – -5.2	-2.7 – -5.5
Slovak Republic	-3.5	-5.2	-7.8 – -9.2	-2.8 – -3.5
Slovenia	-0.9	0.1	0.3 – -2.8	

Source: IMF (2005a), ECB (2005a), Bussière, Müller, and Fratzscher (2004), Doisy and Hervé (2003), and own calculations.

Whether or not the prevailing current account deficits are excessive has been assessed in different empirical studies. According to these studies the current account deficits of most of the CEECs exceed equilibrium levels. For example, Bussière, Müller, and Fratzscher (2004) and Doisy and Hervé (2003) estimate equilibrium current account positions for the CEECs. Bussière, Müller, and Fratzscher (2004) derive a dynamic intertemporal savings-investment model and apply their model to a panel of 33 countries including the CEECs to derive structural current account levels. Doisy and Hervé (2003) derive trend current account levels from a multicountry model for four of the CEECs. A comparison of the results from the empirical literature and the CEECs' actual current account deficits reveals that the deficits of the Czech Republic, Estonia, Hungary, Latvia, and Lithuania exceed equilibrium levels (see Table 4). In the case of Latvia and Estonia, the 2004 current account was more than 2 percentage points of GDP higher than the upper limit of the estimated equilibrium. Poland, the Slovak Republic, and Slovenia experienced current account deficits within the range of the derived equilibrium levels.

Table 5: Net FDI inflows and the current account balance

	Current account balance (in percent of GDP)		Net FDI inflows (in percent of GDP)		FDI inflows plus current account balance (in percent of GDP)	
	2004	Average 2001-2004	2004	Average 2001-2004	2004	Average 2001-2004
Czech Republic	-5.2	-5.6	3.7	6.5	-1.5	0.9
Estonia	-12.6	-10.4	6.0	5.6	-6.6	-4.9
Hungary	-8.8	-7.7	3.6	3.8	-5.2	-3.9
Latvia	-12.3	-8.8	4.0	2.6	-8.3	-6.1
Lithuania	-7.2	-6.0	2.3	2.9	-4.9	-3.1
Poland	-1.6	-2.3	2.2	2.3	0.6	0.0
Slovak Republic	-3.5	-5.2	3.1	7.3	-0.4	2.1
Slovenia	-0.9	0.1	0.1	1.9	-0.8	2.0

Source: IMF (2005a), ECB (2005a), and own calculations.

The structure of net capital inflows necessary to cover the CEECs' current account deficits, during the early 2000s, has shifted from long-term equity flows, i.e., FDI flows, to more short-term debt financing. While FDI flows more than covered the 2001-2004 average current account deficits of the Czech Republic,

Poland, and the Slovak Republic, the average current account deficits of the remaining CEECs were partly financed through portfolio inflows and other financial inflows (see Table 5).

In 2004, however, only Poland received sufficient FDI inflows to fully finance its current account deficit. FDI coverage of the current account deficit is especially weak in Estonia, Hungary, Latvia, and Lithuania, where the difference between current account deficit and FDI inflow reached between 5.2 and 8.3 percent of GDP in 2004. Among these countries Latvia financed most of its 2004 current account deficit through other investment inflows (Figure 6), i.e., currency deposits, loans, and trade credits, which in general are all short-term flows.

Figure 6: Financial account balance and subaccounts balances as percentage of GDP (2004)

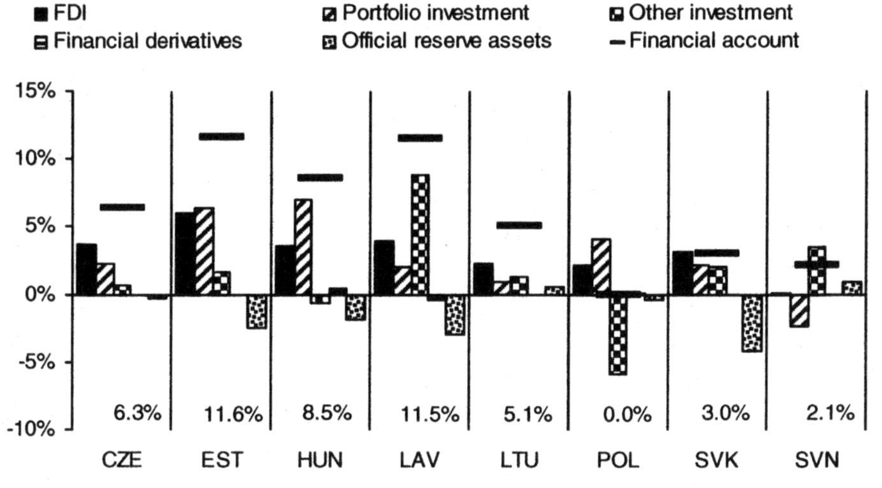

Source: IMF (2005a), ECB (2005a), and own calculations.

The different patterns in current account deficits and their financing across countries are reflected in the different evolution of the CEECs' external indebtedness. Since 1997, the increase in external debt was most pronounced in the Baltic countries (see Figure 7). In Latvia and Estonia, external debt in 2004 reached five and four times the level of 1997, respectively. Over the same period the external debt of Lithuania, Slovenia, and Hungary grew by 208 to 221 percent, while the debt burden of the remaining three CEECs, i.e., Poland, the Czech Republic, and

Slovenia more than doubled. The growth of the external debt burden in the Baltic countries, however, not only reflects the fast increase in the stock of external debt but also a basis effect that is due to the countries' low level of external debt in the beginning of the 1990s.

Figure 7: Evolution of external debt (1997-2004)
(1997 = 100)

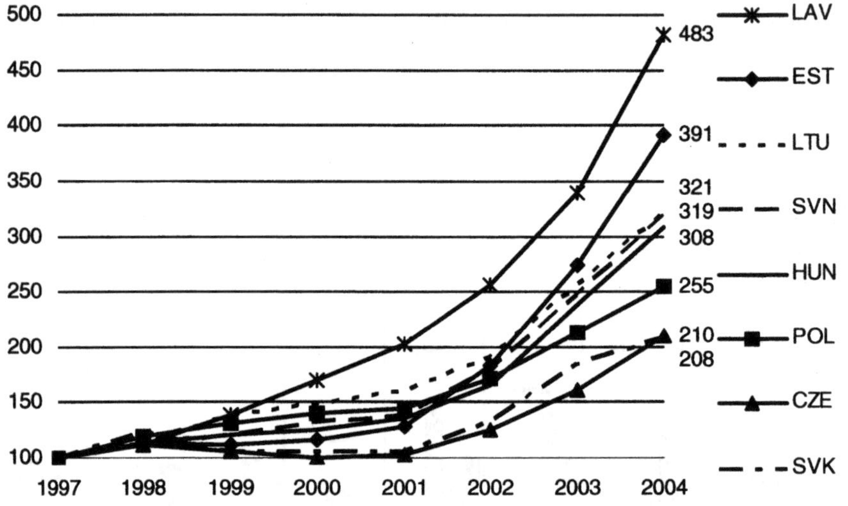

Source: IMF (2005d), ECB (2005a), and own calculations.

Only a few of the former communist countries had high stocks of external debt at the beginning of the transition process. Among these countries were Hungary and Poland, which had borrowed heavily from Western creditors during the communist area. In 1990, Hungary and Poland faced a level of external debt of 62 percent and 84 percent of GDP, respectively (see Figure 8). By the time the former Czechoslovakia was split, two thirds of the country's debt was taken over by the Czech Republic and one third by the Slovak Republic. Due to the prudent fiscal and monetary policy followed by the communist regime of Czechoslovakia, the initial level of external debt of the two succeeding countries was relatively low (27 percent of GDP in 1993[29]). At the break-up of the Soviet Union in 1991,

29 Calculation based on data from World Development Indicators database, World Bank (2005d).

Russia took over 100 percent of the external debt as well as the external assets of the former union. The Baltic countries, therefore, started into the transition process without any external debt.

Figure 8: External debt as percentage of GDP at the beginning of transition (1990-1994) [1)]

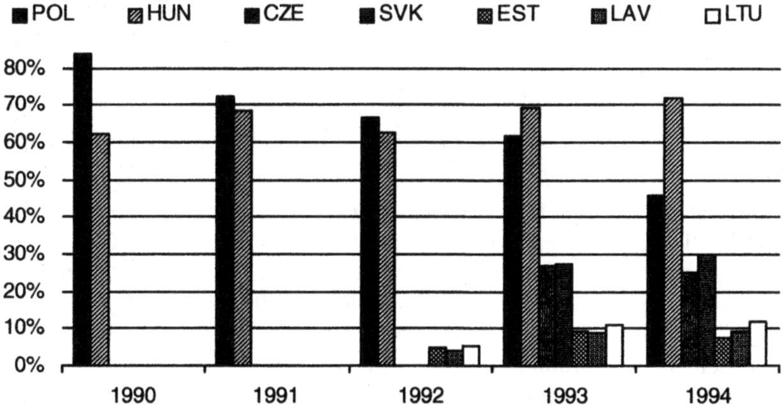

1) Data for Slovenia are not available.
Source: World Bank (2005d) and ECB (2005a).

Hungary and Poland handled their high level of external debt in different ways. Hungary fully serviced its debt at all times and sought to grow out of its debt problems by implementing stabilization and adjustment policies. This allowed the country to reduce its external debt from about 79 percent of GDP in 1995 to about 59 percent of GDP in 1997. Hungary's external debt rose again to over 75 percent of GDP in 2004 (see Figure 9). Poland went through several rounds of debt restructuring.[30] In 1991, official bilateral creditors, the so-called Paris Club[31], cancelled about 50 percent of the stock of debt or the equivalent in scheduled debt services on a net present value (NPV) basis. Furthermore, in 1994 a debt and debt service reduction was agreed with commercial banks (restructur-

---

30 See World Bank (1999, 2002).

31 The Paris Club is an informal group of official creditors who met for the first time to arrange a rescheduling of Argentina's debt payments during the financial crisis in 1956. Members of the Paris Club are Austria, Australia, Belgium, Canada, Denmark, Finland, France, Germany, Ireland, Italy, Japan, the Netherlands, Norway, the Russian Federation, Spain, Sweden, Switzerland, the United Kingdom, and the United States.

ing USD 14.3 billion of debt). In the same year, Poland issued a tranche of so-called Brady bonds[32]. In October of 2000, Poland undertook a buyback operation retiring USD 943 million of Brady bonds, which was equivalent to about 20 percent of the total amount outstanding.[33] As a consequence of these developments Poland reduced the level of external debt from almost 84 percent of GDP in 1990 to about 30 percent of GDP in 1997. Thereafter, the debt level increased again to 52 percent of GDP in 2004.

As a consequence of the high current account deficits—despite their advantageous starting position—Estonia and Latvia, in 2004, faced a stock of external debt equivalent to 91 percent and 97 percent of GDP, respectively (see Figure 9). These are the highest levels among the CEECs.

The Slovak Republic's external debt level grew notably in the late 1990s before stabilizing in the early 2000s and stood at 57 percent of GDP in 2003[34]. Slovenia recently experienced a sharp increase in the debt burden when the external debt ratio surged from 37 percent of GDP in 1999 to above 65 percent of GDP in 2004. The Czech Republic and Lithuania were able to largely stabilize the external debt ratio at around 40 percent of GDP and 45 percent of GDP, respectively.

Figure 9: External debt as percentage of GDP (1996-2004)

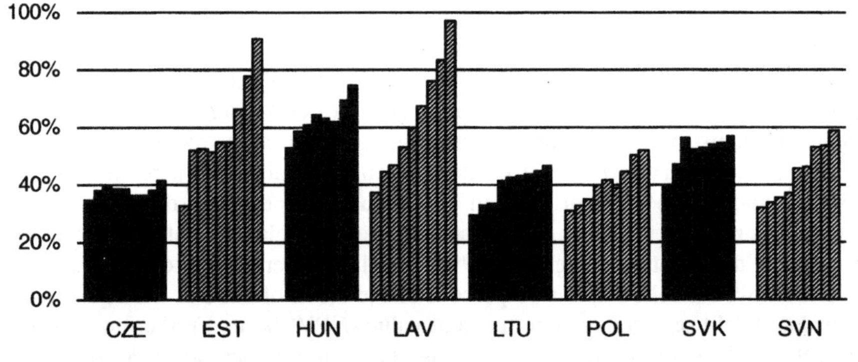

Source: IMF (2005d), ECB (2005a), and own calculations.

32 Brady Bonds are debt securities that resulted from the IMF's and the World Bank's effort to permanently restructure outstanding sovereign loans and interest arrears into liquid debt instruments. They are named after U.S. Treasury Secretary Nicholas Brady, who worked on the structuring of the instrument with the two institutions.

33 See World Bank (2004a).

34 Data for the Slovak Republic's external debt in 2004 are not yet available.

International organizations and EU institutions regard the level of indebtedness of some CEECs as alarming.[35] According to the country classification published by the World Bank[36] (see Table 6), based on economic data on external debt[37] from 2001 through 2003, Estonia and Latvia are considered to be severely indebted. With respect to indebtedness, the World Bank sees them in one group with, among others, Argentina, Brazil, and Turkey, countries that went through severe financial crises in the recent past.

Table 6: World Bank classification [1)] of countries by level of external indebtedness

Severely indebted middle-income	Moderately indebted middle-income	Less indebted middle-income
Argentina	**Hungary**	**Czech Republic**
Brazil	**Lithuania**	Mexico
Estonia	**Poland**	Thailand
Latvia	Russian Federation	
Turkey	**Slovak Republic**	

1) See definition given in the chapter's appendix.
Source: World Bank (2005a).

Against the background of this World Bank scheme, two questions arise: (i) What does the history of financial crises tell about the impact of a crisis on welfare and about how they evolved and spread and (ii) are there developments in the CEECs that are similar to those that prevailed in the countries that experienced a financial crisis. The next subsection addresses these questions by giving a brief overview of some aspects of financial crises and by pointing out both the similarities and the differences between the CEECs and countries that had been struck by a financial crisis.

35 See for example European Commission (2005i).

36 See Table A 2-1 in the chapter's appendix for income and indebtedness classification criteria applied by the World Bank.

37 Indicators taken into account for the classification are the present value of external debt as percentage of exports of goods and services and as percentage of GNI.

2.1.3 Recent financial crises and their impact on economic development

No matter whether a financial crisis starts as a currency crisis, as a debt crisis, or as a banking sector crisis,[38] the damage caused by it in terms of loss of economic welfare is enormous. During the past fifteen years a number of financial crises hit different emerging markets in Latin America (Mexico 1994, Brazil 1999, Argentina 2001-2002), East Asia (1997), and Europe (Russia 1998, Turkey 2000–2001).[39] The resulting tumults in the international financial markets negatively impacted the countries' economic growth as well as the economic development and stability of surrounding regions and even geographically unrelated emerging markets. Due to economic linkages and the behavior of market participants, financial crises starting in one country can spread rapidly, gain in momentum, and affect the global economy.[40]

The economic developments leading to financial crises in emerging economies were the consequence of rapid economic growth, largely financed by short-term foreign capital inflows.[41] The positive economic developments in the emerging economies in the 1980s and the first half of the 1990s were accompanied by large capital inflows and thus by a rapidly increasing stock of external debt. Foreign investors rushed into the countries and financed the high investment needs in a period of fast economic growth. However, at some point—due to an economic slowdown, an unsustainable increase in asset prices, or the huge stock of external debt—investors started to fear that the expected future economic developments would not allow the country to repay the external liabilities it accumulated. This sentiment was fueled by macroeconomic instabilities, fragile financial systems, e.g., unsustainable exchange rate arrangements and weak banking sectors, and a lack of transparency, as well as governance problems, which aggravated the economies' vulnerability. Investors feared that the economy could be destabilized and that the country could default on its debt. As a consequence, they decided to withdraw their capital. This led to a rise in interest rates and an increase in the countries' debt financing costs, which in turn caused a debt

---

38 See Feldstein (2002) for a detailed discussion of the characteristics, the causes, and the effects of the different types of financial crises.

39 Berg (1999), Corsetti, Pesenti, and Roubini (1998), and Radelet and Sachs (1998) discuss the causes and the consequences of the financial crises in Asia.

40 For a discussion of the contagious effects of financial crises and their impact on economic development, see for example Fratzscher (1998) and Singh (2002).

41 Corsetti, Pesenti, and Roubini (1998) discuss the counterintuitive interrelation of high economic growth and a country's vulnerability for financial crisis. Metzger (2001) underlines the role of external debt on the Latin American and Asian crises.

crisis and finally a default on external debt.[42] The reversal in capital flows also resulted in depreciation pressure on the countries' currencies. Since most of the countries' liabilities were denominated in foreign currency, the devaluation of their currencies increased the debt burden in terms of domestic currency. The magnitude of devaluation was even more pronounced in countries where governments hesitated too long to let the currency depreciate, e.g., Mexico (1994) and Thailand (1997). When defending their fixed exchange rate systems, the countries lost their foreign reserves, which led to an even larger devaluation once the reserves were used up and the exchange rate floated.

Financial crises had a substantial impact on the economies of all affected countries.[43] Economic growth is negatively affected by a financial crisis and most of the economies—for a short period after they were hit by a crisis—experienced negative growth. It took Thailand's and Indonesia's economies more than four years after the Asian financial crisis in 1997 to reach the pre-crisis GDP level. Additionally, financial crises not only had a negative one-off impact on the level of economic activity but also dampened long-term economic growth.[44] Not even considering the slowdown in growth following the crisis, Figure 10 shows the impact on economic development due to the downward shift in the level of economic activity. If this negative one-off effect could have been avoided, Indonesia and Thailand in 2004 would have experienced 288 percent and 214 percent of their 1990 GDP levels instead of 250 percent and 189 percent, respectively. The negative impact of the crisis was even more pronounced in the case of Argentina, where the GDP compared to 1990 would have been at 191 percent instead of 151 percent in 2004 if negative growth during the economic crisis in Latin American could have been avoided. Brazil is the only country where the financial crisis had almost no negative impact on the country's GDP level.

42 The linkage between high short-term capital inflows and recent financial crisis is reflected in the statement by Krueger, the first deputy managing director of the IMF: "The headline crises of the 1990s were capital rather than current account crises" (see Krueger 2003).

43 Empirical studies confirm that financial crises have a significant negative impact on the economic development of the affected country. For the case of the Asian financial crisis in the 1990s, Barro (2001) observes that the contraction of real GDP in Indonesia, Malaysia, the Philippines, South Korea, and Thailand—the five Asian economies mainly affected by the crises—was much more severe compared to the slowdown in economic development faced by other countries in the region.

44 Cerra and Saxena (2005), for example, analyze the long-term impact of shocks on economic growth and find that financial crises have a permanent negative impact on economic growth.

Figure 10: Development of GDP in countries hit by financial crisis
(Index 1990=100) [1)]

(a) East Asian emerging economies

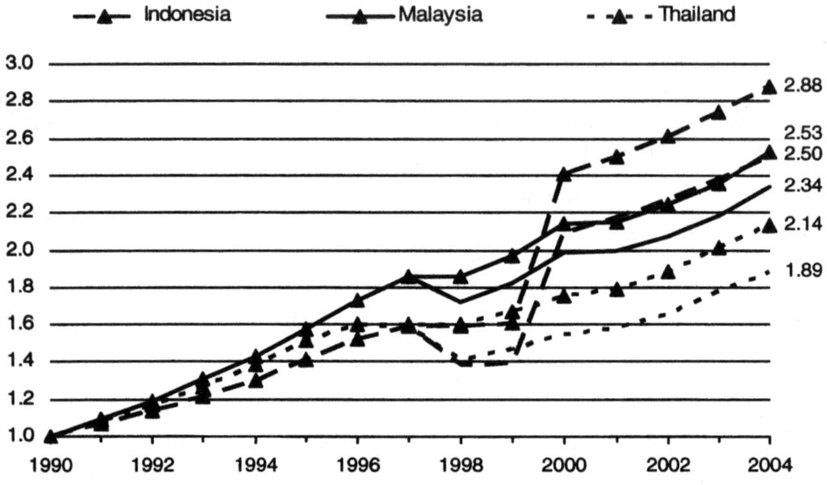

(b) Latin American emerging economies

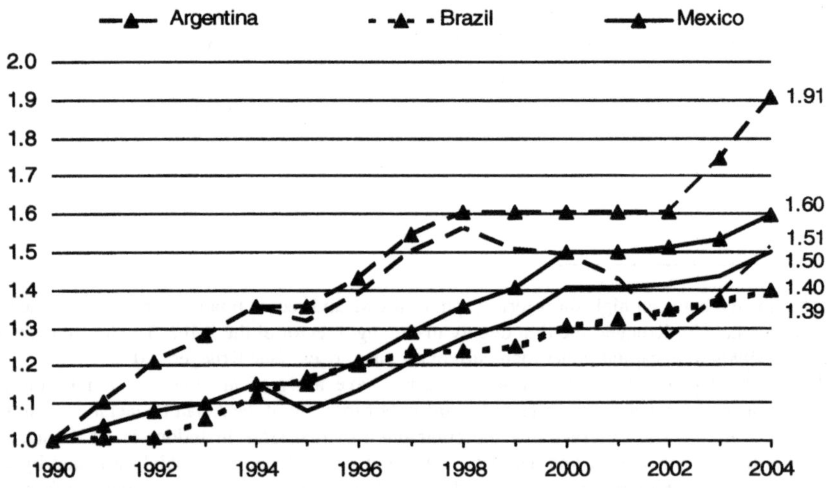

1) Lines show actual path of GDP index and lines with triangles show path after eliminating negative growth.

Source: IMF (2005c) and own calculations.

The CEECs in recent years—like Latin American and Asian emerging economies in the late 1980s and the 1990s—experienced relatively high economic growth and sizable current account deficits. While an external financing of domestic investment might be reasonable in terms of intertemporal optimization, excessive external financing increases the CEECs' vulnerability to light of a potential sudden withdrawal of external financial resources.

The CEECs over the past fifteen years went through a process of economic and political transition, which was accompanied by rapid economic growth and a fast integration into the world trade and financial market. For some of the countries, this development was accompanied by a rapid increase of external liabilities that made the countries more dependent on the sentiments of the international financial market.[45] This evolution is at least to some extent similar to the economic developments experienced by Latin American and East Asian emerging economies during the late 1980s and the 1990s, i.e., before the respective financial crises. However, as indicated above, not all of the CEECs experience notable current account deficits and not all of the CEECs face a high external indebtedness.

A whole body of literature examines the existence and the effects of contagion.[46] According to this research, a crisis occurring in one country might affect other countries, especially in the same region; due to contagion. Even countries that are unlikely to be the origin of a crisis might suffer from the negative consequences of a neighboring country's crisis. Crises spread through two main channels, i.e., trade linkages[47] and financial systems.[48] While trade linkages played an important role in East Asia—about half of Asia's emerging trade was intraregional trade—neither Argentina nor Turkey were important enough in terms of trade linkages with other emerging economies to cause a risk of this sort of contagion. With respect to the financial system, instabilities occurring in one emerging economy might make investors look more closely at other countries with similar economic structures or equivalent problems. This was the case when

45 See Drabek and Griffith-Jones (1998).

46 See Moser (2003) for an overview of relevant publications. Empirical studies confirm that regional contagion leads to a spillover of financial crises from one country to regionally or structurally related emerging economies. Applying an impulse response function, Agénor, Aizenman, and Hoffmaister (1998) show for the case of Argentina and the Mexican peso crisis in 1994 that the cyclical component of output is significantly negatively affected by contagious shocks.

47 For a discussion of the trade channel see, for example, Forbes (2001).

48 For a discussion of the different channels for contagion see, for example, Fratzscher (1998), Forbes and Rigobon (2000), and Moser (2003).

Argentina's trouble, for example, affected Brazil because it had investors focus on Brazil's large debt burden. Furthermore, financial market participants that follow technical investment rules can trigger financial contagion. Such investors might sell assets of an emerging market country to rebalance their portfolios after losing money in another emerging economy that was hit by a crisis.[49] Finally, a general panic caused by a crisis in some part of the world could make investors lose their appetite for risk and thus cause a rush of capital out of emerging economies.[50]

The risk of a regional dispersion of a financial crisis among the CEECs due to trade linkages is very limited. The main trading partners of the CEECs are the EU-15 countries and trade linkages between the CEECs are relatively weak (see Table 7). The Slovak Republic shows the highest dependence on interregional trade; 22 percent of the country's imports and exports are related to other CEECs. Less than 10 percent of the trade of Hungary, Latvia, Poland, and Slovenia are related to intra-CEEC trade. Trade linkages should, therefore, not cause any major contagious impulse among the CEECs in the case of a financial crisis.

Table 7: CEECs' and EU-15 trade with EU-15, CEECs, and Russia, 2004

	CZE	EST	HUN	LVA	LTU	POL	SVK	SVN	EU-15
Trading partner	in percent of total trade [1)]								
EU 15	62%	53%	63%	52%	42%	65%	56%	66%	54%
CEEC 8	15%	12%	7%	7%	16%	9%	22%	8%	5%
Russia	1%	9%	1%	3%	9%	3%	1%	2%	1%
Sum	78%	74%	71%	62%	66%	76%	79%	76%	61%

1) Trade shares are measured as exports plus imports with the respective country or region as a percentage of exports plus imports with the world.
Source: IMF (2005b) and own calculations.

For the CEECs, the threat of contagion through the financial market might be of higher importance than the contagion through trade linkages. Foreign

49 Institutional investors that lost money in the Asian financial crises might withdraw their funds from other emerging economies by selling high-liquidity corporate stocks to meet portfolio rebalancing needs after suffering losses in Asian economies. In the literature on financial contagion this process has been called the liquidity effect (see, e.g., Federal Reserve Bank of San Francisco, 2001).

50 This refers to the tendency for investors to reevaluate firms operating in the same region or regions with similar economic conditions as the crisis country. In the literature this is called the wake-up call effect (see, e.g., Federal Reserve Bank of San Francisco, 2001).

investors might not yet have a differentiated view of the CEECs and, thus, could tend to withdraw their funds from the whole region as soon as the economic situation of one country is destabilized. This mechanism can be especially forceful if a common characteristic of the CEECs is viewed as the cause of the crisis. If financial markets, for example, determine the external debt of one of the CEECs to be unsustainable they might find that other CEECs that face similar high levels of high external debt are subject to the same risk. Even though the overall situation of the other countries might still be sustainable, just the fact that they record a high debt burden and that an excessively high debt burden caused a crisis in a neighboring country could trigger a regional spread of the crisis.

A financial crisis in the CEECs after euro area accession could have a considerably negative impact on the economic situation of the euro area. If investors withdraw their funds from the region and from the euro area—assuming an unchanged level of current account balances—this would lead to a depreciation pressure on the euro. Fluctuations in the exchange rate would impact the economies of all euro area countries.

At least some of the CEECs are severely indebted. Therefore, as a consequence of any kind of financial distress a crisis might occur and spread across the CEECs. Due to the risk of a crisis as well as the likely impact of a crisis on their economic development, monitoring of the development of the CEECs' external balance—external debt position and the current account balance—is considered to be a critical issue for the countries themselves, the EU, and international observers.

2.2 External debt sustainability: Important concepts and definitions

This section and the following section focus on different aspects of external debt. We discuss (i) the determination of external debt, (ii) conditions for external debt sustainability, and (iii) concepts for the assessment of external sustainability. Furthermore, we assess the sustainability of the CEECs' external debt. By placing a special emphasis on the development of the level and the structure of external debt, we follow Frankel (2000, p.1), who points out that "large-scale borrowing by itself need not lead to a crisis. . . . More important than the magnitude of the current account deficit is how it is financed. . . . The composition of the capital inflow matters. East Asian countries, in 1997, relied too much on short-term foreign-currency-denominated debt." Since the composition of the capital flows is reflected in the structure of external liabilities, we take a closer look at the financing structure of the CEECs. This allows us to provide an indicative assessment of whether CEECs—like the East Asian countries—tend to rely too much on short-term external financing and are, therefore, vulnerable to changes in investors' sentiments.

2.2.1 External debt and its linkages to the balance of payments and the international investment position

The annual BOP statistic reflects all international economic flows a country encounters within one year (see Table 8). Due to the double entry of any transaction, the BOP in accounting terms is by definition always balanced. Therefore, a current account deficit must be financed by a surplus in the financial account[51], i.e., an increase in foreign liabilities or a decrease in foreign assets, or by a decrease in foreign reserves. A current account surplus goes hand in hand with a financial account deficit, i.e., a decrease in foreign liabilities or an increase in foreign assets, or an increase in foreign reserves.[52] The transactions recorded in the financial account reflect the change in a country's international assets and liabilities, i.e., foreign direct investment, portfolio investment, financial derivatives, other investments, and reserve assets. A surplus in the financial account reflects financial inflows in excess over financial outflows, i.e., the country's foreign liabilities increased by more than its foreign assets.

While the BOP reflects international economic flows, the stock of a country's external financial assets and liabilities is reported as its international investment position (IIP).[53] The financial items included in the IIP consist of claims on nonresidents, liabilities to nonresidents, and reserve assets (see Table 9 for a standard layout of the IIP). The net international investment position (net IIP) equals the stock of external assets less the stock of external liabilities. It shows the difference between what an economy owns in relation to what it owes. The net worth of the economy therefore consists of the net IIP plus the stock of the economy's nonfinancial assets.

---

51 The capital account covers only transfers that are of minor importance for most countries. Major financial flows are recorded in the financial account. We therefore concentrate on the financial account and exclude the capital account from our further discussion and analysis.

52 Sizable changes in foreign reserves only occur in managed or fixed exchange rate regimes.

53 The IIP is part of the balance of payments statistics as it is published by the IMF. The data included in the IIP are subject to the IMF's special data dissemination standard (SDDS). The statistic provides USD values of the stock of external assets and external liabilities held by a country. Assets as well as liabilities are divided into different categories depending on their nature and the nature of the underlying real economic transaction (see Table 9).

Table 8: Standard layout of the BOP

	Credit	Debit
I Current account		
A Goods and services	Exports	Imports
B Income	Income earned	Income paid
1. Compensation of employees		
2. Investment Income		
Of which: interest on external debt	Interest earned	Interest paid
C Current transfers	Transfers received	Transfers made
II Capital and financial account		
A Capital account		
1. Capital transfers	Transfers received	Transfers made
2. Acquisition / disposal of non-produced, nonfinancial assets		
B Financial account	Imports	Exports
1. Direct investment		
1.1 Equity capital		
1.2 Reinvested earnings		
1.3 Other capital		
2. Portfolio investment		
2.1 Equity securities		
2.2 Debt securities		
3. Financial derivatives		
4. Other investment		
5. Reserve Assets		

Source: IMF (1993).

The BOP and the IIP are closely linked; however, changes in the end-of-period stocks of the IIP do not only reflect financial flows recorded in the BOP for the respective period but also reflect valuation changes and other adjustments that occurred in that period and affected the levels of assets and/or liabilities (see Figure 11). Changes in the value of assets and liabilities can be caused by changes in the exchange rate and/or by changes in market value. Changes in the exchange rate affect both equity and debt instruments. A nominal depreciation of a country's currency causes the value of foreign-currency-denominated assets and liabilities to increase, and the net IIP of a country that is a net debtor (net creditor) decreases (increases) as its currency depreciates. Changes in the market value might occur for equity assets and liabilities as well as for debt assets but not for debt liabilities. A change in the value of equity assets can, for example, be caused by a general change in the economic situation. If an economic downturn occurs, the value of assets that are claims on the economy's equity, i.e., future cash flows, decreases. If the likelihood that one of the country's debtors does not repay a debt increases, the value of the debt assets the country holds against this particular debtor have to be revalued, i.e., written off. The debt obligation a country has to its creditors, however, does not change as long as the contractual agreement that establishes the debt does not change.

Table 9: Standard components of IIP statement and external debt statistics

A. External assets	B. External liabilities
1. Direct investment	1. Direct investment
1.1 Equity capital and reinvested earnings	1.1 Equity capital and reinvested earnings
1.2 Other capital	1.2 Other capital
1.2.1 Claims on affiliated enterprises	1.2.1 Claims on direct investors
1.2.2 Liabilities to affiliated enterprises [1)]	1.2.2 Liabilities to direct investors [1)]
2. Portfolio investment	2. Portfolio investment
2.1 Equity securities	2.1 Equity securities
2.2 Debt securities [2)]	2.2 Debt securities [1) 2)]
3. Financial derivatives	3. Financial derivatives
4. Other investment	4. Other investment
4.1 Trade credits	4.1 Trade credits [1)]
4.2 Loans	4.2 Loans [1)]
4.3 Currency and deposits	4.3 Currency and deposits [1)]
4.4 Other assets	4.4 Other liabilities [1)]
5. Reserve assets	
~ Net international investment position	

1) These components comprise gross external debt.
2) Includes bonds and notes and money market instruments.
Source: IMF (1993).

The IIP takes into account the stock of all external assets and all external liabilities, including equity and debt instruments as well as reserve assets. The external debt position of a country, however, is determined by debt instruments only. This is reflected in the agreed core definition of external debt,[54] which reads as follows: "Gross external debt is the amount, at any given time, of disbursed and outstanding contractual liabilities of residents of a country to non-residents to re-

54 A group of major multilateral economic organizations (World Bank, IMF, Bank for International Settlements [BIS], and Organisation for Economic Co-operation and Development [OECD], 1988, p.25) agreed upon and published this core definition of external debt.

pay principal, with or without interest, or to repay interest with or without principal."

Figure 11: Relationship between the BOP and the IIP

		BOP Current account Capital account Financial account	Other changes in position			
	Position at the beginning of the period	Transactions	Price changes	Exchange rate changes	Other adjustments 1)	Position at the end of the period
International Investment Position	**Assets**	**Assets**				**Assets**
	Direct Investment abroad	Direct Investment abroad	√	√	√	Direct Investment abroad
	Portfolio Investment	Portfolio Investment	√	√	√	Portfolio Investment
	Financial Derivatives	Financial Derivatives	√	√	√	Financial Derivatives
	Other Investment	Other Investment	√	√	√	Other Investment
	Reserve Assets	Reserve Assets	√	√	√	Reserve Assets
	Liabilities	**Liabilities**				**Liabilities**
	Direct Investment in reporting economy	Direct Investment in reporting economy	√ 2)	√	√ 2)	Direct Investment in reporting economy
	Portfolio Investment	Portfolio Investment	√ 2)	√	√ 2)	Portfolio Investment
	Financial Derivatives	Financial Derivatives	√	√	√	Financial Derivatives
	Other Investment	Other Investment	√ 2)	√	√ 2)	Other Investment
	Net International Investment Position					Net International Investment Position

1) Other adjustments are, for example, changes in the value due to write-downs.
2) Debt-creating liabilities included in direct investments, portfolio investments, and other investments are usually not subject to price changes or to write-downs. A debt relief might, however, cause a change in the value of debt liabilities.

Source: IMF (2002b).

External debt is a subset of the liability components recorded in the IIP and can, therefore, be derived from the IIP. The definition explicitly includes only those liabilities for which a contractual obligation for payment of the principal and/or interest exists.[55] Pure equity securities as well as financial derivatives are not subject to such terms and are, therefore, not considered external debt.

Transactions related to foreign direct investments can comprise equity and debt creating financial flows. FDI flows are an important source of external financing and due to the substantial stock of FDI accumulated by some of the CEECs, the financial flows related to these investments gain in importance. The financial flow related to the initial foreign investment normally is a pure equity transaction and does not add to external debt. Once the investment entity receives loans from its foreign owner or generates profits that are to be repatriated to the foreign investor, the obligation for a payment is established and the respective liability is included in the country's external debt.

2.2.2 The valuation of debt liabilities

While a clear definition exists regarding the IIP items that are considered external debt, it is less clear how these liabilities are to be valued. The valuation can be done either according to the face value of debt outstanding or by considering the present value (PV) of future debt service payments[56].[57] In line with finance theory, the cash flow perspective is preferable when valuing the financial burden a commitment puts on an entity.[58] The PV of the future debt service obligations reflects the actual burden of the cash flows related to a country's external debt. In contrast to the PV of debt service obligations, the face value of debt does not take into account the market's perception of the time value of money.[59] Valuing debt at

55 In the interpretation of the definition, it is stated that "obligations to make specified payments, including instances such as a financial obligation stemming from a court ruling, where there may be no contractual agreement" are also subject to this definition (World Bank, IMF, BIS, and OECD, 1988, p. 20).

56 Debt service payments are repayments of the principal plus interest payments.

57 The following considerations focus on the valuation of gross debt, i.e., debt liabilities only. The valuation of debt assets can be done along the same lines. Debt assets might, however, be subject to price changes and write-downs. Once the value of debt liabilities and debt assets is determined, the calculation of the net debt burden is straightforward.

58 For an introduction to the valuation of debt see, for example, Martellini, Priaulet, and Priaulet (2003).

59 According to the World Bank (2005b), the definition the "Present Value (PV) of Debt is the discounted sum of all future debt-service obligations (interest and principal). This measure takes into account the degree of concessionallity of a country's debt stock. Whenever the interest rate on a loan is lower than the market rate, the resulting PV of debt is smaller than its

its face value would imply that a debtor is indifferent between repaying a debt immediately, in ten years, or in 100 years. Since the debtor will be able to earn a return, e.g., interest, on the financial resources at hand, while being obliged to make interest payments on the debt, the timing of payments has an impact on the debtor's economic performance. Therefore, the schedule for disbursement and repayment matters to debtors and must be taken into account when valuing debt obligations.[60]

The PV of external debt is calculated by discounting all future service and interest payments by the world market rate.[61] If the full amount of outstanding debt was repaid in one sum at time *k*, the PV of the current amount of external debt (*PVD*) is equal to its face value (*D*), subject to the agreed interest (*i*), and discounted by the world market rate (*r*):[62]

$$PVD_t = D_t \frac{\prod_{j=1}^{k} (1 + i_{t+j})}{\prod_{j=1}^{k} (1 + r_{t+j})}. \tag{1}$$

If debt service payments are scheduled over time, the present value of these service payments (*PVDS*) equals the sum of the debt service payments (*DS*), which include agreed interest payments and repayment of the principal, discounted by the world market rate (*r*):

$$PVDS_t = \sum_{i=0}^{\infty} \frac{DS_{t+i}}{\prod_{j=1}^{i} (1 + r_{t+j})}. \tag{2}$$

This is equivalent to the sum of all repayments of the principal (*DP*), subject to agreed interest (*i*), and discounted by the world market rate (*r*):

face value, with the difference reflecting the grant element." For a discussion of the present value calculation, see for example Copeland, Weston, and Shastri (2003).

60 The argumentation is the same for the creditor who is also not indifferent with respect to the payment schedule.

61 If the debt is denominated in foreign currency and the present value is determined in local currency terms, the present value of payments also depends on the exchange rate prevailing at the moment of the payment.

62 See IMF (2003).

$$PVDS_t = \sum_{i=0}^{\infty} DP_{t+i} \frac{\prod_{j=1}^{i}(1+i_{t+j})}{\prod_{j=1}^{i}(1+r_{t+j})}. \qquad (3)$$

In those cases in which the interest rate applied to the debt is equivalent to the world market rate, i.e., $i = r$, the PV of debt or debt service payments equals the face value of debt or the sum of debt service payments, respectively. When the interest rate on debt implied by the debt service schedule is lower than the world market rate—as it is often the case for developing countries that are granted financing under concessional terms[63]—the PV is smaller than the face value of external debt. In those cases where the interest rate on debt is higher than the world market rate, the PV of debt is higher than its face value when discounted by the world market rate. This could, for example, be the case for countries that have reached a level of development that no longer qualifies them to receive concessional financing, while—due to political and economic uncertainty—private investors request a risk premium over world market rates on debt for these countries. In those cases where the interest rate on debt does not equal the world market rate—either because the country receives financing under concessional terms or because the country has to pay a risk premium over the world market rate—the PV of debt differs from its face value. In such cases the PV is considered to be the more sensible way to measure a country's debt burden.[64]

The determination of the PV of the external debt is, however, subject to two major problems. First, to exactly calculate the PV, a detailed payment schedule of future debt services payments for each and every debt contract is required. External debt obligations, in most countries, comprise a large number of both private and public debt contracts. Therefore, payment schedules—at least for private contracts—are often not available. The second problem is to choose the appropriate discount rates.[65] According to finance theory, discount rates should reflect the future path of the world market rate.[66] While the future path of the

63 A loan under concessional terms is a loan that is made at more favorable terms that could be obtained commercially, e.g., loans with grant elements or below market interest rates.

64 See, e.g., Copeland, Weston, and Shastri (2003) for a discussion of the time value of money.

65 The most sensitive way to calculate the PV would be to apply a discount rate that reflects the opportunity costs of capital for investors. According to this concept it is assumed that both the holder of debt securities and the debtor would be able to invest any funds (repayments received on debt assets or funds held for future debt services) at the world market rate. The world market rate would, therefore, be the appropriate discount rate.

66 For an introduction into the choice of discount rates and their link to market interest rates, see for example Questa (1999).

interest rate cannot be predicted, the yield curve gives some indication of the market's expectation. Considering the interest rate derived from the yield curve when determining the PV of debt would, however, imply that the calculation is affected by interest rate fluctuations. Movements in the world market interest rate, therefore, lead to fluctuations in the calculated PVs. These fluctuations are undesirable since they are not related to developments in the debtor's economy. Furthermore, a world market rate is not available and must be proxied by some other interest rate.[67]

In practice, different methods are applied to determine the PV of a country's debt. The World Bank (2004a, 2005c), for example, publishes PVs of debt calculated by applying a flat discount rate of 10 percent, while the IMF (2003) uses the historical averages of currency-specific commercial interest reference rates to determine the PV of debt in the context of the heavily indebted poor countries (HIPC) initiative.[68]

While the PV would be the more sensible measure for the external debt burden from a theoretical point of view, data on the face value are more broadly used in the context of debt sustainability analysis. This is due to both limitations regarding the availability of data on debt service payments and the undesirable impact of the choice of the discount rate on the assessment. As discussed above, the difference between the face value of debt and the PV of debt service payments is negligible as long as the interest rate (i) and the discount rate (r) do not diverge, i.e., as long as a country is not granted financing under concessional terms and the country does not have to pay a significant risk premium over the world market rate.

2.2.3 A definition of external debt sustainability

Before we are able to assess whether a country's external debt is sustainable, the conditions under which a country's external position is considered sustainable need to be defined. There is not one single definition for debt sustainability. According to the widely used definition by the IMF (2002a, p.4), debt sustainability is a "situation in which a borrower is expected to be able to continue

---

67 See IMF and International Development Association (IDA) (2004) for a discussion of a possible approximation of the world market rate.

68 The currency-specific commercial interest reference rate corresponds to secondary market yields on sovereign bonds in industrial countries and is, therefore, close to some kind of world market interest rate. United Nations Conference on Trade and Development (UNCTAD, 2004a) provides an overview of the pros and cons regarding the application of the different currency-specific commercial interest rates in the context of the HIPC initiative.

servicing its debts without an unrealistically large future correction to the balance of income and expenditure." This definition comprises two important requirements for a financial situation to be called sustainable: First, a country has to be able to serve its future debt obligations, and second, the country has to be able to do so without undertaking a drastic policy shift.

Whether a country can be expected to be able to service its debt obligations depends on its solvency and on its liquidity. An economy is said to be solvent if the PV of its external debt service payments (*DS*) does not exceed the PV of the future path of net national savings, i.e., the present value of future trade surpluses (*TB*). This intertemporal budget constraint is binding for countries and can be formalized as follows:

$$\sum_{i=0}^{\infty} \frac{DS_{t+i}}{\prod_{j=1}^{i}\left(1+r_{t+j}\right)} \leq \sum_{i=0}^{\infty} \frac{TB_{t+i}}{\prod_{j=1}^{i}\left(1+r_{t+j}\right)}, \tag{4}$$

where r_{t+j} is the discount rate prevailing in the market in period $t + j$.

An economy is said to be liquid if it is able to meet or roll over its maturing liabilities through its own liquid assets or through borrowing, regardless of whether it is solvent. Liquidity is determined by the actual ability to borrow, which in turn depends on the country's specific market cost of credit. In a functioning financial market an insolvent country will face a prohibitively high cost of credit. Therefore, insolvency causes illiquidity. The distinction between solvency and liquidity is sometimes blurred. A country might become illiquid, which is manifested in rising interest rates—in the limiting case that no further financing is available, the marginal interest rate becomes infinite—which eventually calls into question the country's solvency. Solvency is, thus, a necessary but not a sufficient condition for debt sustainability.

A simpler and more pragmatic approach to define debt sustainability is to require the debt to GDP ratio to not increase, i.e., to stabilize at a given level or to decline over time.[69] With D_t for the stock of external debt at the end of period t and Y_t for the GDP of period t this condition can be expressed as follows:

$$\frac{D_t}{Y_t} \geq \frac{D_{t+1}}{Y_{t+1}} \geq \frac{D_{t+2}}{Y_{t+2}} \geq \ldots \geq \frac{D_{t+n}}{Y_{t+n}}. \tag{5}$$

To satisfy this condition, external debt must grow at a lower rate or at most at the same rate as GDP, after translating both into the same currency. In a

69 See Roubini (2001) and Loser (2004).

simplified world, where we abstract for example from changes in the valuation of debt, the stock of debt changes by the amount of the current account deficit. Two sub-balances of the current account determine the change of external debt: the balance of the trade account, which records trade in goods and services, and the balance of the income account, which among others records interest payments and, thus, also depends on the existing amount of debt outstanding.[70] In this way, requiring a constant debt-to-GDP ratio for sustainability combines the flow and stock perspective—current account balance and stock of external debt—of the external balance.

However, while the economic conditions required for a constant debt-to-GDP ratio are straightforward, no rule specifies the level at which the debt-to-GDP ratio would have to stabilize in order to be sustainable. If the simple rule of a non-increasing debt-to-GDP ratio would be applied to a country no matter what the initial debt situation of the country was, this would lead to inconsistent results: On the one hand, a country that has no external debt and no external assets at all would not be allowed to run a current account deficit since this would increase the debt-to-GDP ratio above the initial level of zero. On the other hand, a country with a high debt to GDP ratio would be allowed to run a current account deficit as long as this does not cause the stock debt to grow at a higher rate than GDP. According to this line of argumentation, requiring a constant debt-to-GDP ratio allows the indebted country to further increase the stock of external debt while it prohibits the country without any external liabilities form accumulating any external debt. Economically this result is not sensible. The approach of a constant debt-to-GDP ratio does not provide a clear guidance for the assessment of the sustainability of current debt levels. It, therefore, needs to be supplemented by further considerations that allow the level of the debt-to-GDP ratio to be assessed.

The debt-to-GDP ratio is only one among many indicators that can be applied to monitor different aspects of a country's vulnerability to a situation of financial distress. In the following section, we derive the economic conditions that are required to allow for a constant debt-to-GDP ratio and discuss different debt indicators and their application in practice. We also illustrate the determination of relevant threshold values for these indicators.

---

70 For simplicity we assume that the deficit is completely financed through debt inflows. Furthermore, we abstract from transfers.

2.3 Assessing the sustainability of the external balance

2.3.1 Concepts for the assessment of debt sustainability

A long and intense debate on how to judge whether a country is vulnerable to financial distress has been going on since the first financial crisis erupted in emerging economies in the early 1980s.[71] Major international organizations, e.g., World Bank, IMF, United Nations (UN), and OECD, looked for practicable concepts that could be applied to assess the sustainability of external debt especially after Russia (1998) and Argentina (2002) defaulted on their debt and the launch of the HIPC initiative.[72]

The most appropriate way to assess a country's debt sustainability—comparing the PV of a country's debt obligations and the PV of its future current account surpluses—is difficult or even impossible to implement in practice. Such an analysis requires the projection of the balance of payments, especially the current account and the financial account in relation to the prevailing level of the exchange rate. Such projections would allow for a forecast of the associated debt/liabilities dynamics. Projecting the BOP touches upon diverse stock-flow and trade elasticity linkages; this makes this exercise complex and the outcome vulnerable to assumptions. Macroeconomic variables, e.g., interest rates and growth rates, as well as policy decisions, e.g., expenditure and tax policies, need to be projected. This adds further uncertainty to the forecasts; results of the sustainability analysis depend to a large extent on assumptions underlying the forecasts of macroeconomic and financial market developments. Furthermore, the assessment must rely on very long-term projections—theoretically covering an infinite horizon—of the balance of payment. Moreover, such an assessment focuses on the analysis of a country's solvency and does not identify potential liquidity problems. As discussed above, this approach is, therefore, less useful for practical purposes.

Since forward looking methods, i.e., concepts based on BOP projections, are not practical to assess the sustainability of external debt, alternative approaches that rely on current economic data have been developed. In the following, we present two approaches. The first approach is based on the notion of a stable debt burden; the second approach assesses the burden of external

71 For a more general discussion of the assessment of financial vulnerability and the lessons learned from financial past crises see Goldstein, Kaminsky, and Reinhart (2000) and Bisignano, Hunter, and Kaufman (2000).

72 See for example World Bank (2004a), IMF (2002a, 2000), IMF and IDA (2004), United Nations Economic Commission for Africa (UNECA, 2003), and Loser (2004).

through debt indicators, which compare a country's obligations from external debt with the economic capacity to meet these obligations.

2.3.1.1 *Stabilization of the debt burden*

As discussed above, one way to assess external debt sustainability is to require the economic burden of external debt—measured by the debt-to-GDP ratio—to not increase. The development of the debt-to-GDP ratio is determined by several economic variables: the initial debt-to-GDP ratio, economic growth, the interest rate, and the trade balance.[73] The linkage between a constant debt-to-GDP ratio and these variables can be derived as shown in equations (6) through (10), where i is the nominal interest rate applied to the external debt, g is the nominal GDP growth rate, and TB_{t+1} reflects the trade balance in period $t+1$. The stock of external debt at the end of period $t+1$ equals the stock of external debt observed at the end of period t plus interest on external debt accrued during period $t+1$, minus the trade account balance of period $t+1$:

$$D_{t+1} = (1+i)D_t - TB_{t+1}. \qquad (6)$$

Expressing equation (6) in percentage of GDP yields:

$$\frac{D_{t+1}}{Y_{t+1}} = \frac{(1+i)D_t}{(1+g)Y_t} - \frac{TB_{t+1}}{Y_{t+1}}, \qquad (7)$$

where g is the GDP growth rate. When defining d_t as the debt-to-GDP ratio in period t and tb_{t+1} as the trade account to GDP ratio observed in period t + 1, equation (7) becomes

$$d_{t+1} = \frac{(1+i)}{(1+g)} d_t - tb_{t+1}. \qquad (8)$$

The change in the debt ratio (Δd) is calculated as the difference between the debt-to-GDP ratio (d_{t+1}) at the end of period $t+1$ and the debt-to-GDP ratio (d_t) at the end of period t:

$$\Delta d = d_{t+1} - d_t = \frac{(i-g)}{(1+g)} d_t - tb_{t+1}. \qquad (9)$$

---

73 We abstract from changes in the valuation of debt, transfers, and items covered by the income account other than interest payments on external debt. We also assume that a deficit in the current account will be financed entirely through debt-creating financial inflows.

Applying the condition that the debt-to-GDP ratio (d) must not increase implies that the change in the debt-to-GDP ratio must be zero or smaller than zero ($\Delta d \leq 0$):

$$\Delta d \leq 0 \Rightarrow \frac{(i-g)}{(1+g)} d_t - tb_{t+1} \leq 0 \Rightarrow \frac{(i-g)}{(1+g)} d_t \leq tb_{t+1}. \tag{10}$$

Whenever the interest rate is higher than the growth rate ($i > g$), the left-hand side of the last part of equation (10) becomes positive and an equivalent surplus in the trade balance is required to keep the debt-to-GDP ratio constant. The required size of trade surplus $\left[\overline{tb_{t+1}}\right]$ depends negatively on the nominal GDP growth rate (g) and positively on the interest rate (i) and on the debt-to-GDP ratio (d_t) in the beginning of the period:

$$\overline{tb_{t+1}} = f\left(\overset{-}{g}, \overset{+}{d_t}, \overset{+}{i}\right). \tag{11}$$

Whether the debt-to-GDP ratio can be kept constant depends on the GDP growth, the interest rate, the trade balance, and the debt-to-GDP ratio itself. If the growth potential of a country can be determined and the interest rate is either given by debt contracts or can be projected, the level of the debt-to-GDP ratio that is in line with the requirements of the above-discussed notion of sustainability can be determined by projecting a feasible path of the trade balance.

While the concept of a constant debt-to-GDP ratio is straightforward, the analytical determination of the sustainable level of the debt-to-GDP ratio again depends on the future path of the trade account. Taking a purely analytical approach, the definition of sustainability based on a constant debt-to-GDP ratio is, therefore, not more practical than the one derived from the intertemporal budget constraint as discussed before. Threshold values for the sustainable level of the debt-to-GDP ratio can, however, be determined empirically. This empirical determination of threshold values and their limitations is discussed below.

Taking into account a country's actual economic performance regarding the trade account, economic growth, and interest rates as well as the actual debt-to-GDP ratio allows us to determine whether the debt-to-GDP ratio will stay constant or decrease under current economic conditions.

2.3.1.2 *The construction of debt indicators: Debt burden vs. repayment capacity*

A second possibility to assess a country's debt situation in practice is to look at debt indicators. This approach is based on the observation of indicators that provide an impression of a country's debt burden relative to its repayment capacity. These indicators are meant to reflect the relation between external debt service obligations and funds available to meet these obligations as is also done in equation (4), which defines debt sustainability. While a sustainability assessment according to the definition of equation (4) would require the trade balance to be projected, debt indicators rely on measures for actual economic developments. However, this simplification does not come without a price; since indicators compare future debt-service obligations with macroeconomic factors that reflect the current repayment capacity, they do not take into account that the macroeconomic situation of countries can change, i.e., that countries might grow or that their investment-savings balance might change over time. These aspects are particularly relevant when debt maturity periods are long.

Debt indicators take the following general form:

$$Debt\ indicator = \frac{Measure\ of\ debt}{Measure\ of\ repayment\ capacity}. \tag{12}$$

The higher the indicator value, the higher is a country's debt burden relative to its repayment capacity and the higher is the country's vulnerability to a situation of financial distress.

Some important aspects have to be taken into account when constructing and applying indicators, which provide reliable information about the relation between a country's debt and its payment capacity: (i) the most appropriate measures for a country's debt burden and (ii) the most appropriate measure for a country's capacity to service its debt have to be determined. (iii) Critical values—against which the actual values of the indicators are assessed—have to be established through an empirical analysis for each indicator. The remainder of this subsection addresses the first two issues when outlining the construction of sensible debt indicators. The determination of threshold values for the assessment of debt indicators will be discussed in the subsection 2.3.1.3.

With respect to the measurement of the debt burden that external debt puts on a country, the stock and the flow perspective are to be considered. From the stock perspective, the appropriate measure is the PV of the stock of gross external debt.[74] Gross debt is taken instead of net debt since gross debt is the debt aggregate that reflects the country's debt obligations. Though net debt is a useful analytical concept to assess a country's wealth, it adds complexity as well as uncertainty to the sustainability assessment. This is mainly due to the risk of default of a country's creditors. A prudent debt sustainability assessment is therefore based on gross debt while using data on net external debt as an additional source of information when analyzing a country's financial situation. Besides the total stock of debt, some subcategories of external debt can be important measures for specific aspects of a country's debt burden. Different characteristics of external debt, such as currency denomination, maturity, or the status of debtor,[75] i.e., whether the debtor is public or a private entity,[76] can be employed to reflect the structure of repayment requirements. The structure of external debt is, therefore, of major importance for the construction of sensible debt indicators. While the total stock of external debt is most appropriate to assess a country's solvency, indicators based on short-term debt can provide an impression of the country's liquidity situation. Foreign-currency-based indicators allow the need for international reserves and the country's vulnerability to exchange rate fluctuations to be assessed.

Taking a flow perspective, debt service payments are the appropriate measure for the funds needed per period to meet payment obligations.[77] Due to the agreed repayment schedule, e.g., agreed grace periods, debt service obligations can be volatile and might not always portray a realistic picture of the accumulated debt burden. Debt service payments can, however, be used to assess a country's ability to meet repayment requirements in a timely manner.

---

74 Gross debt is the sum of all debt liabilities to foreigners. Net debt is the equivalent to gross debt minus the sum of all debt assets.

75 For middle-income countries a clear delineation between private and public external debt on one hand and external and domestic public debt on the other exists. Many low-income countries have little private sector external debt and little domestic public debt. In these cases the distinction between private and public external debt is of less importance. Furthermore, private external debt is often either explicitly or implicitly publicly guaranteed and is, therefore, a contingent claim on the public sector (see IMF, 2003).

76 Occasionally, it has been argued that foreign indebtedness should not be concerned as long as the liabilities are private as compared to government sector driven. This notion is sometimes referred to as the Lawson Doctrine (see Reisen, 1998). Experience during the Asian crisis, however, suggests that such discrimination is to a large extent futile as private sector debt could be considered as liabilities of the government contingent on the outburst of a financial crisis.

77 See World Bank, IMF, BIS, and OECD (1988).

Both short-term debt and debt service payments as a measure for a country's debt burden focus on short-term considerations and, therefore, on liquidity issues. While short-term debt allows for a forward looking perspective, debt service payments are a more backward oriented measure. Short-term debt obligations equal the amount of short-term external debt, i.e., debt with a maturity of one year and less. Repayment of these obligations is required within the year ahead; the measure is, therefore, forward looking. By taking debt service payments as a measure for the short-term debt burden, the payments made over the past year are considered, which is a backward oriented approach.

Debt indicators can be based on every meaningful subcategory of the stock of external debt or debt service payments. It is important to relate the measure for the debt burden to a meaningful measure for the country's repayment capacity. The measure for the repayment capacity must be chosen in such a way that it corresponds to the characteristics of the measure of debt obligation.

Turning to measures of a country's repayment capacity, a country has to generate current account surpluses, i.e., generate positive net national savings, to meet debt obligations. The repayment capacity of a country is, therefore, reflected in economic variables that determine the country's ability to generate net national savings. In this context the overall production (GDP) is the total amount of income, which can be used for either consumption or savings. Savings net of investment equal net national savings and correspond to the current account balance. While GDP determines the country's capacity to generate savings, this does not automatically correspond to the capability to generate current account surpluses. High savings with low net exports might lead to a buildup of inventory, i.e., unplanned investment. Exports are a major factor determining the current account balance and—at least in the short run—they are only partly determined by national policies. A country's ability to sell goods and services abroad reflects the country's ability to generate external resources. Therefore, exports are employed as a measure for a country's debt repayment capacity. For middle-income countries, the repayment capacity is typically best captured by the size of the entire economy. In such cases the debt-to-GDP ratio provides the most meaningful debt indicator. In cases where a country primarily faces foreign-exchange constraints[78], the gross external debt-to-exports ratio would be the appropriate indicator.[79]

78 To service foreign currency debt, foreign currency funds must be available. These funds can be generated through exports, by capital imports, or through a decrease of foreign exchange reserves. The most commonly used variable to control for the availability of the required foreign exchange funds is exports—in some cases adjusted for required imports and reexports.

79 See IMF (2003).

External debt-to-GDP ratios and external debt-to-exports ratios are widely used in debt sustainability assessments.[80] A further source from which external debt can be serviced is the country's international reserve assets. Finally, the government can be seen as the ultimate instance in the repayment of a country's external debt. Government revenues reflect the public sector's capacity for payment and are, therefore, a further indicator of the country's repayment capacity. The fundamental issue when choosing an indicator for the payment capacity is to determine who pays for the debt or the debt service and how are the funds generated that can be used to pay for debt related obligations.

The export capacity, the stock of foreign reserve assets, and government revenues reflect both the country's short-term repayment capacity and its ability to repay its outstanding debt, i.e., to meet long-term obligations. In the case of lagging exports, the GDP can give an indication of the country's production and its export potential; a transformation of local into export-oriented production can only be achieved in the long run. The GDP, therefore, gives more of an indication of a country's long-term payment capacity. Table 10 gives an overview of the most relevant long- and short-term debt indicators. Each indicator provides information on a special aspect of the sustainability of a country's external debt.

A country might get into a situation with either multiple constraints or constraints in a specific area, e.g., a shortfall of the government's ability to repay debt or to jump in for the private sector in the event of a financial crisis. If the government has no external debt liabilities and the private sector is healthy and can, thus, be expected to meet its obligations, a single debt indicator based on government revenues would not provide a complete picture of the country's debt situation. It is therefore necessary to base the debt sustainability assessments on an analysis of the whole range of debt indicators.

Some caveats with respect to the information value of debt indicators are to be considered. (i) While debt creates a future burden on the country's economy, the economic variables used to assess the repayment capacity are backward looking. Changes in the economy's performance, competitiveness, or fiscal policy will lower the quality of an assessment based on past observations. (ii) External debt in many cases is dominated in foreign currency while national income and government revenues, which are employed as measures for the repayment capacity, are denominated in local currency. Therefore, fluctuations in the exchange rate cause fluctuations in the debt indicator even if neither the debt nor the income or revenue level has changed.[81] (iii) While the comparison of the PV of debt

80 See, e.g., Loser (2004) and IMF and IDA (2004).
81 IMF (2002a).

service obligation and the PV of future current account surpluses would provide a clear indication of debt sustainability, debt indicators as such do not provide this information.

Table 10: Most relevant debt indicators

Horizon and focus of assessment	Source payments	Debt indicator
Long-term sustainability: solvency	GDP	PV of debt / GDP
	Exports	PV of debt / exports
	Government revenues	PV of debt / government revenues
	International reserve assets	
Short-term sustainability: liquidity	International reserve assets	Short-term debt / reserve assets Debt service / reserve assets
	Exports	Short-term debt /exports Debt service / exports
	Government revenues	Short-term debt / government revenues Debt service / government revenues

A debt sustainability assessment can employ debt indicators in two ways: (i) it can be based on the analysis of the behavior of different indicators or (ii) it can compare the actual value of the indicator with some defined threshold that allows discriminating between supposedly sustainable and unsustainable debt levels. These thresholds are in general determined by correlating indicators with the actual occurrence of financial distress.[82] The most difficult judgment is to choose the appropriate threshold for assessing whether a country's current or projected debt burden is sustainable. This judgment needs to be substantiated by the experience of countries that suffered from debt-servicing problems with varying frequency and while having different levels of external debt. We discuss the determination of threshold values for the different indicators by drawing on the recent empirical literature, which has examined episodes of debt distress in low- and middle-income countries.

82 See Loser (2004).

2.3.1.3 *Determining critical threshold values for the assessment of debt indicators*

A straightforward approach to determine threshold values against which to assess debt indicators is to use past observations on indicator levels of countries that actually experienced financial distress. In recent years, numerous studies analyzed the relationship between debt indicators and the occurrence of financial distress.[83] These studies face two problems related to the determination of the thresholds themselves and to the application in the debt sustainability assessment of a given country or a given set of countries. First, an appropriate measure for financial distress needs to be defined. Different authors use diverse definitions for financial distress, e.g., the default on or the restructuring of external debt, the change in foreign reserve assets, or changes in the exchange rate. Depending on the definition, a country might be judged to be under distress or not. Second, another problem arises since the level of debt that is manageable for a country varies across countries with different characteristics. For example, Reinhart, Rogoff, and Savastano (2003) show that emerging economies are able to manage only smaller debt levels than advanced economies, and IMF and IDA (2004) find that the quality of the political and institutional environment has an impact on a country's debt management capacity. The empirical assessment of indicator thresholds should, therefore, be based on a group of homogenous countries.[84] Furthermore, thresholds derived from an empirical analysis of countries that share common characteristics should be applied to assess the debt sustainability of countries with the same or at least similar characteristics.

Since empirical thresholds can only be determined by analyzing countries that actually experienced a situation of financial distress in the past, any possible peer group is by definition limited to such countries.[85] It is, therefore, difficult to use debt indicators to assess the debt sustainability of countries that have themselves not yet experienced any financial distress and that do not share the relevant characteristics of other countries that experienced financial distress.

A review of the empirical literature on debt sustainability and debt indicators reveals that most of the research focuses on analyzing the explanatory power of different debt indicators and further macroeconomic and policy variables for financial distress.[86] A translation of the results from such regression analysis

---

83 See, IMF and IDA (2004).

84 See, for example, IMF (2000a).

85 IMF and IDA (2004).

86 See for example McFadden, Eckhaus, Feder, Hajivassiliou, and O'Connell (1985), Cohen (1996), and Detragiache and Spilimbergo (2001).

into thresholds values for debt indicators can only be done by assuming a specific distress probability. Since the choice of a specific probability is arbitrary, most researchers do not take this step but limit themselves to the assessment of the original regression results. For some practical purposes—especially in the light of policy discussions—it is, however, of interest to determine such threshold values. Kraay and Nehru (2004) (World Bank officials) and IMF and IDA (2004) are among the few that derive debt indicator thresholds. Kraay and Nehru (2004) use three different indicators for financial distress, i.e., significant arrears on external debt, Paris Club rescheduling, and nonconcessional IMF lending in support of the BOP to estimate a probit regression. They include different debt indicators, i.e., debt-to-exports, debt service-to-exports, debt service-to-government revenues, and debt service-to-reserve assets, as well as further macroeconomic indicators, and find that the debt burden, the quality of policies and institutions,[87] and economic shocks explain a substantial portion of incidences of financial distress. The results are robust to a variety of alternative specifications and the core specifications reveal substantial out-of-sample predictive power—when including debt indicators in their model, Kraay and Nehru are able to predict between 70 percent and 90 percent of all distress events correctly.[88] IMF and IDA (2004) closely relate to the work of Kraay and Nehru but include some modifications, i.e., debt distress is defined as the occurrence of significant arrears to official creditors. Furthermore, a smaller country sample and a different database are employed in the empirical analysis. The results of the analysis, however, broadly corroborate the findings of Kraay and Nehru (2004). Thresholds for the most relevant solvency indicators derived from the estimations of the two analyses are given in Table 11.

While the ranges given by Kraay and Nehru (2004) correspond to a 25 percent distress probability, the results of the IMF and the World Bank refer to a distress probability of 20 percent. The lower and the upper values correspond to the threshold for countries in the 25 and 75 percentile of the World Bank's CPIA, respectively. The considerable difference between the lower and the upper value point to the importance of the political and institutional environment for a country's debt management capacity.

87 Kraay and Nehru (2004) include the World Bank's Country Policy and Institutional Assessment (CPIA) rating to measure the quality of the political and institutional environment.

88 False alarms occurred in 13 percent to 55 percent of all cases.

Table 11: Empirically determined ranges for threshold values of debt indicators

	Kraay and Nehru (2004) 1)	IMF and IDA (2004) 2)
PV of debt / GDP	21 - 49%	26 - 58%
PV of debt / exports	79 - 300%	83 - 276%
PV of debt / revenues	142 – 235%	138 - 264%

1) Values correspond to a probability of distress of 25 percent.
2) Values correspond to a probability of distress of 20 percent.
Source: IMF and IDA (2004).

IMF and IDA (2004) translate the indicator ranges given in Table 11 as well as results for further debt indicators into indicator thresholds for three country groups, i.e., countries with poor, medium, and strong political and institutional environment (see Table 12). According to these results countries with a strong political and institutional environment are able to manage debt levels that lead to debt indicators two times higher than those manageable for countries with a poor political and institutional environment.

Table 12: Debt indicator threshold values by country characteristics 1)

	Quality of the political and institutional environment		
	Poor	Medium	Strong
PV of debt / GDP	30	45	60
PV of debt / exports	100	200	300
PV of debt / revenues	150	200	250
Debt service / exports	15	25	35
Debt service / government revenues	20	30	40

1) Threshold values correspond to a probability of distress of 20 percent.
Source: IMF and IDA (2004).

Focusing on financial market access instead of debt sustainability—thus considering financial distress only indirectly—Reinhart, Rogoff, and Savastano (2003) assess the impact of external debt on the Institutional Investor Rating (IIR).[89] In their analysis they use the IIR as the dependent variable and external debt-to-GDP ratio as well as time dummies as independent variables in a pooled fixed effects least square regression. Looking for an assessment of debt

89 The IIR is a rating that provides an indicator for country risk. It is published by the Institutional Investor.

sustainability, they divide their country sample into three groups depending on the IIR—the countries with the highest IIR are comprised in Club A and those with the lowest IIR in Club C —and further distinguish Club B countries by their external debt-to-GDP ratio. The results are translated into a continuum reflecting the countries' access to the capital market. Club A countries have continuous access to the capital market and Club C countries do not have capital market access at all (see Figure 12).[90]

Figure 12: Debtors clubs, debt intolerance, and financial market access

Club A	Club B				Club C
IIR $\geq$ 67.7	24.2 < IIR < 67.7				IIR $\leq$ 24.2
	Region I	Region II	Region III	Region IV	
	45.9 $\leq$ IIR < 67.7	45.9 $\leq$ IIR < 67.7	24.2 < IIR < 45.9	24.2 < IIR < 45.9	
	ext. debt / GDP < 35	ext. debt / GDP $\geq$ 35	ext. debt / GDP < 35	ext. debt / GDP $\geq$ 35	
	Least debt intolerant	Quasi-debt intolerant	Quasi-debt intolerant	Most debt intolerant	
Continuous access to capital markets (least debt intolerant)	←			→	No access to capital markets (most debt intolerant)

Source: Reinhart, Rogoff, and Savastano (2003), p. 27.

As discussed above, the empirical assessment of sustainability thresholds can only be based on countries that experienced financial distress in the past. While Kraay and Nehru (2004) and IMF and IDA (2004), as well as many other studies on debt sustainability, focus on low-income countries—in a few cases also middle-income countries—Reinhart, Rogoff, and Savastano (2003) include countries of all different states of development in their analysis. In the analysis of Reinhart, Rogoff, and Savastano debt indicators are, however, only applied to differentiate between the degree of capital market access the country falls into given a specific rang of the IIP rating, which is not an indicator-based debt sustainability assessment.

Though evidence exists that debt indicators provide some information on possible debt crises, due to the limited information on the economic performance of a country included in debt indicators, debt indicators have to be interpreted

90 Reinhart, Rogoff, Savastano (2003) include the Czech Republic, Hungary, and Poland in their sample. All three CEECs are part of Club B.

cautiously.[91] Indicators work with variable lags and do not provide reliable and consistent signals in all cases. A debt sustainability assessment, therefore, needs to be based on several indicators and, in addition to debt indicators, further information, e.g., macroeconomic indicators or sovereign credit ratings, can add to a rounded assessment of a country's financial vulnerability.

2.3.2 Assessing the CEECs' external debt sustainability

2.3.2.1 The CEECs' potential for debt stabilization

To assess the external debt sustainability of the CEECs we apply some of the concepts discussed above. While it would be most sensible to take a forward looking approach and to assess whether the PV of the CEECs' external debt exceeds the present value of their current account surpluses, no reliable projections of future current account developments are available. We therefore mainly rely on those approaches to sustainability assessments that are based on current data, namely on a debt-indicator-based assessment.

Before turning to debt indicators, we analyze the debt sustainability of the CEECs by assessing under which circumstances the debt-to-GDP ratio of the countries would stabilize. We determine the current account balance-FDI balance—current account balance plus FDI inflows—that would be required to keep the debt-to-GDP ratio constant. If the actual current account-FDI balance is lower (higher) than the calculated value, the debt-to-GDP ratio decreases (increases). The calculation is based on an adjusted version of the stability condition formulated in equation (10). Since the CEECs in the past financed their current account deficits at least partly through FDI inflows, we give up the assumption of a pure debt financing of the deficits (see footnote 70). Furthermore, we take into account that in addition to the trade account deficit, repatriated income of foreign investors, which is not reflected in interest payments, needs to be financed through capital inflows. The available data, however, do not allow to distinguish between income flows due to interest payments and income flows caused by the repatriation of the income of foreign investors. The current account balance of most of the CEECs is dominated by the trade account and the two countries for which the income account plays a major role—the Czech Republic and Hungary—face high-income balance deficits that are mainly due to the repatriation of foreign investors' income. Therefore, it seems reasonable to neglect interest payments recorded in the income balance and to consider the overall

91 See Loser (2004).

current account balance (*CA*) as the relevant measure for the need of external financing.[92] The calculation is thus based on the stability condition

$$\frac{(i-g)}{(1+g)}d_t \leq ca_{t+1} + fdi_{t+1}, \tag{13}$$

where fdi_{t+1} is the ratio of FDI inflows in period t to GDP of the same period. If we define the current account-FDI balance (bal_{t+1}) as the net resources available to finance interest payments, i.e., the sum of the current account balance and FDI inflows ($ca_{t+1} + fdi_{t+1}$), the condition becomes

$$\frac{(i-g)}{(1+g)}d_t \leq bal_{t+1}. \tag{14}$$

To calculate the minimum level of the current account-FDI balance that would be required to keep the debt-to-GDP ratio constant, assumptions regarding the interest rate (i), the growth rate (g), and the debt ratio (d) have to be made. For the growth rate we employ the country-specific real GDP growth rate of 2004 and the four-year average rate of 2001 through 2004, alternatively. As an interest rate we take the latest available twelve-month average of long-term government bond rates. We consider end-2004 actual gross debt-to-GDP ratios.

A calculation based on the assumptions given above is conservative in the sense that the calculated minimum level of the current account-FDI balance is probably too low. This is mainly due to two factors: (i) The CEECs are still in the catching-up process. Therefore, their economies currently grow at higher rates than those of developed economies. At some point—once convergence occurs—their growth rates will decline to the level of developed countries' rates.[93] Regarding a medium-term outlook, the Vienna Institute for International Economic Studies (2005) expected average growth rates of the CEECs to come out at below 4 percent in 2005 and not to accelerate too much in 2006. The actual growth rates that we use for the calculations are, therefore, above long-term potential growth

---

92 Current transfers are also recorded in the current account. Transfers are counter entries for transactions without quid pro quo. A positive transfer balance can counterbalance a deficit in the trade account or the income account. Current transfer balances of the CEECs show surpluses (see country tables in the chapter's appendix) that are small compared to most countries' trade account deficits. In our analysis we take the overall current account balance into account and, thus, reflect that current transfers partly cover trade account or income account deficits.

93 The euro area, for example, grew at 1.9 percent in 2004 and at 1.2 percent on average between 2001 and 2004.

rates and even above medium-term expectations. (ii) The interest rate we employ is equivalent to the risk-free country-specific interest rate, which is lower than the average interest rate foreign creditors request especially from private sector debtors. As stated in equation (11), the minimum level of the current account-FDI balance depends negatively on the growth rate and positively on the interest rate. Assuming relatively high growth rates and relatively low interest rates, therefore, causes the required minimum balance to be rather too small than too large for any given debt-to GDP ratio. We, nevertheless, rely on these assumptions since they allow us to base the calculations on consistent and observable data without requiring any projections, which would again be based on assumptions and thus add extra uncertainty to the analysis.

Table 13: Debt stabilizing current account deficit

	Long-term interest rate (*i*) 2004/2005	GDP growth rate (*g*) 2004	GDP growth rate (*g*) 2001-2004	Debt-to-GDP ratio (*d*) 2004	Stabilizing balance 2004	Actual balance 2004	Surplus(+) / Gap(-) 2004	Stabilizing balance 2001-2004	Actual balance 2001-2004	Surplus(+) / Gap(-) 2001-2004
	(a)	(b)	(c)	(d)	**(e)**	(f)	**(g)**	**(h)**	(i)	**(j)**
Czech Republic	4.0%	4.4%	2.9%	42%	**-0.2%**	-1.5%	**-1.3%**	**0.4%**	0.9%	**+0.5%**
Estonia	4.1%	7.8%	7.1%	91%	**-3.1%**	-6.6%	**-3.5%**	**-2.5%**	-4.9%	**-2.4%**
Hungary	7.2%	4.2%	3.6%	75%	**2.1%**	-5.2%	**-7.3%**	**2.6%**	-3.9%	**-6.5%**
Latvia	4.2%	8.5%	7.6%	97%	**-3.8%**	-8.3%	**-4.5%**	**-3.0%**	-6.2%	**-3.1%**
Lithuania	4.0%	6.7%	7.4%	47%	**-1.2%**	-4.9%	**-3.7%**	**-1.5%**	-3.1%	**-1.6%**
Poland	5.9%	5.4%	2.9%	51% 1)	**0.2%**	0.6%	**+0.4%**	**1.5%**	0.0%	**-1.5%**
Slovak Republic	4.1%	5.5%	4.6%	57% 1)	**-0.8%**	-0.4%	**+0.4%**	**-0.3%**	2.1%	**+2.4%**
Slovenia	4.1%	4.6%	3.3%	59% 2)	**-0.3%**	-0.8%	**-0.5%**	**0.5%**	2.0%	**+1.5%**

1) Based on latest available data: 2003
2) Data taken from IMF (2005f).
Source: ECB (2005a), IMF (2005h), and own calculations.

The debt stabilizing current account-FDI balances are given in columns (e) and (h) of Table 13. This calculated value for the stabilizing balance reflects a minimum level of the current account-FDI balance that is in line with a non-increasing debt-to-GDP ratio.[94] Due to the assumptions on which the calculation is based, the value is too low rather than too high; this means the current account balance required at a given level of FDI inflows is rather underestimated.

To assess the current external balance of the CEECs, we compare the calculated current account-FDI balance with the actual balance that prevailed in 2004 and the average of the actual balance of 2001 through 2004, respectively. Columns (g) and (j) of Table 13 show the difference of the calculated and the actual balance, i.e., a surplus or a gap. As the results show, despite Poland and the Slovak Republic, all CEECs in 2004 experienced a gap. In the case of Estonia, Hungary, Latvia, and Lithuania the size of the gap surpassed 3 percent of GDP. More specifically, Hungary, in 2004, would have had to lower its current account deficit or to increase FDI inflows by 7.3 percent of GDP in order to stabilize its debt-to-GDP ratio. Since the calculated minimum balance levels are rather on the low side, the reduction in the current account deficit or the extra FDI flows required to achieve a stable debt-to-GDP ratio would be rather higher than the values given in columns (e) and (j), respectively. Overall, due to the recent decrease in FDI inflows, prevailing gaps are lower when considering the average of 2001 through 2004 instead of 2004 data only.[95] Going forward, the prevailing gaps between debt stabilizing current account-FDI balances and actual current account-FDI balances can be expected to increase further, since FDI inflows will most likely decrease further once the privatization of public assets is finalized.

2.3.2.2 Debt indicator for the CEECs

Turning to the indicator-based approach, we assess the external debt sustainability by applying the major solvency and liquidity oriented debt indicators, i.e., gross debt to GDP, gross debt to exports, gross debt to government revenues, debt to reserve assets, short-term debt to exports, short-term debt-to-government revenues, short-term debt-to-reserve assets, and debt service to reserve assets.

While the PV of debt is the preferable measure for a country's debt burden, the difference between PV and face value is of minor importance for the debt of the CEECs, which—with the exception of Poland, which agreed to a debt

94 A negative value for the minimum current account-FDI balance indicates that the debt stabilizing condition as given in equation (14) is fulfilled even if the current account deficit is not fully covered by FDI inflows.

95 While multiple-year averages take out some of the volatility of the data, they might hide the effects of recent trends. It is therefore sensible to look at both multiperiod averages and the most recent period.

restructuring with the Paris Club in 1991[96]—did not receive substantial concessional lending.[97] Figure 13 shows that, due to the minor role played by concessional debt in the CEECs, no major differences exist between the PV and the face value of gross debt. Since data on the PV of the CEECs' external debt are not available, our debt sustainability assessment will be based on the face value of the countries' gross external debt.

As discussed before, contingent claims are an important factor in the assessment of the financial vulnerability of the public sector. They become effective if private sector debtors are no longer able to repay their debt and the government is either committed to or decides to take over existing obligations from the private sector. As long as the analysis concentrates on the assessment of the sustainability of a country's external debt, it is, however, irrelevant whether debt services have to be paid by the private or the public sector. Contingent claims are, therefore, not considered in the analysis.

Figure 13: Face value and PV of the stock of gross external debt of the CEECs
Total external debt in 2002 (current USD) [1)]

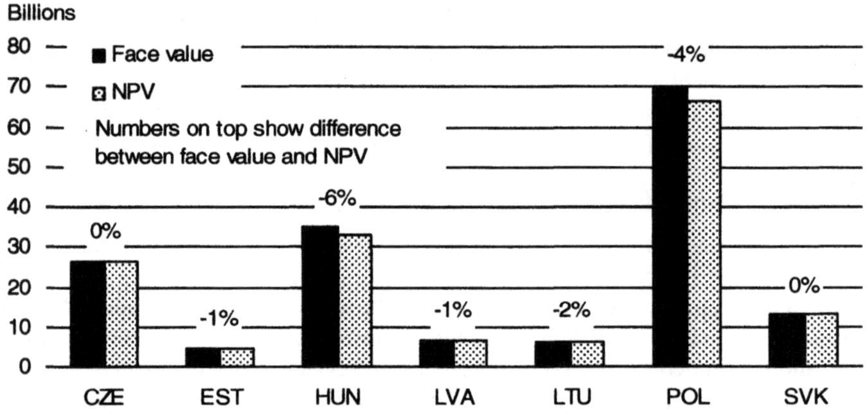

1) The graph reflects the latest available data. Data for Slovenia are not available.
Source: World Bank (2004b) and own calculations.

---

96 From 1993 through 1997 Poland on average received official flows (including grants) of USD 1,677 million per year. From 1997 through 2001 Poland on average repaid USD 473 million of official loans per year. (World Bank, 2000, 2004a)

97 Over the past ten years all CEECs received loans from the International Bank for Reconstruction and Development (IBRD, World Bank Group).

It would be useful not only to analyze the external debt sustainability for a country as a whole but also for different sectors or categories of economic activity within the economy—distinguishing between public and private external debt and separately looking at trade-related external debt—and to relate the different sector or activity specific external debt to indicators for the repayment capacity of the relevant debtors. However, no comprehensive data set is available that would allow such an analysis to be performed for the CEECs. The following assessment for the CEECs therefore concentrates on assessing external debt sustainability on the country level. Information on the split-up of external debt and an assessment of this information is considered whenever available.

As discussed above, debt indicators as such do not allow a country's financial vulnerability to be assessed. To put the calculated debt indicators into perspective, a set of sensible threshold values needs to be determined. Subsection 2.3.1.3 above discusses the empirical assessment of such thresholds and the difficulties related to their application. As mentioned, an empirical analysis of the link between certain threshold values and financial distress can only be done for countries that experienced financial distress. The characteristics of a reference group determined by this selection criterion might not exactly reflect the characteristics of the country or region under examination. Since the CEECs—with the exception of Poland—did not experience incidences that could be seen as financial distress, it is not possible to determine debt indicator thresholds in an empirical analysis of the CEECs. Therefore, a debt sustainability analysis of the CEECs has to be based on thresholds determined through an empirical analysis of a sample of countries that are mostly unrelated to the CEECs.

We start our debt sustainability assessment by applying the thresholds determined by IMF and IDA (2004) and Kraay and Nehru (2004). The assessment is enhanced by taking into account further variables, i.e., indicators for the institutional and political environment, and so forth. Since the CEECs all received the maximum rating of 5 points in the recent World Bank's CPIA, the relevant thresholds for the countries under examination are those calculated for the countries of the upper percentile of the rating, i.e., countries with a strong political and institutional environment (see Table 12).

As a basis for our assessment we determine the value for the different debt indicators on an annual basis for 1998 through 2004.[98] Values for all indicators

98 The starting point has been selected due to data availability considerations. Data sources and definitions are described in the Appendix to Chapter 2. For some countries, e.g., Poland, the Slovak Republic, and Slovenia, recent data on external debt are not yet available. Whenever possible we fill data gaps by using additional sources besides our data framework.

and the applied threshold values are given in country tables in the Appendix to Chapter 2. Table 14 provides a summary of the CEECs' performance with respect to different debt indicators for 2004. The simple discrimination between indicator levels below the respective threshold value[99] and indicator levels surpassing the critical hurdle value—as it is done in Table 14—reveals a relatively positive picture of the CEECs' debt sustainability; only for Latvia and Lithuania do more than two indicator(s) breach the critical level in 2004.

Table 14: CEECs debt indicators' performance compared to empirical thresholds [1)]

	CZE	EST	HUN	LAV	LTU	POL [2)]	SVK	SVN
Gross debt to GDP	+	-	-	-	+	+	+ [1)]	+
Gross debt to exports	+	+	+	+	+	+	+ [1)]	+
Gross debt to government revenues	+	+	+	-	+	+	+ [1)]	+ [3)]
Debt service to exports	+	+	+	-	-	+	+	+
Debt service to government revenues	-	+	+	-	-	+	+	+
Debt service to reserve assets	+	+	+	-	-	+	+ [2)]	+ [3)]
Short-term debt to reserve assets	+	-	-	+	-	+	+	+ [3)]

1) "-" ("+") means that a country breached (did not breach) the threshold level for the respective debt indicator.
2) Based on latest available data: 2003
3) Based on latest available data: 2002.

Since the results as presented in Table 14 neither provide information on how close the actual indicator levels are to the threshold levels nor provide information on trends in the development of the different debt indicators over time, a more detailed look at the different indicators, their level relative to the employed threshold and to the other countries', and their evolution over time is required.

Panels (a) through (c) in Figure 14 show the development of the stock of gross external debt relative to different measures of the repayment capacity over the past seven years. The evolution of the debt-to GDP ratios reveals that the debt of Latvia, Estonia, and Hungary grew significantly faster than their respective GDPs. While the debt-to-GDP ratios of Latvia and Estonia increased constantly quickly over the observation period, in the case of Hungary the ratio remained relatively stable until 2002 before increasing notably for the next two years. The

99 As mentioned above, we consider the threshold values estimated by IMF and IDA (2004) for countries with strong political and institutional environments.

indicator surpassed the 60 percent threshold level notably for all three countries. Debt-to-GDP ratios increased slowly for all other CEECs and remained below critical levels.

The development of debt-to-export ratios as presented in panel (b) shows that the indicator values remain well below the critical level of 300 percent. While the indicator remained stable below or slightly above 100 percent, the increase in Latvia's debt stock is reflected in the trend of the country's indicator and Poland's relatively low export orientation (see export-to-GDP ratio in the country tables in the chapter's appendix) leads to an indicator level of around 150 percent. The generally low level of the debt-to-export ratio reflects the CEECs' high degree of integration into the world market—also reflected in export-to-GDP ratios of between 39 percent (Poland) and 81 percent (Estonia). High exports from Estonia led to a relatively low indicator value despite the country's high debt burden.

It can be argued that the debt-to-government revenue ratio might be less relevant for the assessment of the CEECs' external sustainability. First, the CEECs' external debt comes through the private sector and public sector. Compared to other emerging economies, the private portion of external debt is relatively high and the repayment capacity measured by government revenues is primarily relevant for public debt. Second, the estimation of critical thresholds for the debt-to-government revenue ratio have been based on a country sample including developing countries and emerging economies that have a small public sector relative to developed countries. The size of the CEECs' government sector is more comparable to that of developed countries than to that of developing countries or other emerging economies.[100] The indicator calculated for a CEEC is therefore consistently lower than the indicator values one would expect for a developing country. Looking at debt-to-government revenue ratios (see panel (c)) reveals a somewhat similar picture to the one drawn by the debt-to-GDP ratio. However, only Latvia's indicator value breaches the critical level while Estonia's indicator increased over time without yet surpassing the threshold.

Figure 15 shows the development of the CEECs' debt service ratios over the observation period. The strong increase in Latvia's external debt is also reflected in the development of short-term indicators. Panel (a) of Figure 15 displays the development of debt-service-to-export ratios. Indicator values have been relatively stable and below the critical threshold for Estonia, Poland, the Slovak Republic, and Slovenia. Debt service payments in relation to exports decreased constantly and fell below critical levels in the Czech Republic and

100 See Table A 2-2 in the appendix.

Hungary. Latvia and Lithuania are the only countries with continuously increasing indicator values that surpassed the threshold level of 35 percent in 2001. While Latvia's high debt-service-to-export ratio reflects the country's high overall debt burden, Lithuania faced the second lowest debt-to-GDP ratio but the highest debt-service-to-exports ratio.

Figure 14: Development of gross debt ratios

(a) Debt-to-GDP ratio

(b) Debt-to-export ratio

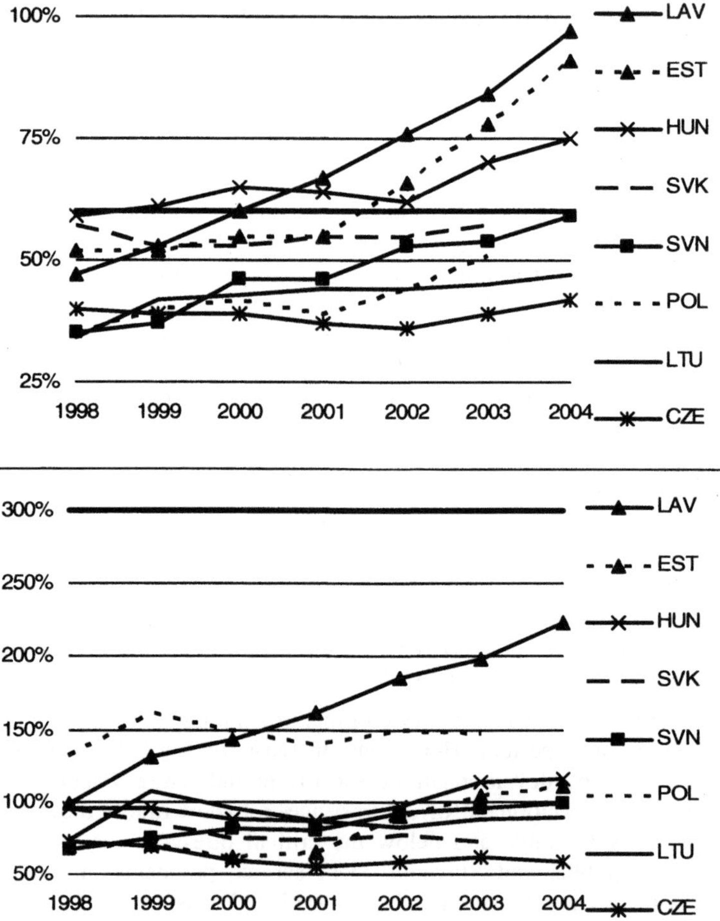

Figure 14: Development of gross debt ratios (concluded)

(c) Debt-to-government revenue ratio

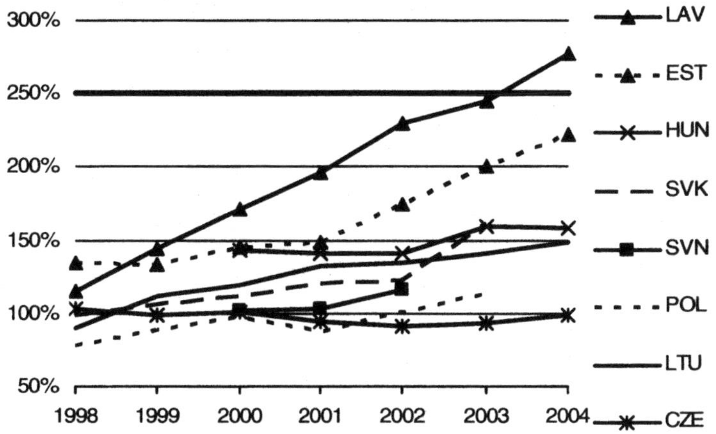

Source: ECB (2005a), IMF (2005a), IMF (2005d), and own calculations.

Figure 15: Development of debt service ratios

(a) Debt-service-to-export ratio

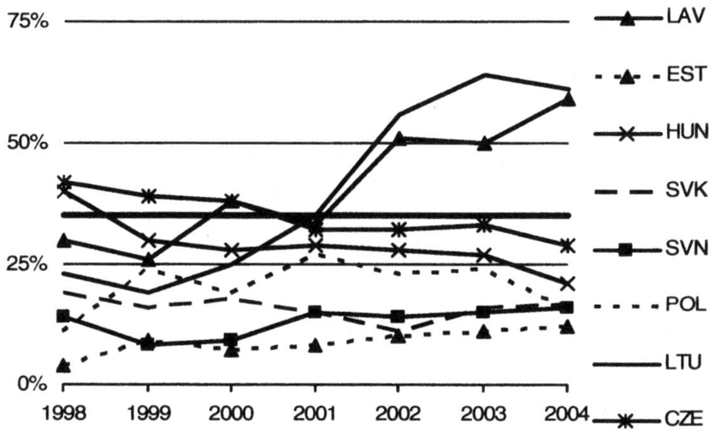

Figure 15: Development of debt service ratios (concluded)

(b) Debt-service-to-government revenue ratio

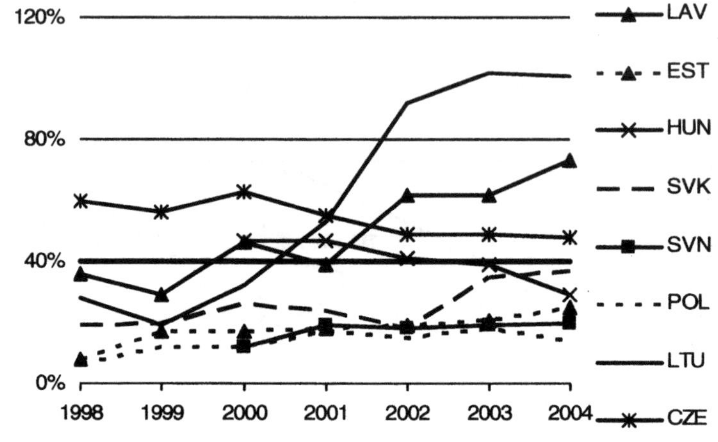

(c) Debt-service-to-reserve assets ratio

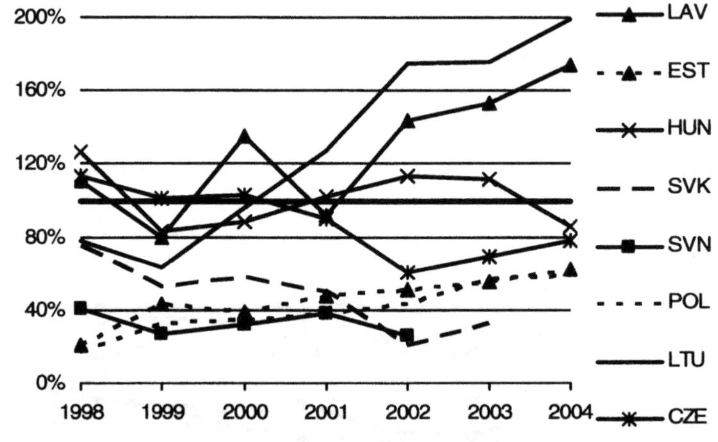

Source: ECB (2005a), IMF (2005d), IMF (2005h), and own calculations.

The high burden of Lithuania's debt service payments is also reflected in the debt-service-to-government revenue ratio (panel (b)) and the debt-service-to-reserve assets ratio (panel (c)). Together with Lithuania, Latvia records increasing values for both indicators and the indicators of both countries are well above the respective threshold levels. The other six CEECs experience stable or declining values for the government revenue and the reserve-based short-term indicator. In 2004 reserve assets more than covered the debt service obligations of the Czech Republic, Estonia, Hungary, Poland, the Slovak Republic, and Slovenia.

At first glance it can be argued that debt service indicators based on exports and government revenues for the CEECs are closer to critical levels than debt-stock-based indicators. It can therefore be inferred that the level of the countries' debt service obligations is high relative to their stock of external debt. This reflects the recent inflow of short-term financing and the resulting increase in short-term debt liabilities.[101] The maturity structure of external debt shown in Figure 16 reveals the high dependence of some of the CEECs on short-term financing. While Hungary's and Poland's external debt is more long term, over 50 percent of Latvia's external debt is financed short term.

Figure 16: Maturity structure of external debt as of 2003

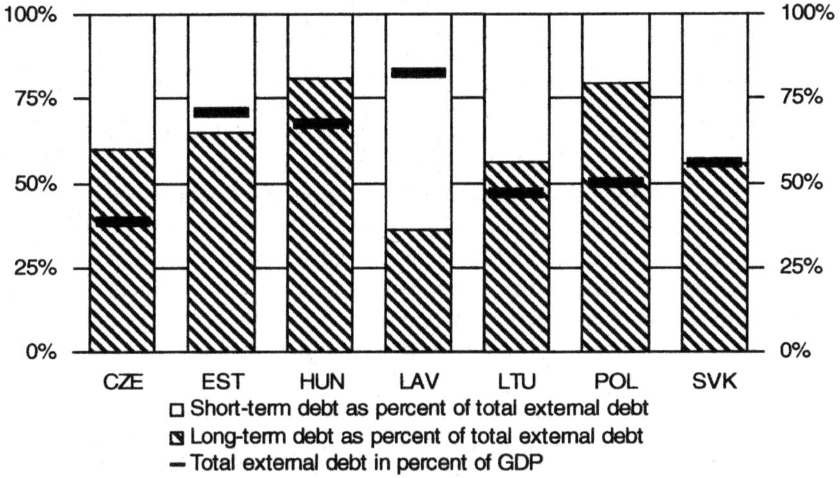

Source: ECB (2005a), IMF (2005d), World Bank (2005d), and own calculations.

Latvia, more than any other CEEC, financed its external debt through short-term capital inflows. A significant fraction of this short-term debt is, how-

101 Short-term external debt is defined as debt that has an original maturity of one year or less; accordingly, long-term external debt is defined as debt that has an original or extended maturity of more than a year.

ever, due to nonresident deposits (over 30 percent of all external liabilities, see country table (d) in the appendix), which are reinvested abroad.[102] Considering gross debt instead of net debt and disregarding the use of the financial inflows hides these facts and leads to the impression that the country faces a significant risk of becoming illiquid. The extent of this effect is, however, not assessable.

Overall, indicators based on external debt stocks suggest some weaknesses in the solvency especially for Estonia and Latvia and to a lesser extend also for Hungary. More short-term-oriented indicators based on debt service payments reveal that besides Latvia, Lithuania might be threatened by liquidity problems while Estonia—with respect to liquidity—seems to be on relatively safe ground.

The assessment of a country's debt sustainability based on debt indicators has some limitations. The analysis is mostly based on information on current and past economic data while debt sustainability is determined by future debt service obligation and a country's future repayment capacity. It is important not only to look at the actual level of such indicators, i.e., a snapshot of the external debt situation, but also to assess the indicators' development over time, which allows detecting possible trends. The aforementioned problems related to an indicator-based sustainability analysis also underline that a purely mechanical examination based on the chosen indicators will provide only a partial picture of a country's vulnerability. If debt indicators reveal possible threats to a country's external sustainability, additional information on other economic fundamentals—including the soundness of the financial system—as well as economic and political developments needs to be considered to obtain a realistic view on the overall vulnerability to economic shocks. In our analysis we focus on the indicator-based and debt-stability-oriented assessment of external debt. We detect possible vulnerabilities of the CEECs due to external debt but we do not assess whether other macroeconomic factors and the political and institutional environment are strong enough to prevent the vulnerabilities from materializing.

The results of the debt-indicator and debt-stabilization-based approaches as well as the insights from the discussion on the CEECs' current account and the financial account are summarized in the following section, which brings the different aspects of external sustainability together and provides an indication for the CEECs' overall external sustainability.

102 For a discussion of this issue see Beguna (2002) or Burges, Fabrizio, and Xiao (2003).

2.4 Assessment of the CEECs' overall external sustainability

Taking into account all three dimensions of the external sector suggests that the current external situation of the CEECs can be considered to be broadly sustainable in most countries. According to the available data on developments for the past several years, Slovenia does not face a risk of running into an unsustainable external balance situation in the foreseeable future. The country's current account has been close to balance or in surplus and well in line with estimated equilibrium levels and FDI flows on average more than covered prevailing deficits over the past four years. The Slovak debt indicators, solvency- as well as liquidity-related indicators, are well below critical levels and remained on a stable level over the past four years.

The Slovak Republic faces a relatively high level of external debt and current account deficits have been substantial and above equilibrium levels in the past. The current account deficits, however, decreased sharply in 2003 and remained below estimated equilibrium levels since then. Furthermore, debt ratios were stable or declined since 1998. High export rates and substantial foreign reserves lead to debt stock and debt service indicators well below critical thresholds. If the external balance continues to develop along the trend of recent years, the Slovak Republic can be expected to maintain external sustainability despite the relatively high level of external debt.

Poland's current account deficit decreased over recent years and remained within equilibrium ranges since 2001. Debt indicators reflect Poland's relatively high debt burden. After observing decreasing indicator levels until the early 2000s, indicators increased again. Over the observation period, however, no indicator surpassed a critical level. Poland's situation is probably best characterized as stable but vulnerable to adverse future developments especially in the current account deficit.

The Czech Republic's current account deficit, however, increased in the past four years and exceeded equilibrium levels. Debt indicators, however, suggest that the country carries a stable and relatively low external debt burden, partly reflecting strong inflows of non-debt-generating means of financing. According to short-term indicators, i.e., liquidity-oriented indicators, the Czech Republic reveals some weaknesses. The export and reserve asset-related indicators decreased over the observation period and fell below their respective threshold levels in the beginning of the 2000s. Debt service obligations are, however, still critically high in relation to government revenues. Whether this factor should be a matter of concern depends on the participation of the public sector in external debt. If external debt is mostly held against the private sector, and the private sector—for example through exports—can service its debt obligations, high government revenue based debt ratios should not matter for the country's external sustainability.

Lithuania's current account deficit has breached equilibrium levels since the beginning of the observation period. After financing its 2000 and 2001 current account deficit almost entirely with FDI inflows, over the past two years—mainly due to a drop in FDI inflows—the deficit exceeded FDI inflows by more than 5 percent of GDP. While the stock of external debt does not exceed critical levels, debt service indicators increased over time and by 2004 surpassed threshold values by about 100 percent. While the country might not run the risk of becoming insolvent, its liquidity seems to be vulnerable. Investors—due to observing short-term obligations that exceed short-term repayment capacity—could question the country's capacity to service scheduled debt payments. In this case short-term capital inflows that financed the current account deficit in recent years might cease and the country becomes incapable of covering its short-term financing needs; i.e., it becomes illiquid. While Lithuania's external sustainability might not be at acute risk, the development of short-term debt indicators and of the current account should be monitored closely to detect an aggravation of the external sustainability early.

Estonia, Hungary, and Latvia are probably the CEECs with the highest risk of financial distress. Hungary's stock of external debt over the past years grew notably faster than its economy. Growth of local production (GDP) as well as of the export sector did not manage to hold up with the fast buildup of external debt. The debt-to-GDP ratio increased by more than 5 percent in 2003 and 2004 and has breached critical levels since 1999. In contrast to debt stock indictors, short-term debt indicators improved in recent years. Debt service ratios declined and after recording several years of high or excessive debt-service-to-reserve asset ratios, in 2004 the indicator fell again below critical levels; i.e., reserve assets were high enough to cover debt service obligations. Hungary's major problem is the high stock of external debt, but the current account deficits are also high—between 7 and 8 percent of GDP in 2002 through 2004—and in 2004 they exceeded the range of estimated equilibrium levels. The fast increase in external debt is caused by the financing of the deficit, which relies heavily on debt generating portfolio inflows; the difference between current account deficit and FDI inflows in 2004 exceeded 5 percent of GDP. In 2004 the current account-FDI balance (current account balance plus FDI inflows) fell short of the level that would be in line with a stabilization of the debt-to-GDP ratio by 7.3 percent of GDP. While the debt-indicator-based analysis of Hungary's external balance suggests that the country's liquidity does not pose reasons for major concern, the level external debt is substantial. The development of current account deficits and the structure of the capital inflows that are needed to finance the deficit have to be monitored.

Estonia and Latvia face both a high and increasing stock of external debt and an excessive current account—reaching levels of above 12 percent of GDP in 2004. In both countries the current account deficit in 2004 surpassed equilibrium levels by about 3 percent of GDP. Furthermore, current account deficits exceeded FDI inflows by more than 6.6 and 8.3 percent of GDP in Estonia and Latvia, respectively. To stabilize debt-to-GDP ratios a minimum current account-FDI balance of about -3 and -4 percent, respectively, would be required. The indicator-based assessment of debt sustainability reflects that the stock of external debt of both countries, over the past years, grew more rapidly than their GDP; as a consequence debt-to-GDP ratios surpassed critical thresholds. While short-term debt indicators suggest that Estonia is not threatened by liquidity risks, Latvia's debt service obligations surpass reserve assets by more than 70 percent and debt-service-to-export as well as debt-service-to-government-revenue ratios over the past several years breached critical levels notably. Latvia's debt indicators are affected by the high stock of nonresident deposits, which are reinvested abroad. The exact extent of the impact of these financial flows that are more led through the country than stuck in the country is not observable. Therefore, we conclude that, according to the data, external sustainability might be at risk in Estonia and Latvia. As a consequence the developments in the external balance of these countries should be monitored closely and both countries should seek policy measures that counter a further deterioration of their external sustainability.

Taking into account the negative effects a financial crisis would have on affected countries, the threat of a regional spread of a crisis, and possible effects on the former EU countries, a continuous monitoring of the external sustainability of the CEECs is an important aspect for the process of European integration. While the current external balance of most of the CEECs seems to be in reasonably safe ranges, some countries, especially Estonia, Hungary, and Latvia, face high levels of external debt and excessive current account deficits, which could lead to a situation of financial distress. Close monitoring and appropriate countermeasures, e.g., restrictive fiscal policies, will be necessary to relax the situation especially in these three countries.

Due to the effects of the catching-up process and the related consumption smoothing equilibrium, current account levels for the CEECs are relatively high. To finance these deficits without risking an unsustainable debt situation, the CEECs need to attract long-term equity capital, i.e., FDI inflows. The countries are, therefore, interested in implementing policy measures that make their country an attractive location for foreign investors. While the CEECs established diverse investment promotion agencies to attract FDI flows to their countries,[103] especially by offering fiscal and financial incentives, other macroeconomic factors might play a major role for the long-term engagement of investors. To concentrate political efforts on the most effective measures, policy makers need to know the country characteristics that impact an economy's ability to attract FDI. The following chapter addresses this issue by analyzing the factors that determine FDI inflows to the CEECs and other emerging market regions.

103 The relevant investment promotion agencies in the eight CEECs are: CzechInvest, Estonian Investment Agency (EIA), Hungarian Investment and Trade and Development Agency (ITDH), Latvian Development Agency (LDA), Lithuanian Development Agency (LDA), Polish Information and Foreign Investment Agency (PAIiIZ) Slovak Investment and Trade Development Agency (SARIO), Slovenian Trade and Investment Promotion Agency (TIPO).

2.5 Appendix to Chapter 2

Table A 2-1: Income and indebtedness classification criteria

<table>
<tr><td></td><td></td><td colspan="3">Indebtedness classification</td></tr>
<tr><td></td><td></td><td>PV/XGS less than 220 percent or PV/GNI higher than 80 percent</td><td>PV/XGS lower than 220 but higher than 60 percent or PV/GNI less than 80 percent but higher than 60 percent</td><td>PV/XGS less than160 percent and PV/GNI less than 60 percent</td></tr>
<tr><td rowspan="2">Income classification</td><td>Low-income: GNI per capita is $735 or less</td><td>Severely indebted low-income countries</td><td>Moderately indebted low-income countries</td><td>Less indebted low-income countries</td></tr>
<tr><td>Middle-income: GNI per capita between $736 and $9,385</td><td>Severely indebted middle-income countries</td><td>Moderately indebted middle- income countries</td><td>Less indebted middle-income countries</td></tr>
</table>

Note: PV/XGS is the present value of debt service to exports of goods and services. PV/GNI is the present value of debt service to gross national income.
Source: World Bank (2005a).

Table A 2-2: Public sector size across countries

	Revenue, excluding grants in percent of GDP	Year of observation
Slovenia	43.39	2003
Hungary	37.29	2003
European Monetary Union	35.86	2002
Slovak Republic	35.32	2003
Czech Republic	33.16	2003
Poland	29.55	2002
Lithuania	28.09	2003
Estonia	28.05	2001
Latvia	26.33	2003
Indonesia	20.98	2001
Thailand	19.51	2003
Mexico	14.75	2000
Argentina	13.66	2002
Philippines	3.72	2004
Turkey	0.01	2004

Source: World Bank (2005d).

Data Sources

The data used for the calculation of the relevant indicators are taken from different sources including databases of ECB, IMF, and World Bank. The use of diverse data sources cannot be avoided since no source provides data on all economic variables required for a comprehensive analysis. We are aware of possible inconsistencies in the data due to differences in the measurement of variables, currency transformations, and so forth. A maximum level of consistency is, however, achieved by using the same sources for the determination of debt indicators over time and across countries. Likewise, consistency across different indicators is achieved by using the same data source for the numerator and the denominator of indicators whenever possible.

Data used for the calculation of gross external debt are taken from the IIP of the IMF's Balance of Payments Statistics (BPS).[104] Gross external debt is calculated as the sum of all debt components as defined by World Bank, IMF, BIS, and OECD (1988).[105]

Data for annual values of GDP, exports, and government revenues are taken from the ECB's AMECO database. While government revenue data in AMECO consider general government revenues, IFS data cover central government revenues only. Since the distribution of government revenues among different public entities is a political decision and therefore varies across countries, general government revenue is the more consistent and therefore preferred measure. Since debt data in the BPS are given in USD and AMECO data are available in national currency values only, the latter have to be converted into USD. The exchange rate used for the currency conversion is the average USD exchange rate provided in the ECB's AMECO database. Data for reserve assets are taken from the IIP of the IMF's BPS.

The BPS does not allow for a consistent differentiation of external debt by maturity nor does it provide data on debt service payments. Data on both short-term debt as well as debt service payments are, therefore, taken from the IMF's

---

104 The IMF's IIP data are almost (small differences for most recent data points are possible due to differences in the frequency / timing of database updates) identical to the BOP data of the ECB's BOP database and the BOP data provided on the national central bank's Web sites. The IMF however also provides quarterly data if available. Furthermore, the IMF data cover a larger range of countries. Using this database therefore allows a comparative analysis even with countries outside the EU.

105 External debt there is defined as the sum of liabilities to direct investors (item 1.2.2), debt securities (item 2.2), and other investment (item 4). Information in parentheses refers to the enumeration used in Table 9 on page 66.

World Economic Outlook (WEO) data base. For consistency, data on export and general government revenues in the case of short-term debt and debt service indicators are also taken from the WEO database. Since data on reserve assets are not available from this source, this variable is taken from the IIP of the IMF's BPS. The table below provides an overview of variables and databases used in the CEECs' debt sustainability assessment.

Table A 2-3: Variables and data sources

Data base	Variables
AMECO (ECB)	GDP
	Exports
	General government revenues
IIP, BPS (IMF)	Gross external debt
	Reserve assets
WEO (IMF)	Exports
	General government revenues
	Short-term external debt
	Debt service payments

Table A 2-4: External balance and sustainability indicators—Czech Republic

Balance of payments, main items (in percent of GDP)

	1998	1999	2000	2001	2002	2003	2004
Current account	-2.1%	-2.5%	-4.9%	-5.4%	-5.6%	-6.3%	-5.2%
Goods	-4.3%	-3.2%	-5.6%	-5.0%	-3.0%	-2.7%	-0.8%
Service	3.2%	2.0%	2.5%	2.5%	0.9%	0.5%	0.5%
Income	-1.8%	-2.3%	-2.5%	-3.6%	-4.8%	-4.7%	-5.1%
Transfers	0.8%	1.0%	0.7%	0.8%	1.2%	0.6%	0.2%
Financial account	1.6%	2.4%	5.4%	4.6%	5.4%	5.7%	6.3%
FDI	5.9%	10.6%	8.9%	9.0%	11.2%	2.1%	3.7%
Portfolio investment	1.8%	-2.4%	-3.2%	1.5%	-1.9%	-1.4%	2.3%
o/w *Portfolio equity*	0.0%	-3.2%	-4.0%	0.2%	-3.1%	-3.3%	-2.2%
Portfolio debt	1.8%	0.8%	0.9%	1.3%	1.2%	1.9%	4.5%
Other investment	-2.9%	-3.0%	1.2%	-2.9%	5.3%	5.3%	0.7%
Official reserve assets	-3.2%	-2.8%	-1.5%	-2.9%	-9.0%	-0.5%	-0.2%

Balance of payments, main items (in percent of GDP)

	03 Q4*	04 Q1*	04 Q2*	04 Q3*	04 Q4*
Current account	-6.3%	-6.4%	-6.3%	-6.4%	-5.2%
Goods	-2.7%	-2.5%	-2.3%	-1.8%	-0.8%
Service	0.5%	0.5%	0.5%	0.5%	0.5%
Income	-4.7%	-4.7%	-5.1%	-5.5%	-5.1%
Transfers	0.6%	0.3%	0.5%	0.4%	0.2%
Financial account	5.7%	4.6%	5.3%	6.0%	6.3%
FDI	2.1%	2.1%	2.2%	2.3%	3.7%
Portfolio investment	-1.4%	0.9%	2.5%	3.0%	2.3%
o/w *Portfolio equity*	-3.3%	-1.6%	-1.9%	-1.4%	-2.2%
Portfolio debt	1.9%	2.4%	4.4%	4.5%	4.5%
Other investment	5.3%	1.8%	0.8%	0.9%	0.7%
Official reserve assets	-0.5%	-0.3%	-0.3%	-0.3%	-0.2%

Table A 2-4: External balance and sustainability indicators—Czech Republic (concluded)

Debt indicators

	1998	1999	2000	2001	2002	2003	2004	Threshold
Gross debt to GDP	40%	39%	39%	37%	36%	39%	42%	60%
Gross debt to exports	73%	69%	60%	55%	59%	62%	59%	300%
Gross debt to government revenues	103%	99%	101%	94%	91%	93%	99%	250%
Gross debt to reserve assets	193%	178%	164%	155%	114%	129%	159%	
Debt service to exports	**42%**	**39%**	**38%**	32%	32%	33%	29%	35%
Debt service to government revenues	**60%**	**56%**	**63%**	**55%**	**49%**	**49%**	**48%**	40%
Debt service to reserve assets	**113%**	**101%**	**103%**	90%	61%	69%	78%	100%
Short-term debt to reserve assets	97%	93%	96%	84%	57%	63%	53%	100%
Memo item: exports to GDP	55%	56%	64%	66%	62%	62%	71%	
Memo item: net external debt to GDP	3%	1%	-1%	-4%	5%	7%	12%	

IIP (in USD billions) and composition of liabilities (in percent of total liabilities)

	1998	1999	2000	2001	2002	2003	2004
Net IIP (billions USD)	-3.93	-3.08	-5.07	-6.73	-13.18	-20.56	-36.89
NET IIP as % of GDP	-6%	-5%	-9%	-11%	-18%	-23%	-34%
Assets (billions USD)	36.43	37.47	38.30	42.61	52.42	59.93	68.64
Assets as % of GDP	60%	63%	69%	70%	71%	66%	64%
Liabilities (billions USD)	40.36	40.55	43.38	49.34	65.60	80.49	105.52
Liabilities as % of GDP	66%	69%	78%	81%	89%	89%	98%
Foreign direct investment	36%	43%	50%	55%	59%	56%	53%
Portfolio investment	14%	11%	10%	10%	10%	11%	16%
o/w Equity securities	68%	59%	70%	71%	64%	63%	55%
Debt securities	32%	41%	30%	29%	36%	37%	45%
Financial derivatives	0%	0%	0%	1%	1%	1%	1%
Other investment	51%	45%	40%	34%	30%	32%	29%
o/w Trade credits	12%	12%	14%	13%	13%	9%	12%
Loans	54%	53%	51%	55%	56%	57%	60%
Currency and deposits	30%	30%	31%	31%	29%	31%	25%
Other liabilities	3%	4%	3%	2%	2%	3%	3%
Memo item: Gross external debt**	60%	56%	50%	45%	41%	43%	43%

* Four quarter moving average.

** Debt securities, other investment plus debt creating liabilities associated with FDI.

Source: ECB (2005a), IMF (2005a, 2005d, 2005h), World Bank (2005d), and own calculations.

Table A 2-5: External balance and sustainability indicators—Estonia

Balance of payments, main items (in percent of GDP)	1998	1999	2000	2001	2002	2003	2004
Current account	-8.6%	-4.4%	-5.5%	-5.6%	-10.2%	-13.2%	-12.6%
Goods	-20.1%	-14.8%	-14.2%	-13.2%	-15.4%	-17.4%	-17.7%
Service	10.3%	10.2%	10.3%	9.7%	8.3%	9.3%	10.3%
Income	-1.5%	-1.8%	-3.8%	-4.7%	-4.6%	-6.3%	-6.6%
Transfers	2.7%	2.0%	2.1%	2.5%	1.6%	1.2%	1.4%
Financial account	8.6%	5.0%	5.1%	5.3%	9.8%	12.8%	11.6%
FDI	10.2%	3.9%	6.0%	5.7%	2.2%	8.3%	6.0%
Portfolio investment	0.0%	0.2%	1.5%	-0.6%	2.1%	1.9%	6.4%
o/w *Portfolio equity*	-0.2%	-2.3%	0.2%	-2.0%	-2.7%	-4.3%	-3.2%
Portfolio debt	0.1%	2.5%	1.4%	1.4%	4.8%	6.2%	9.6%
Other investment	-1.4%	3.1%	0.0%	-0.4%	6.4%	4.5%	1.7%
Official reserve assets	-0.2%	-2.2%	-2.4%	0.7%	-0.8%	-1.8%	-2.5%

Balance of payments, main items (in percent of GDP)	03 Q4*	04 Q1*	04 Q2*	04 Q3*	04 Q4*
Current account	-13.2%	-12.1%	-14.3%	-13.0%	-12.6%
Goods	-17.4%	-16.3%	-18.1%	-17.7%	-17.7%
Service	9.3%	9.6%	9.8%	10.1%	10.3%
Income	-6.3%	-6.6%	-7.2%	-6.6%	-6.6%
Transfers	1.2%	1.1%	1.3%	1.2%	1.4%
Financial account	12.8%	11.8%	13.6%	12.5%	11.6%
FDI	8.3%	6.0%	6.1%	4.6%	6.0%
Portfolio investment	1.9%	-2.6%	5.0%	4.0%	6.4%
o/w *Portfolio equity*	-4.3%	-4.9%	-3.3%	-3.8%	-3.2%
Portfolio debt	6.2%	2.2%	8.4%	7.8%	9.6%
Other investment	4.5%	9.4%	4.1%	6.7%	1.7%
Official reserve assets	-1.8%	-0.9%	-1.7%	-2.7%	-2.5%

Table A 2-5: External balance and sustainability indicators— Estonia (concluded)

Debt indicators

	1998	1999	2000	2001	2002	2003	2004	Threshold
Gross debt to GDP	52%	52%	55%	55%	**66%**	**78%**	**91%**	60%
Gross debt to exports	70%	71%	62%	65%	90%	104%	111%	300%
Gross debt to government revenues	134%	133%	145%	148%	175%	200%	222%	250%
Gross debt to reserve assets	358%	335%	324%	399%	467%	511%	553%	
Debt service to exports	4%	9%	7%	8%	10%	11%	12%	35%
Debt service to government revenues	8%	17%	17%	18%	19%	21%	25%	40%
Debt service to reserve assets	21%	43%	39%	48%	51%	55%	62%	100%
Short-term debt to reserve assets	**111%**	**111%**	**121%**	**140%**	**163%**	**175%**	**184%**	100%
Memo item: exports to GDP	75%	72%	88%	84%	74%	75%	81%	
Memo item: net external debt to GDP	28%	26%	27%	25%	30%	35%	41%	

IIP (in USD billions) and composition of liabilities (in percent of total liabilities)

	1998	1999	2000	2001	2002	2003	2004
Net IIP (billions USD)	-2.15	-2.78	-2.78	-3.10	-4.41	-7.29	-11.40
NET IIP as % of GDP	-39%	-50%	-51%	-52%	-63%	-80%	-104%
Assets (billions USD)	2.30	2.42	2.61	2.92	4.08	6.08	8.69
Assets as % of GDP	41%	43%	48%	49%	58%	67%	79%
Liabilities (billions USD)	4.45	5.20	5.39	6.02	8.49	13.37	20.10
Liabilities as % of GDP	80%	93%	99%	101%	120%	147%	183%
Foreign direct investment	41%	47%	49%	53%	50%	52%	50%
Portfolio investment	16%	15%	14%	13%	16%	18%	22%
o/w Equity securities	43%	65%	57%	53%	46%	40%	43%
Debt securities	57%	35%	43%	47%	54%	60%	57%
Financial derivatives	n.a.	n.a.	0%	0%	0%	0%	0%
Other investment	43%	38%	37%	35%	34%	30%	27%
o/w Trade credits	17%	16%	19%	17%	16%	15%	13%
Loans	60%	58%	51%	54%	51%	49%	45%
Currency and deposits	18%	20%	24%	22%	28%	33%	40%
Other liabilities	6%	5%	6%	7%	6%	3%	2%
Memo item: Gross external debt**	65%	55%	55%	55%	55%	52%	49%

* Four quarter moving average.

** Debt securities, other investment plus debt creating liabilities associated with FDI.

Source: ECB (2005a), IMF (2005a, 2005d, 2005h), World Bank (2005d), and own calculations.

Table A 2-6: External balance and sustainability indicators—Hungary

Balance of payments, main items (in percent of GDP)

	1998	1999	2000	2001	2002	2003	2004
Current account	n.a.	n.a.	-8.7%	-6.2%	-7.1%	-8.7%	-8.8%
Goods	n.a.	n.a.	-6.3%	-4.3%	-3.2%	-4.0%	-3.0%
Service	n.a.	n.a.	2.4%	2.8%	0.9%	-0.5%	0.0%
Income	n.a.	n.a.	-5.5%	-5.5%	-5.6%	-5.0%	-6.1%
Transfers	n.a.	n.a.	0.8%	0.8%	0.8%	0.8%	0.3%
Financial account	n.a.	n.a.	8.4%	5.5%	6.6%	8.4%	8.5%
FDI	n.a.	n.a.	4.6%	6.9%	4.2%	0.6%	3.6%
Portfolio investment	n.a.	n.a.	-0.9%	2.7%	2.6%	3.6%	7.0%
o/w *Portfolio equity*	n.a.	n.a.	-0.6%	-0.3%	-0.1%	0.0%	-0.4%
Portfolio debt	n.a.	n.a.	-0.2%	3.0%	2.7%	3.6%	7.4%
Other investment	n.a.	n.a.	6.8%	-4.4%	-3.3%	4.4%	-0.6%
Official reserve assets	n.a.	n.a.	-2.3%	0.1%	2.9%	-0.5%	-1.9%

Balance of payments, main items (in percent of GDP)

	03 Q4*	04 Q1*	04 Q2*	04 Q3*	04 Q4*
Current account	-8.7%	-8.3%	-8.7%	-9.1%	-8.8%
Goods	-4.0%	-3.6%	-3.8%	-3.5%	-3.0%
Service	-0.5%	-0.1%	-0.1%	-0.1%	0.0%
Income	-5.0%	-5.2%	-5.3%	-5.8%	-6.1%
Transfers	0.8%	0.7%	0.4%	0.3%	0.3%
Financial account	8.4%	8.2%	8.6%	9.0%	8.5%
FDI	0.6%	1.4%	1.7%	3.4%	3.6%
Portfolio investment	3.6%	3.5%	4.0%	4.4%	7.0%
o/w *Portfolio equity*	0.0%	0.0%	-0.1%	0.0%	-0.4%
Portfolio debt	3.6%	3.4%	4.1%	4.4%	7.4%
Other investment	4.4%	0.0%	2.4%	0.3%	-0.6%
Official reserve assets	-0.5%	3.0%	0.4%	0.7%	-1.9%

Table A 2-6: External balance and sustainability indicators— Hungary (concluded)

Debt indicators

	1998	1999	2000	2001	2002	2003	2004	Threshold
Gross debt to GDP	59%	**61%**	**65%**	**64%**	**62%**	**70%**	**75%**	60%
Gross debt to exports	95%	95%	88%	87%	97%	114%	116%	300%
Gross debt to government revenues	n.a.	n.a.	143%	141%	141%	159%	158%	250%
Gross debt to reserve assets	295%	269%	270%	307%	389%	458%	469%	
Debt service to exports	**40%**	30%	28%	29%	28%	27%	21%	35%
Debt service to government revenues	n.a.	n.a.	**47%**	**47%**	**41%**	39%	29%	40%
Debt service to reserve assets	**126%**	83%	88%	**102%**	**113%**	**112%**	86%	100%
Short-term debt to reserve assets	71%	81%	85%	99%	85%	**105%**	**104%**	100%
Memo item: exports to GDP	62%	64%	74%	73%	64%	62%	65%	
Memo item: net external debt to GDP	44%	47%	52%	46%	46%	53%	56%	

IIP (in USD billions) and composition of liabilities (in percent of total liabilities)

	1998	1999	2000	2001	2002	2003	2004
Net IIP (billions USD)	-30.84	-34.03	-33.38	-35.91	-49.57	-70.71	-94.36
NET IIP as % of GDP	-66%	-71%	-71%	-69%	-76%	-85%	-95%
Assets (billions USD)	16.99	19.84	19.63	22.74	24.29	32.12	42.28
Assets as % of GDP	36%	41%	42%	44%	37%	39%	42%
Liabilities (billions USD)	47.83	53.87	53.01	58.65	73.85	102.83	136.64
Liabilities as % of GDP	102%	112%	113%	113%	114%	124%	137%
Foreign direct investment	43%	43%	43%	47%	49%	47%	45%
Portfolio investment	30%	31%	28%	27%	28%	27%	32%
o/w Equity securities	16%	26%	20%	19%	18%	20%	26%
Debt securities	84%	74%	80%	81%	82%	80%	74%
Financial derivatives	0%	0%	1%	1%	1%	2%	2%
Other investment	26%	25%	28%	26%	22%	24%	22%
o/w Trade credits	6%	4%	3%	2%	1%	1%	0%
Loans	86%	88%	88%	86%	92%	95%	95%
Currency and deposits	8%	8%	9%	12%	7%	4%	5%
Other liabilities	0%	0%	0%	0%	0%	0%	0%
Memo item: Gross external debt**	58%	55%	57%	56%	55%	57%	55%

* Four quarter moving average.
** Debt securities, other investment plus debt creating liabilities associated with FDI.
Source: ECB (2005a), IMF (2005a, 2005d, 2005h), World Bank (2005d), and own calculations.

Table A 2-7: External balance and sustainability indicators—Latvia

Balance of payments, main items (in percent of GDP)

	1998	1999	2000	2001	2002	2003	2004
Current account	-9.7%	-9.0%	-4.6%	-7.7%	-6.7%	-8.3%	-12.3%
Goods	-17.0%	-14.2%	-13.6%	-16.3%	-16.0%	-18.0%	-20.2%
Service	4.6%	4.6%	6.1%	6.2%	5.8%	5.2%	4.4%
Income	0.8%	-0.8%	0.2%	0.7%	0.6%	-0.2%	-1.6%
Transfers	1.9%	1.3%	2.5%	1.7%	2.9%	4.8%	5.0%
Financial account	8.0%	8.3%	5.3%	7.1%	7.3%	7.4%	11.5%
FDI	4.6%	4.6%	5.2%	1.4%	2.7%	2.4%	4.0%
Portfolio investment	-0.1%	3.8%	-4.2%	1.6%	-2.2%	-2.0%	2.0%
o/w *Portfolio equity*	-0.5%	0.8%	-4.5%	-0.7%	-2.4%	-2.6%	0.0%
Portfolio debt	0.4%	3.0%	0.3%	2.3%	0.2%	0.6%	2.0%
Other investment	4.2%	1.5%	4.2%	7.9%	6.6%	7.5%	8.8%
Official reserve assets	-0.6%	-1.6%	0.1%	-3.7%	0.0%	-0.6%	-2.9%

Balance of payments, main items (in percent of GDP)

	03 Q4*	04 Q1*	04 Q2*	04 Q3*	04 Q4*
Current account	-8.3%	-9.1%	-11.7%	-12.8%	-12.3%
Goods	-18.0%	-18.4%	-20.1%	-20.1%	-20.2%
Service	5.2%	4.7%	4.7%	4.5%	4.4%
Income	-0.2%	-0.4%	-1.1%	-1.7%	-1.6%
Transfers	4.8%	4.9%	4.8%	4.4%	5.0%
Financial account	7.4%	8.8%	10.4%	10.9%	11.5%
FDI	2.4%	2.3%	2.7%	3.6%	4.0%
Portfolio investment	-2.0%	-0.7%	1.4%	1.0%	2.0%
o/w *Portfolio equity*	-2.6%	-1.3%	-1.1%	-1.1%	0.0%
Portfolio debt	0.6%	0.7%	2.5%	2.1%	2.0%
Other investment	7.5%	8.7%	8.0%	8.1%	8.8%
Official reserve assets	-0.6%	-1.6%	-1.6%	-1.7%	-2.9%

Table A 2-7: External balance and sustainability indicators— Latvia (concluded)

Debt indicators

	1998	1999	2000	2001	2002	2003	2004	Threshold
Gross debt to GDP	47%	53%	**60%**	**67%**	**76%**	**84%**	**97%**	60%
Gross debt to exports	99%	131%	143%	162%	185%	198%	223%	300%
Gross debt to government revenues	115%	144%	171%	196%	230%	245%	**277%**	250%
Gross debt to reserve assets	355%	404%	506%	457%	530%	608%	657%	
Debt service to exports	30%	26%	**38%**	33%	**51%**	**50%**	**59%**	35%
Debt service to government revenues	36%	29%	**46%**	39%	**62%**	**62%**	**73%**	40%
Debt service to reserve assets	**111%**	80%	**135%**	92%	**144%**	**153%**	**174%**	100%
Short-term debt to reserve assets	**121%**	**111%**	**108%**	88%	93%	81%	96%	100%
Memo item: exports to GDP	47%	40%	42%	42%	41%	42%	43%	
Memo item: net external debt to GDP	19%	23%	24%	33%	36%	39%	46%	

IIP (in USD billions) and composition of liabilities (in percent of total liabilities)

	1998	1999	2000	2001	2002	2003	2004
Net IIP (billions USD)	-1.20	-1.83	-2.10	-3.05	-3.98	-5.14	-7.41
NET IIP as % of GDP	-18%	-25%	-27%	-37%	-43%	-46%	-54%
Assets (billions USD)	3.05	3.28	3.96	4.12	5.12	6.65	9.21
Assets as % of GDP	46%	46%	51%	50%	55%	60%	67%
Liabilities (billions USD)	4.25	5.11	6.06	7.17	9.11	11.79	16.62
Liabilities as % of GDP	64%	71%	78%	87%	98%	106%	121%
Foreign direct investment	37%	35%	34%	32%	30%	28%	27%
Portfolio investment	1%	5%	4%	6%	6%	6%	6%
o/w Equity securities	97%	21%	16%	10%	14%	18%	15%
Debt securities	3%	79%	84%	90%	86%	82%	85%
Financial derivatives	0%	0%	0%	0%	0%	0%	0%
Other investment	62%	60%	61%	61%	64%	66%	67%
o/w Trade credits	17%	15%	13%	12%	11%	10%	9%
Loans	41%	38%	29%	49%	44%	44%	47%
Currency and deposits	31%	41%	49%	37%	43%	45%	43%
Other liabilities	10%	7%	9%	2%	1%	1%	1%
Memo item: Gross external debt**	73%	75%	77%	78%	77%	79%	80%

* Four quarter moving average.

** Debt securities, other investment plus debt creating liabilities associated with FDI.

Source: ECB (2005a), IMF (2005a, 2005d, 2005h), World Bank (2005d), and own calculations.

Table A 2-8: External balance and sustainability indicators—Lithuania

Balance of payments, main items (in percent of GDP)

	1998	1999	2000	2001	2002	2003	2004
Current account	n.a.	n.a.	-5.9%	-4.7%	-5.2%	-6.9%	-7.2%
Goods	n.a.	n.a.	-9.7%	-9.2%	-9.4%	-9.2%	-10.4%
Service	n.a.	n.a.	3.3%	3.8%	3.8%	3.4%	4.1%
Income	n.a.	n.a.	-1.7%	-1.5%	-1.2%	-2.7%	-2.4%
Transfers	n.a.	n.a.	2.1%	2.1%	1.6%	1.6%	1.5%
Financial account	n.a.	n.a.	4.8%	3.5%	3.7%	5.6%	5.1%
FDI	n.a.	n.a.	3.3%	3.6%	5.0%	0.8%	2.3%
Portfolio investment	n.a.	n.a.	2.3%	2.2%	0.1%	1.5%	0.9%
o/w *Portfolio equity*	n.a.	n.a.	-1.2%	0.2%	-0.9%	0.2%	-1.0%
Portfolio debt	n.a.	n.a.	3.6%	2.0%	1.0%	1.3%	1.9%
Other investment	n.a.	n.a.	0.3%	0.3%	1.7%	6.4%	1.3%
Official reserve assets	n.a.	n.a.	-1.1%	-2.7%	-3.1%	-2.9%	0.6%

Balance of payments, main items (in percent of GDP)

	03 Q4*	04 Q1*	04 Q2*	04 Q3*	04 Q4*
Current account	-6.9%	-7.6%	-8.0%	-8.4%	-7.2%
Goods	-9.2%	-10.4%	-10.7%	-11.2%	-10.4%
Service	3.4%	3.3%	3.4%	3.8%	4.1%
Income	-2.7%	-2.4%	-2.3%	-2.5%	-2.4%
Transfers	1.6%	1.9%	1.5%	1.4%	1.5%
Financial account	5.6%	5.6%	7.4%	7.0%	5.1%
FDI	0.8%	0.7%	0.9%	2.4%	2.3%
Portfolio investment	1.5%	0.6%	1.3%	1.7%	0.9%
o/w *Portfolio equity*	0.2%	-0.2%	-0.6%	-0.7%	-1.0%
Portfolio debt	1.3%	0.9%	1.9%	2.4%	1.9%
Other investment	6.4%	5.2%	6.9%	4.4%	1.3%
Official reserve assets	-2.9%	-0.8%	-1.7%	-1.4%	0.6%

Table A 2-8: External balance and sustainability indicators— Lithuania (concluded)

Debt indicators

	1998	1999	2000	2001	2002	2003	2004	Threshold
Gross debt to GDP	34%	42%	43%	44%	44%	45%	47%	60%
Gross debt to exports	74%	107%	95%	87%	83%	88%	89%	300%
Gross debt to government revenues	90%	112%	119%	132%	134%	141%	148%	250%
Gross debt to reserve assets	256%	364%	357%	316%	256%	242%	291%	
Debt service to exports	23%	19%	25%	**35%**	**56%**	**64%**	**61%**	35%
Debt service to government revenues	28%	19%	32%	**53%**	**92%**	**102%**	**101%**	40%
Debt service to reserve assets	78%	63%	96%	**127%**	**175%**	**176%**	**199%**	100%
Short-term debt to reserve assets	85%	89%	82%	93%	88%	95%	**100%**	100%
Memo item: exports to GDP	46%	39%	45%	50%	53%	52%	53%	
Memo item: net external debt to GDP	25%	31%	31%	32%	32%	33%	31%	

IIP (in USD billions) and composition of liabilities (in percent of total liabilities)

	1998	1999	2000	2001	2002	2003	2004
Net IIP (billions USD)	-2.46	-3.66	-4.02	-4.21	-5.15	-6.86	-8.54
NET IIP as % of GDP	-22%	-34%	-35%	-35%	-37%	-37%	-38%
Assets (billions USD)	2.47	2.45	2.68	3.13	4.23	5.72	7.41
Assets as % of GDP	22%	23%	24%	26%	30%	31%	33%
Liabilities (billions USD)	4.93	6.11	6.69	7.33	9.37	12.58	15.95
Liabilities as % of GDP	44%	56%	59%	61%	67%	68%	72%
Foreign direct investment	33%	34%	35%	36%	42%	39%	40%
Portfolio investment	7%	14%	17%	18%	16%	17%	18%
o/w Equity securities	18%	7%	11%	7%	7%	7%	6%
Debt securities	82%	93%	89%	93%	93%	93%	94%
Financial derivatives	0%	0%	0%	0%	0%	0%	0%
Other investment	60%	53%	48%	46%	41%	44%	42%
o/w Trade credits	22%	21%	23%	26%	30%	26%	24%
Loans	72%	71%	70%	64%	59%	64%	64%
Currency and deposits	5%	6%	5%	5%	6%	7%	10%
Other liabilities	1%	2%	2%	5%	6%	3%	1%
Memo item: Gross external debt**	76%	74%	73%	72%	66%	66%	66%

* Four quarter moving average.

** Debt securities, other investment plus debt creating liabilities associated with FDI.

Source: ECB (2005a), IMF (2005a, 2005d, 2005h), World Bank (2005d), and own calculations.

Table A 2-9: External balance and sustainability indicators—Poland

Balance of payments, main items (in percent of GDP)

	1998	1999	2000	2001	2002	2003	2004
Current account	n.a.	n.a.	-6.0%	-2.9%	-2.6%	-2.2%	-1.6%
Goods	n.a.	n.a.	-7.4%	-4.1%	-3.8%	-2.7%	-2.3%
Service	n.a.	n.a.	0.9%	0.4%	0.4%	0.2%	0.3%
Income	n.a.	n.a.	-0.9%	-0.7%	-1.0%	-1.7%	-1.9%
Transfers	n.a.	n.a.	1.4%	1.6%	1.7%	2.0%	2.3%
Financial account	n.a.	n.a.	5.7%	1.9%	3.4%	1.1%	0.0%
FDI	n.a.	n.a.	5.7%	3.1%	2.0%	1.9%	2.2%
Portfolio investment	n.a.	n.a.	1.9%	0.6%	1.0%	1.2%	4.0%
o/w *Portfolio equity*	n.a.	n.a.	-0.1%	0.0%	-0.6%	-0.6%	-0.5%
Portfolio debt	n.a.	n.a.	2.0%	0.6%	1.6%	1.8%	4.5%
Other investment	n.a.	n.a.	-1.6%	-1.8%	1.2%	-0.9%	-5.9%
Official reserve assets	n.a.	n.a.	-0.4%	0.2%	-0.4%	-0.6%	-0.5%

Balance of payments, main items (in percent of GDP)

	03 Q4*	04 Q1*	04 Q2*	04 Q3*	04 Q4*
Current account	-2.2%	-1.7%	-1.9%	-2.0%	-1.6%
Goods	-2.7%	-2.4%	-2.6%	-2.6%	-2.3%
Service	0.2%	0.3%	0.3%	0.2%	0.3%
Income	-1.7%	-1.7%	-1.7%	-1.9%	-1.9%
Transfers	2.0%	2.1%	2.0%	2.2%	2.3%
Financial account	1.1%	1.0%	1.6%	1.1%	0.0%
FDI	1.9%	2.0%	2.2%	1.8%	2.2%
Portfolio investment	1.2%	1.4%	2.9%	4.1%	4.0%
o/w *Portfolio equity*	-0.6%	-0.9%	-0.8%	-0.5%	-0.5%
Portfolio debt	1.8%	2.3%	3.7%	4.5%	4.5%
Other investment	-0.9%	-0.8%	-1.9%	-3.5%	-5.9%
Official reserve assets	-0.6%	-1.2%	-1.3%	-1.0%	-0.5%

Table A 2-9: External balance and sustainability indicators— Poland (concluded)

Debt indicators

	1998	1999	2000	2001	2002	2003	2004	Threshold
Gross debt to GDP	35%	40%	42%	39%	44%	51%	n.a.	60%
Gross debt to exports	132%	161%	150%	140%	150%	147%	n.a.	300%
Gross debt to government revenues	78%	89%	98%	88%	101%	114%	n.a.	250%
Gross debt to reserve assets	209%	239%	253%	271%	285%	310%	n.a.	
Debt service to exports	11%	24%	19%	27%	23%	24%	16%	35%
Debt service to government revenues	6%	12%	12%	17%	15%	18%	14%	40%
Debt service to reserve assets	17%	33%	35%	38%	43%	57%	59%	100%
Short-term debt to reserve assets	55%	64%	75%	81%	95%	97%	n.a.	100%
Memo item: exports to GDP	26%	25%	28%	28%	30%	34%	39%	
Memo item: net external debt to GDP	29%	32%	32%	27%	34%	38%	n.a.	

IIP (in USD billions) and composition of liabilities (in percent of total liabilities)

	1998	1999	2000	2001	2002	2003	2004
Net IIP (billions USD)	-41.79	-49.16	-55.33	-57.83	-73.43	-92.24	n.a.
NET IIP as % of GDP	-25%	-30%	-33%	-31%	-38%	-44%	n.a.
Assets (billions USD)	38.40	40.10	44.67	49.30	51.70	61.30	n.a.
Assets as % of GDP	23%	24%	27%	27%	27%	29%	n.a.
Liabilities (billions USD)	80.19	89.26	100.00	107.13	125.13	153.55	n.a.
Liabilities as % of GDP	47%	54%	60%	58%	65%	73%	n.a.
Foreign direct investment	28%	29%	34%	39%	39%	36%	n.a.
Portfolio investment	17%	16%	18%	18%	19%	21%	n.a.
o/w Equity securities	36%	34%	30%	23%	18%	19%	n.a.
Debt securities	64%	66%	70%	77%	82%	81%	n.a.
Financial derivatives	0%	0%	0%	0%	0%	0%	n.a.
Other investment	55%	54%	48%	44%	42%	43%	n.a.
o/w Trade credits	8%	11%	12%	14%	16%	19%	n.a.
Loans	84%	80%	82%	79%	77%	71%	n.a.
Currency and deposits	8%	9%	6%	7%	6%	10%	n.a.
Other liabilities	n.a.	n.a.	n.a.	1%	1%	1%	n.a.
Memo item: Gross external debt**	74%	73%	69%	67%	68%	69%	n.a.

* Four quarter moving average.

** Debt securities, other investment plus debt creating liabilities associated with FDI.

Source: ECB (2005a), IMF (2005a, 2005d, 2005h), World Bank (2005d), and own calculations.

Table A 2-10: External balance and sustainability indicators—Slovak Republic

Balance of payments, main items (in percent of GDP)

	1998	1999	2000	2001	2002	2003	2004
Current account	n.a.	n.a.	n.a.	-8.4%	-8.0%	-0.8%	-3.5%
Goods	n.a.	n.a.	n.a.	-10.2%	-8.8%	-2.0%	-3.5%
Service	n.a.	n.a.	n.a.	2.3%	1.9%	0.7%	0.7%
Income	n.a.	n.a.	n.a.	-1.5%	-1.9%	-0.4%	-1.0%
Transfers	n.a.	n.a.	n.a.	1.0%	0.8%	0.8%	0.3%
Financial account	n.a.	n.a.	n.a.	7.5%	6.3%	1.0%	3.0%
FDI	n.a.	n.a.	n.a.	7.4%	16.5%	2.1%	3.1%
Portfolio investment	n.a.	n.a.	n.a.	-1.3%	2.3%	-1.7%	2.1%
o/w *Portfolio equity*	n.a.	n.a.	n.a.	-2.4%	1.1%	-2.2%	-2.0%
Portfolio debt	n.a.	n.a.	n.a.	1.1%	1.2%	0.5%	4.1%
Other investment	n.a.	n.a.	n.a.	2.0%	2.1%	4.8%	2.0%
Official reserve assets	n.a.	n.a.	n.a.	-0.7%	-14.6%	-4.3%	-4.2%

Balance of payments, main items (in percent of GDP)

	03 Q4*	04 Q1*	04 Q2*	04 Q3*	04 Q4*
Current account	-0.8%	-0.2%	-1.8%	-2.6%	-3.5%
Goods	-2.0%	-1.5%	-2.1%	-2.8%	-3.5%
Service	0.7%	0.8%	0.8%	0.7%	0.7%
Income	-0.4%	-0.2%	-0.9%	-1.0%	-1.0%
Transfers	0.8%	0.7%	0.4%	0.4%	0.3%
Financial account	1.0%	0.3%	1.5%	3.2%	3.0%
FDI	2.1%	2.1%	2.9%	3.3%	3.1%
Portfolio investment	-1.7%	-1.6%	2.4%	2.5%	2.1%
o/w *Portfolio equity*	-2.2%	-2.6%	-1.8%	-1.5%	-2.0%
Portfolio debt	0.5%	1.0%	4.2%	4.0%	4.1%
Other investment	4.8%	3.5%	-0.3%	3.1%	2.0%
Official reserve assets	-4.3%	-3.9%	-3.5%	-5.6%	-4.2%

Table A 2-10: External balance and sustainability indicators— Slovak Republic (concluded)

Debt indicators

	1998	1999	2000	2001	2002	2003	2004	Threshold
Gross debt to GDP	57%	53%	53%	55%	55%	57%	n.a.	60%
Gross debt to exports	95%	86%	75%	74%	77%	73%	n.a.	300%
Gross debt to government revenues	99%	106%	112%	120%	122%	161%	n.a.	250%
Gross debt to reserve assets	388%	287%	246%	255%	145%	154%	n.a.	
Debt service to exports	19%	16%	18%	15%	11%	16%	17%	35%
Debt service to government revenues	19%	20%	26%	24%	18%	35%	37%	40%
Debt service to reserve assets	75%	53%	58%	50%	21%	33%	n.a.	100%
Short-term debt to reserve assets	86%	**101%**	98%	**105%**	76%	**116%**	81%	100%
Memo item: exports to GDP	60%	61%	71%	73%	72%	78%	77%	
Memo item: net external debt to GDP	27%	30%	27%	27%	34%	38%	n.a.	

IIP (in USD billions) and composition of liabilities (in percent of total liabilities)

	1998	1999	2000	2001	2002	2003	2004
Net IIP (billions USD)	-4.33	-4.55	-4.28	-5.42	-5.83	-8.70	n.a.
NET IIP as % of GDP	-20%	-22%	-21%	-26%	-24%	-27%	n.a.
Assets (billions USD)	10.32	8.65	10.09	10.54	14.68	19.48	n.a.
Assets as % of GDP	47%	42%	50%	50%	60%	60%	n.a.
Liabilities (billions USD)	14.66	13.20	14.37	15.96	20.51	28.18	n.a.
Liabilities as % of GDP	66%	65%	71%	76%	84%	87%	n.a.
Foreign direct investment	20%	24%	31%	35%	42%	42%	n.a.
Portfolio investment	11%	15%	20%	18%	16%	15%	n.a.
o/w Equity securities	7%	17%	9%	14%	15%	12%	n.a.
Debt securities	93%	83%	91%	86%	85%	88%	n.a.
Financial derivatives	0%	0%	0%	0%	0%	0%	n.a.
Other investment	70%	60%	49%	47%	42%	43%	n.a.
o/w Trade credits	18%	22%	23%	21%	23%	21%	n.a.
Loans	64%	71%	69%	72%	61%	55%	n.a.
Currency and deposits	12%	3%	5%	7%	11%	13%	n.a.
Other liabilities	5%	3%	4%	1%	5%	11%	n.a.
Memo item: Gross external debt**	86%	81%	75%	71%	65%	66%	n.a.

* Four quarter moving average.

** Debt securities, other investment plus debt creating liabilities associated with FDI.

Source: ECB (2005a), IMF (2005a, 2005d, 2005h), World Bank (2005d), and own calculations.

Table A 2-11: External balance and sustainability indicators—Slovenia

Balance of payments, main items (in percent of GDP)

	1998	1999	2000	2001	2002	2003	2004
Current account	-0.6%	-3.3%	-2.8%	0.2%	1.4%	-0.4%	-0.9%
Goods	-3.8%	-5.8%	-5.9%	-3.1%	-1.1%	-2.2%	-3.2%
Service	2.4%	1.6%	2.4%	2.4%	2.6%	2.2%	2.6%
Income	0.3%	0.3%	0.1%	0.2%	-0.6%	-0.7%	-0.4%
Transfers	0.6%	0.6%	0.6%	0.7%	0.6%	0.4%	0.1%
Financial account	0.3%	3.1%	2.6%	-0.7%	0.1%	0.8%	2.1%
FDI	1.1%	0.3%	0.4%	1.1%	6.8%	-0.5%	0.1%
Portfolio investment	0.4%	1.6%	0.9%	0.3%	-0.3%	-0.9%	-2.4%
o/w *Portfolio equity*	-0.1%	0.0%	-0.3%	-0.5%	-0.4%	-0.8%	-2.3%
Portfolio debt	0.6%	1.6%	1.2%	0.9%	0.1%	-0.1%	-0.1%
Other investment	-0.4%	0.8%	2.3%	4.5%	1.7%	3.2%	3.4%
Official reserve assets	-0.8%	0.5%	-0.9%	-6.6%	-8.1%	-1.1%	1.0%

Balance of payments, main items (in percent of GDP)

	03 Q4*	04 Q1*	04 Q2*	04 Q3*	04 Q4*
Current account	-0.4%	0.0%	-0.5%	-0.8%	-0.9%
Goods	-2.2%	-2.0%	-2.7%	-3.0%	-3.2%
Service	2.2%	2.1%	2.2%	2.4%	2.6%
Income	-0.7%	-0.6%	-0.4%	-0.4%	-0.4%
Transfers	0.4%	0.4%	0.4%	0.2%	0.1%
Financial account	0.8%	0.6%	1.5%	2.2%	2.1%
FDI	-0.5%	-0.6%	-0.5%	-0.2%	0.1%
Portfolio investment	-0.9%	-1.1%	-2.5%	-2.7%	-2.4%
o/w *Portfolio equity*	-0.8%	-1.0%	-1.5%	-1.9%	-2.3%
Portfolio debt	-0.1%	-0.2%	-1.0%	-0.8%	-0.1%
Other investment	3.2%	3.4%	3.5%	3.8%	3.4%
Official reserve assets	-1.1%	-1.1%	1.1%	1.3%	1.0%

Table A 2-8: External balance and sustainability indicators— Slovenia (concluded)

Debt indicators***

	1998	1999	2000	2001	2002	2003	2004	Threshold
Gross debt to GDP	35%	37%	46%	46%	53%	54%	59%	60%
Gross debt to exports	67%	75%	81%	80%	92%	95%	99%	300%
Gross debt to government revenues	n.a.	n.a.	102%	103%	116%	n.a.	n.a.	250%
Gross debt to reserve assets	203%	248%	271%	206%	167%	n.a.	n.a.	
Debt service to exports	14%	8%	9%	15%	14%	15%	16%	35%
Debt service to government revenues	n.a.	n.a.	12%	19%	18%	19%	20%	40%
Debt service to reserve assets	41%	27%	32%	38%	26%	n.a.	n.a.	100%
Short-term debt to reserve assets	74%	**106%**	**127%**	92%	64%	n.a.	n.a.	100%
Memo item: exports to GDP	53%	49%	56%	58%	58%	56%	60%	
Memo item: net external debt to GDP	13%	16%	21%	21%	27%	n.a.	n.a	

IIP (in USD billions) and composition of liabilities (in percent of total liabilities)

	1998	1999	2000	2001	2002	2003	2004
Net IIP (billions USD)	-0.99	-1.98	-2.37	-1.28	-1.47	n.a.	n.a.
NET IIP as % of GDP	-5%	-9%	-12%	-7%	-7%	n.a.	n.a.
Assets (billions USD)	8.45	7.86	8.30	9.94	13.63	n.a.	n.a.
Assets as % of GDP	41%	37%	44%	51%	61%	n.a.	n.a.
Liabilities (billions USD)	9.44	9.83	10.67	11.22	15.10	n.a.	n.a.
Liabilities as % of GDP	45%	46%	56%	57%	68%	n.a.	n.a.
Foreign direct investment	29%	27%	27%	23%	27%	n.a.	n.a.
Portfolio investment	15%	17%	17%	17%	15%	n.a.	n.a.
o/w Equity securities	10%	10%	9%	9%	5%	n.a.	n.a.
Debt securities	90%	90%	91%	91%	95%	n.a.	n.a.
Financial derivatives	0%	0%	0%	0%	0%	n.a.	n.a.
Other investment	56%	56%	56%	60%	58%	n.a.	n.a.
o/w Trade credits	35%	32%	30%	23%	20%	n.a.	n.a.
Loans	56%	59%	63%	67%	69%	n.a.	n.a.
Currency and deposits	8%	7%	6%	7%	8%	n.a.	n.a.
Other liabilities	2%	2%	1%	2%	3%	n.a.	n.a.
Memo item: Gross external debt**	78%	80%	81%	81%	78%	n.a.	n.a.

* Four quarter moving average.

** Debt securities, other investment plus debt creating liabilities associated with FDI.

*** Information partly taken from IMF (2005f) since data are not available from IIP.

Source: ECB (2005a), IMF (2005a, 2005d, 2005h), World Bank (2005d), and own calculations.

3 Foreign direct investment flows to emerging economies

3.1 Introduction

3.1.1 The role of FDI in the CEECs

Attracting FDI is an important issue for the central and eastern European economies, as they need long-term capital inflows to be able to maintain the relatively high investment rates needed to restructure the industry and to build an efficient infrastructure.[106] As discussed in the previous chapter, the structure of capital inflows is of major importance for the sustainability of a country's external liabilities. Long-term financing with a high-equity and low-debt component allows a country to minimize the threat of a sudden flight of foreign capital and therefore reduces the likelihood of a financial crisis.[107] Equity inflows can either be portfolio investment or FDI. Of these two forms of equity financing, direct investment is on average more long-term oriented than portfolio flows.[108]

Beside its long-term character and the resulting impact on financial stability, an additional attractive feature of FDI is the positive effect it has on the economy of the host[109] country.[110] It is widely recognized that FDI triggers technology spillovers, assists in human capital formation, contributes to international trade integration, helps to create a more competitive business environment, and enhances enterprise development.[111] With respect to the situation of the CEECs, recent empirical research shows that FDI inflows had a positive effect on the restructuring process and on productivity growth in these countries.[112] It has also been shown that a positive correlation exists between foreign ownership and the propensity to invest in tradables, i.e., to export. This

106 See World Trade Organization (1998) for an assessment of the need for external financing in the CEECs.

107 See Rogoff (1999) for an assessment of the stabilizing effect of equity capital compared to debt financing for emerging markets. The arguments brought forward in the context of emerging economies also accommodate the situation of the central and eastern European transition countries.

108 See Singh (2002) for an assessment of the implication of the long-term characteristic of FDI.

109 Home country is the country from which FDI flows originate. Host country is the country in which FDI takes place.

110 See Borensztein, De Gregorio, and Lee (1998) for an analysis of the link between FDI and economic growth.

111 See OECD (2002) for an assessment of the benefits and costs of FDI for economic development.

112 Damijan and Rojec (2004) show that FDI has had a positive impact on the catching-up process of the new EU member states.

aspect is an important issue for emerging economies and transition countries for which the integration into international markets is a major driver for [high] economic growth and where the sustainability of the external balance—which is of special importance for the CEECs—depends on the growth of exports. The economic situation of the transition countries and the economic benefits associated with FDI make FDI the preferred form of external financing, especially in the case of the CEECs where the long-term sustainability of external financing, progress in the economic restructuring, and export growth are the factors that are expected to accelerate the process of sustainable economic convergence toward the EU-15.

To attract foreign capital, countries need to be mindful about the attractiveness of their economies to foreign investors. Determining such factors of attractiveness in relation to FDI inflows is of vital importance for policy makers. The size of FDI inflows to a specific country most likely depends on both host country specific macroeconomic and political factors as well as developments in the international economic environment. If a country wants to increase its attractiveness for foreign investors it first needs to determine the country characteristics that can be altered to affect FDI inflows positively. This chapter addresses this issue by analyzing the macroeconomic and political factors that determine the magnitude of FDI flows to CEECs and major countries of the two other main emerging market regions, i.e., Asia and Latin America.

The remainder of this chapter is structured as follows. Subsection 3.1.2 presents some stylized facts on world FDI flows and FDI flows to the three emerging market regions. Subsection 3.1.3 gives an overview of the literature on FDI. The model used in the empirical analysis is specified in subsection 3.2.1. A description of the data employed in the empirical analysis is given in subsection 3.2.2. Subsection 3.2.3 discusses the regression results. Section 3.3 summarizes the main results and offers some conclusions for the CEECs.

3.1.2 Stylized facts

Private capital flows from developed countries to developing countries and CEECs[113] grew significantly throughout the 1990s (see Figure 17). While equity

113 In this paper, we follow the classification of country groups as used by UNCTAD. UNCTAD uses three broader country groups: developed countries, developing countries, and the CEECs. Emerging markets are, thus, part of the developing countries and part of the CEECs. Developing countries according to the World Bank definition cover low-income to upper-middle-income economies. Emerging markets and transition countries are also included in this group of countries. While we also use World Bank data, the references to country

and debt flows at the beginning of the period were of about equal size, the relative importance of equity flows compared to debt flows increased in the second half of the 1990s. During that period net debt flows dropped dramatically and in 2001 they even turned negative before increasing again in 2002 and thereafter. Net equity flows continued to grow in the second half of the 1990s and remained at a high level in the late 1990s and the early 2000s.

The growth of equity flows was driven by a notable surge in net FDI flows to developing countries and CEECs, which increased from about USD 25 billion in 1990 to almost USD 175 billion in 2001. Over the same period net equity portfolio flows fluctuated around levels below USD 50 billion. Since 1997, net foreign investment had been more or less constant and dropped even slightly in the early 2000s. For 2005, the World Bank projects an increase in these flows to developing countries and the CEECs.

Figure 17: Net private financial flows to developing countries

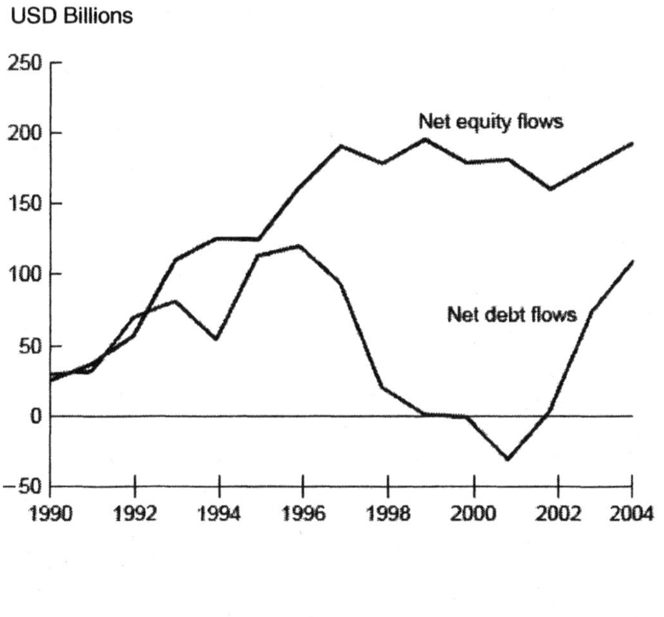

---

classifications used in the text reflect the UNCTAD definition. The expression *emerging markets* in this chapter refers to the group of host countries considered for the empirical analysis.

Figure 17: Net private financial flows to developing countries (concluded)

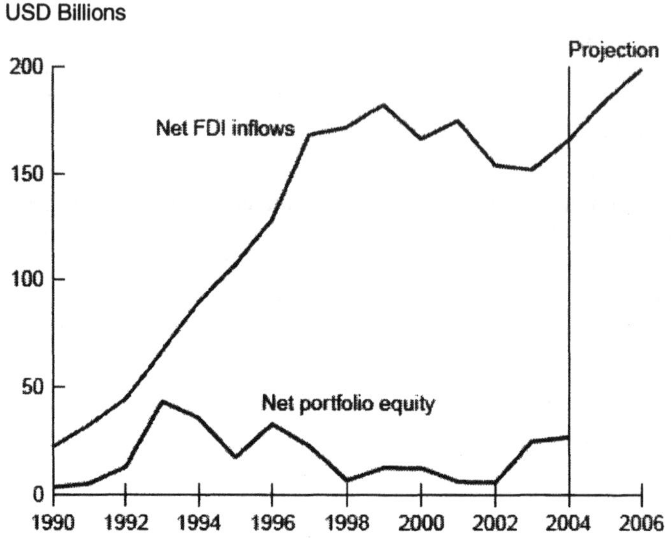

Source: World Bank (2005a).

Figure 18: Development of total worldwide FDI outflows and relative contribution by relevant home country groups

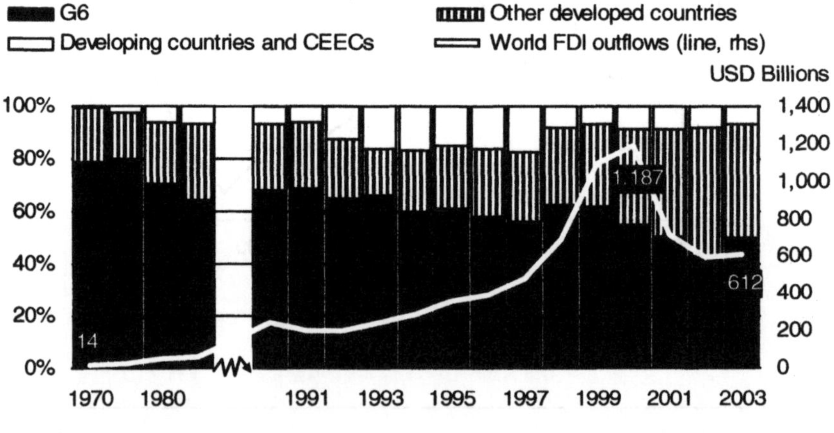

Note: The G6 include France, Germany, Italy, Japan, the United Kingdom, and the United States. These are the countries that we consider as home countries for FDI flows in our empirical study.
Source: UNCTAD (2005) and own calculations.

FDI flows played only a minor role before the 1990s, but grew rapidly thereafter (see Figure 18 and Figure 19). Worldwide FDI flows reached a peak level of about USD 1.2 trillion in 2000.[114] This was almost five times the amount of FDI outflows recorded in the beginning of the 1990s. After 2000, FDI flows fell sharply by almost 50 percent and stabilized at about USD 600 billion per year.

Figure 19: Development of total worldwide FDI inflows and relative absorption by relevant host country groups

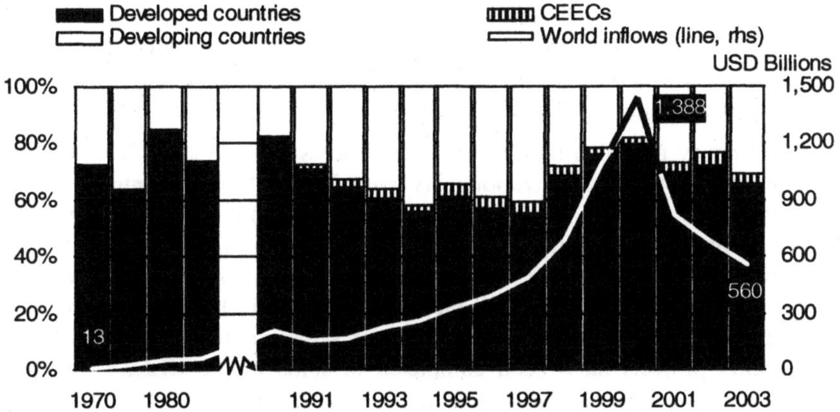

Note: The CEECs include the Czech Republic, Hungary, Poland, Slovakia, and Slovenia. Out of the group of the eight central and eastern European countries these are the countries for which data on bilateral FDI flows are available.
Source: UNCTAD (2005) and own calculations.

The sharp drop of world FDI flows in 2001 was a result of the decline in cross-border mergers and acquisitions (M&As) that usually account for the majority of total FDI flows. However, the amount of FDI flows recorded in 2001 was still slightly higher than the level of 1998 and well above 1990–2000 average FDI flows.[115] The slowdown in M&A activities in 2001 and thereafter has been

114 From an accounting point of view worldwide FDI inflows and worldwide FDI outflows should be the same. The reported numbers of FDI inflows and outflows differ, however, notably. This is due to the fact that FDI inflows and outflows are reported by host and home countries, respectively. Differences in the definition of FDI and divergent timing in the recording can be the cause for these discrepancies.

115 The significant increase in FDI flows in 1999 and 2000 was caused by large M&A deals, e.g., the USD 200 billion acquisition of Mannesmann by VodafoneAirTouch in 2000.

attributed to the sluggish macroeconomic performance and a weak economic recovery as well as to concerns about international security.[116]

FDI flows to the CEECs and to a lesser extent also to emerging markets have not been affected as severely by the 2001 drop in world FDI as were flows to developed economies. Since most of the FDI in emerging market regions involve greenfield investment, FDI flows to these regions are not as closely linked to cross-border M&A activities as the flows to developed countries. The situation of the CEECs is somewhat special. Over the transition process, FDI inflows to most of the CEECs have been related to the privatization of state-owned assets. The amount of FDI received by a central and eastern European transition country depended more on the privatization process than on private sector M&A activity.

The way in which the privatization process was managed differed across countries and not all privatizations involved FDI.[117] Some countries, e.g., the Czech Republic and the Slovak Republic, actively promoted privatization to local investors. Others, e.g., Hungary and Poland, privatized via stock market flotation, which was associated with portfolio inflows instead of FDI inflows. The pace of privatization also had an impact on the amount of FDI inflows. Slowly reforming countries attracted less FDI than more progressive countries. Since large-scale privatization projects have been completed in some of the CEECs, fewer FDI inflows are absorbed by these activities and greenfield investment gained in importance over the past couple of years. Greenfield investments have, however, not been able to fully replace privatization-related FDI inflows, which led to a significant decrease in FDI inflows to the CEECs in 2003.[118]

The vast majority of FDI has traditionally involved developed countries as the home and/or the host country of these capital flows. During the period 1990-2003, FDI outflows from developed countries accounted for 83 percent to 93 percent of worldwide FDI outflows annually (Table 15). During the same period, FDI inflows focused to a lesser extent on developed countries. Their share,

---

116 See UNCTAD (2003).

117 See Hunya (2004) and Kaminsky (2001) for a discussion of the differences in the privatization processes across countries and for an assessment of the impact of the privatization process on FDI inflows.

118 According to the *World Investment Report 2004* (UNCTAD, 2004b), the plunge in FDI inflows to the CEECS in 2003 is mainly the result of the end of privatization in the Czech Republic and Slovakia. In Hungary and in Poland this trend started at the end of the 1990s. Although only about 30 percent of FDI in Poland were greenfield investments in 1998, whereas the rest were mostly related to the privatization of state-owned enterprises, in 1999 greenfield investments accounted already for over 50 percent of total FDI inflows (Republic of Poland, Ministry of Economic Affairs & Labor, 2001).

however, still ranged from between 56 percent and 80 percent of annual worldwide FDI inflows. As a consequence, although only a smaller portion of FDI outflows from developed countries were directed toward developing countries and the CEECs, these FDI flows nevertheless represented the vast majority of FDI inflows to these two country groups.[119]

During the 1990s, FDI flows to countries outside the group of developed countries concentrated mainly on Asia, Latin America, and the CEECs. Countries in these regions received about 95 percent of all FDI flows to countries outside the group of developed countries. The high share of FDI flows going to these regions can be explained by region-specific factors. The emerging markets in Asia showed impressive economic growth in the 1990s despite the 1997/98 crisis with its temporary setback for international private capital flows. As a consequence, Asia attracted more than half of all FDI inflows that occurred in the developing countries and the CEECs (Table 15). Many of the Latin American countries implemented significant policy reforms in the 1990s including macroeconomic stabilization, trade liberalization, privatization, and deregulation. As mentioned above, the CEECs pursued ambitious privatization and transition process during the same period.

Given that most of the FDI flows to countries outside the developed world were to emerging markets in Asia, Latin America, and central and eastern Europe, we focus our analysis on FDI inflows into these regions. Regarding the home country of the flows, we concentrate on the G-6, i.e., Germany, France, Italy, Japan, United Kingdom, and the United States.[120] Figure 20 illustrates the magnitude of FDI outflows from these countries to the three main emerging market regions, i.e., the CEECs, Asia, and Latin America.[121] As pointed out by the OECD (2000), FDI outflows from all major developed countries to emerging markets increased throughout the 1990s. The general trend in the development of world FDI flows is also reflected in the regional panels (see Figure 20). FDI inflows from the G-6 countries to all three emerging market regions increased throughout the 1990s before dropping more or less sharply in the early 2000s.

119 According to Hull and Tesar (2001) the predominance of FDI flows to developing countries is partly due to the surge of FDI to China, where other private capital inflows are subject to fairly tight restrictions. For a detailed study of FDI flows into the Chinese economy see also Li, Liu, and Parker (2001).

120 Canada could not be included in the empirical analysis since the availability of data on bilateral FDI flows from Canada is very limited.

121 For reasons of data availability, FDI flows shown in Figure 20 only include host countries that we consider in our host country sample. However, as we argue later, this sample is representative of the three emerging market regions studied in this paper.

Table 15: Total world FDI flows

		2000	2001	2002	2003
Total Outflows	World (USD millions)	1,186,838	721,501	596,487	612,201
	Developed countries (USD millions)	1,083,885	658,094	547,603	569,577
	... as % of world	*91%*	*91%*	*92%*	*93%*
	G6 (USD millions)	653,876	367,155	257,979	304,737
	... as % of developed countries	*60%*	*56%*	*47%*	*54%*
	Other developed countries (USD millions)	430,008	290,939	289,624	264,839
	... as % of developed countries	*40%*	*44%*	*53%*	*46%*
	Developing countries and central and eastern European countries (USD millions)	102,953	63,407	48,884	42,625
	... as % of world	*9%*	*9%*	*8%*	*7%*
Total Inflows	World (USD millions)	1,387,953	817,574	678,751	559,576
	Developing countries and central and eastern European countries (USD millions)	279,967	246,091	188,844	193,003
	... as % of world	*20%*	*30%*	*28%*	*34%*
	Central and eastern European countries (USD millions)	27,508	26,371	31,232	20,970
	... as % of developing countries and central and eastern European countries	*10%*	*11%*	*17%*	*11%*
	Developing countries (USD millions)	252,459	219,721	157,612	172,033
	... as % of developing countries and central and eastern European countries	*90%*	*89%*	*83%*	*89%*
	Asia (USD millions)	146,195	111,966	94,474	107,278
	... as % of developing countries and central and eastern European countries	*52%*	*45%*	*50%*	*56%*
	Latin America (USD millions)	97,537	88,139	51,358	49,722
	... as % of developing countries and central and eastern European countries	*35%*	*36%*	*27%*	*26%*
	Africa (USD millions)	8,728	19,616	11,780	15,033
	... as % of developing countries and central and eastern European countries	*3%*	*8%*	*6%*	*8%*
	Developed countries (USD millions)	1,107,987	571,483	489,907	366,573
	... as % of world	*80%*	*70%*	*72%*	*66%*

Source: UNCTAD (2005) and own calculations.

There are some significant differences in the relative importance of the six home countries across emerging market regions. In the CEECs, FDI flows from

Germany and France play a dominant role, while flows from the United States and Japan are of less importance. Inflows from the two large EU countries dropped sharply in the beginning of the 2000s. Inflows from the United States—apart from 2000—were relatively stable. This might be due to the fact that privatization-related flows came mostly from neighboring EU countries, while inflows from the United States went into greenfield investment and are thus not affected by the finalization of the privatization process. FDI flows to Asia originate mainly from Japan and the United States and flows to Latin America are dominated by the United States. In this context, it is important to note that the data shown in Figure 20 reflect the level of FDI inflows from the respective countries. Total FDI outflows originating from the United States between 1990 and 2003 were on average more than two times the outflow recorded for Germany or France. Over the same period FDI inflows to the CEECs from Germany and France were on average more than three times higher than from the United States.[122] This underlines the relative importance of Germany and France for the CEECs.

Figure 20: FDI flows of the G6 countries to CEECs, Asia, and Latin America

FDI flows to central and eastern European host countries (in USD millions)

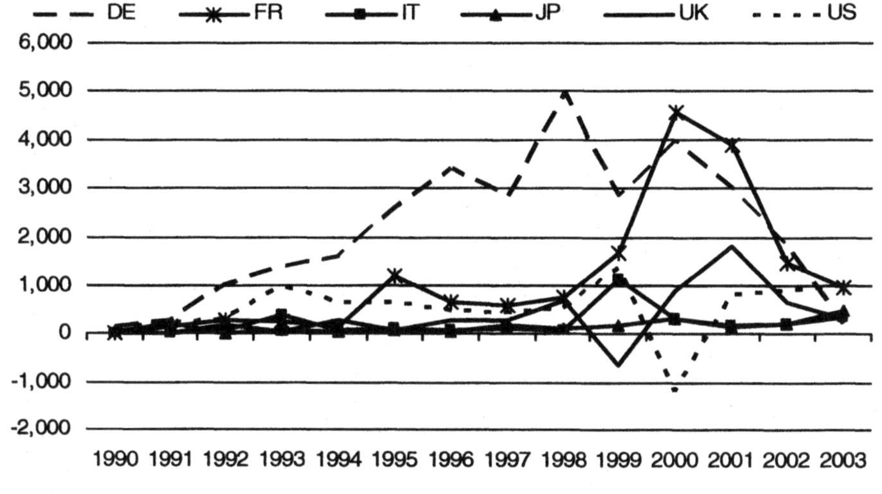

122 The amount of FDI flows from Italy to the CEECs is relatively small compared to the amount coming from Germany and France. The proportion of total Italian flows that go to the CEECs is, however, approximately as high as the proportion of total German FDI flows.

Figure 20: FDI flows of the G6 countries to CEECs, Asia, and Latin America (concluded)

FDI flows to Asian host countries (in USD millions)

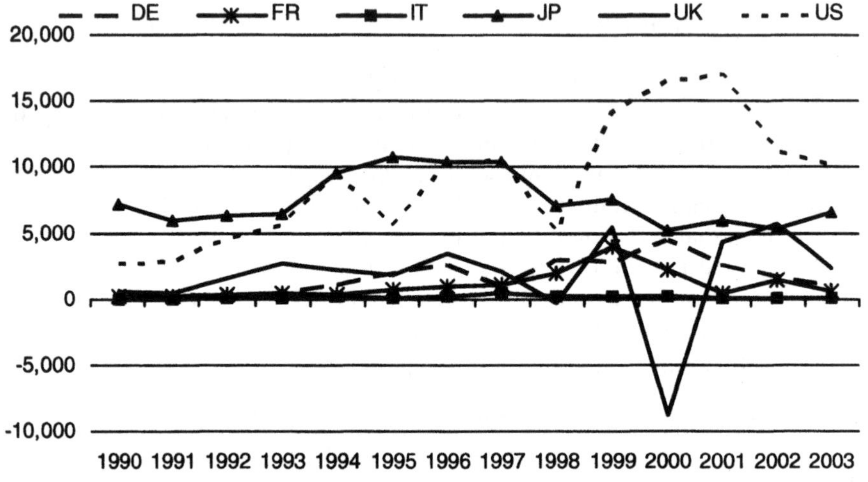

FDI flows to Latin American host countries (in USD millions)

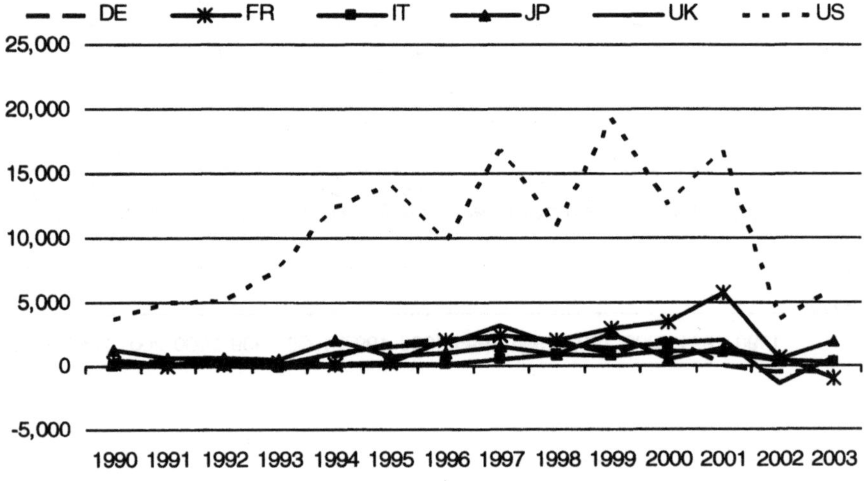

Source: OECD (2005a).

The pattern of FDI flows between host country regions and the different home countries suggests that regional proximity may be an important factor for FDI flows. Using data on bilateral FDI flows allows us to examine the impact and the importance of this factor for FDI inflows in the empirical analysis in more detail.

3.1.3 Literature overview

In recent years, private capital flows to transition economies and emerging markets have been the topic of a number of studies. The high volatility of some of these flows, the observed fragility of financial systems in emerging markets associated with this volatility, and the adverse effects of the financial crises in Asia, Russia, and Latin America can be seen as reasons for the increasing attention this topic has received. Among the three categories of private capital flows, i.e., bank loans, portfolio investment, and FDI, the latter has developed into the most important category since the mid-1990s. Its share in total private capital flows to emerging markets increased significantly, while, in particular, portfolio investment decreased, reflecting a more cautious attitude of international stock market investors.

The different causes of FDI represent an important focus of the literature on both FDI flows and stocks. Early contributions to the FDI literature date back to the first half of the 20th century and are mostly concerned with why investment is undertaken abroad rather than at home. Heckscher (1919) and Ohlin (1933) emphasize differences in the endowment of production factors resulting in differences in relative factor prices. Nurske (1933) and Ivers (1935) discuss international capital flows in the context of portfolio theory and interest rate arbitrage. Using related arguments, Branson (1970) and Corden (1974), among others, explain international capital flows as a means for equilibrating the marginal productivity of capital and labor between enterprises of the same multinational corporation. These approaches were able to explain the occurrence of international capital flows in general but they did not provide any reasoning for the form these capital flows would take. For example, whether a difference in the endowment of production factors will be equilibrated by portfolio flows or by FDI cannot be explained on the basis of the arguments given in this early literature on FDI.

The more recent FDI literature has usually concentrated on either why a company engages in FDI, i.e., why FDI outflows take place, or which factors make a country an attractive location for FDI, i.e., why FDI inflows occur in a particular country. When answering the first question, mainly firm-specific assets in the context of FDI decisions are discussed. In this more microeconomic perspective, Williamson (1975), Hymer (1976), and Dunning (1993) emphasize know-how and patents, while Hood and Young (1979) also point to management skills, superior organizational set-up, and monopolistic power as important firm-specific assets. Brainard (1993) adds to the discussion by highlighting the potential trade-off between the advantage of market proximity and the concentration of production facilities. When answering the second question, i.e., which factors make a country an attractive FDI location, the analyses take the willingness of corporations to invest internationally for granted and apply a more macroeconomic perspective. Vernon (1966) points to specific characteristics of a country that can pull production facilities to a specific location during a particular phase in the life cycle of a product. Aliber (1970) emphasizes differences in economic stability as an important factor in attracting FDI. Rugman (1979) reasons that some locations are particularly useful for firms in meeting their need to diversify businesses risks. Dunning (1977, 1988) provides an approach that is an attempt to include both microeconomic and macroeconomic perspectives by combining arguments of ownership advantages, location advantages, and internalization advantages. His so-called OLI paradigm states that FDI is undertaken if ownership-specific advantages ("O") such as proprietary technology exist together with location-specific advantages ("L") in host countries, e.g., low factor costs, and potential benefits from internalization ("I") of the production process abroad.[123]

Observations of pattern in bilateral FDI flows showed that additional aspects, e.g., geographical proximity, besides the macroeconomic and microeconomic factors influence the location decision of investors. More recent empirical studies of FDI flows are, therefore, also based on the gravity model approach, which had been introduced by Tinbergen (1962) in the context of trade flow analyses. The model explains flows, e.g., trade flows or capital flows, between two countries as being proportional to the size of the economies, i.e., national income, and inversely proportional to the distance between the countries. A gravity argument is used by Brenton and DiMauro (1999), who examine bilateral FDI flows of four home countries to thirty-five host countries from 1992 to 1995. Wei (2000) applies an extended gravity model to FDI flows. He assesses the impact of corruption in host countries on FDI inflows and finds that the three gravity factors have significant impact of the expected direction. Furthermore, his results show that corruption in host countries negatively affects FDI inflows. Levy-Yeyati, Panizza, and Stein (2003) use an extended gravity model to investigate the impact of economic cycles on north-south FDI flows. Their results suggest that FDI flows to southern countries tend to increase during recessions in

123 For a discussion of this approach, see Resmini (2000) and Buch, Kotka, and Piazolo (2003).

industrialized countries. Bénassy-Quéré, Coupert, and Mayer (2005) apply the gravity framework to determine the impact of the quality of institutions in host countries on FDI inflows. Their analysis reveals that institutions, e.g., the efficiency of the tax system, transparency, and lack of corruption, have a positive impact on FDI even if the state of economic development, i.e., GDP per capita, is also taken into account.

The development of FDI flows to transition economies and the impact of EU accession on these flows received some attention in recent economic research.[124] Estimating an ordinary least squares (OLS) regression, Lansbury, Pain, and Smidkova (1996) find that private sector size, the intensity of the bilateral trade relation, research and development, and relative labor costs have an effect on FDI flows to the four major CEECs while country risk and energy consumption have no significant impact. Bevan and Estrin (2000) apply an extended gravity model in which FDI flows from eighteen established market economies to eleven transition economies are determined by a country risk variable and factors that affect either profitability or costs of an investment. The results of OLS estimations reveal that besides two of the gravity factors, i.e., host country GDP and distance, country risk and unit labor costs significantly affect FDI inflows to transition countries. Brada, Kutan, and Yigit (2003) estimate the effects of transition and political instability in transition economies on FDI inflows to these countries. Their results reveal that both economic transition and political instability have a negative impact on foreign investment. Bos and von de Laar (2004)—among others—apply an extended gravity model to investigate the determinants of FDI in ten central and eastern European countries. The results reveal that FDI flows are driven by economic fundamentals rather than by the fact that a country enters the EU. Assessing the effect of announcements regarding the accession process on FDI, Clausing and Dorobantu (2005) find that announcements related to EU accession as well as market size and cost factors have a significant impact on FDI.[125]

---

124 Previous studies on FDI in the central and eastern European transition economies took either a macroeconomic perspective or a sectoral perspective. Since we focus on the macroeconomic view, we only review the economic literature taking a macroeconomic approach. For an overview including also sectoral studies we refer to the broader literature review in Clausen and Dorobanto (2005).

125 Other studies investigated the impact of EU enlargement on intra-European FDI flows. Also using a gravity model framework, Buch, Kokta and Piazolo (2001) for example analyze the impact of EU enlargement on FDI flows within the enlarged EU. The results show no evidence of FDI diversion between southern European countries and the CEECs.

This study contributes to the analysis of FDI flows from industrial countries to emerging economies by examining in more detail, on a macroeconomic level, the empirical evidence for bilateral capital flows to the major emerging market regions.[126] We apply an extended gravity model to bilateral data on FDI flows from six industrial countries to twenty-two emerging market economies. While we are especially interested in drawing conclusions regarding the factors that will determine future FDI flows to the CEECs, we do include other major emerging market economies in our empirical study. This allows us to make a regional differentiation when comparing the driving factors behind FDI inflows to emerging markets.

Due to the political and economic transition under way, the situation of the CEECs to some extent is unique compared to Asian and Latin American emerging markets. Several studies show that the transition process, especially through the privatization of state-owned assets, had and—to a decreasing extent—still has an impact on FDI flows to the CEECs. Furthermore, FDI was affected by the integration of the CEECs into the European goods market and EU accession. The three emerging market regions, i.e., central and eastern Europe, Asia, and Latin America, are, however, competitors when it comes to attracting FDI. Once the transition process fades out and once the shift of investments to the CEECs due to EU membership reaches a steady state, the CEECs must stand the competition for foreign investors with other emerging market regions. It is, therefore, of interest to see which factors other than the transition process have an impact on FDI flows from industrial countries to these three regions.

3.2 Empirical analysis

3.2.1 The empirical model

It has often been argued that international investment flows are driven by factors that push capital out of a country as well as by factors that pull capital into a country, i.e., factors that determine the attractiveness of a country as a location for international investments. Using a comprehensive data set on bilateral FDI flows, we study factors related to the home country as well as factors related to the host country. The latter can be seen as reflecting the macroeconomic aspect of Dunning's idea of location-specific advantages. The data set also enables us to

126 This analysis is an extension of Frenkel, Funke, and Stadtmann (2004). Due to better data availability we are able to include further relevant factors; e.g., unite labour costs, and to extend the time period covered in our analysis.

examine the importance of proximity between the home country and the host country of FDI activities. Given that the main source of FDI flows to emerging markets is the industrial countries, we concentrate on the G-6 as the countries of FDI outflows. In addition, we are interested in the main emerging market regions and therefore focus on several countries in East Asia, Latin America, and central and eastern Europe.

More recent empirical studies on determinants of FDI take advantage of data on bilateral FDI flows that are now available from different sources.[127] This allows taking a macroeconomic perspective while considering both home and host country factors when analyzing the determinants of FDI. The earlier empirical literature on this topic either focused on FDI outflows or on FDI inflows.[128] This was mainly due to the fact that bilateral data on FDI flows were not available. The distinction is a matter of focus as well as of the analytical approach chosen: Inward studies more or less ignore the micro factors behind the FDI decisions and take the micro foundations for granted. Thus, these studies concentrate on macroeconomic characteristics of the host countries.[129] Empirical work on FDI outflows focuses on firm-specific characteristics to explain why some companies invest in real assets abroad, while others do not.[130]

In our study of FDI activities, we focus on FDI flows rather than stocks and investigate the factors that influence the magnitude of such capital flows from major industrial countries to a number of emerging economies.[131] We use data for the period 1992 through 2003 and apply a panel analysis to annual FDI flows. We particularly take into account two aspects of FDI flows. One aspect reflects the profit maximization objective of the firm. We therefore examine country-specific factors of host countries that could influence the profitability of FDI projects. The second aspect reflects economic developments in the home country of the FDI flows. This is based on the hypothesis that, to some extent, host countries cannot

---

127 Data on bilateral FDI flows are available from different sources, e.g., the OECD provides data on FDI flows from all OECD countries to OECD countries and several non-OECD countries, a database on FDI to central and eastern Europe is provided by the Vienna Institute for International Economic Studies. The German Bundesbank maintains a database on bilateral flows involving Germany as home or host country.

128 A further direction of research in the context of FDI is the impact of these capital flows on the development of host economies. For a recent example see Hunya (2002).

129 See, e.g., Ancharaz (2002).

130 See, e.g., Grubaugh (1987).

131 We are aware of the fact that FDI flows are more volatile than FDI stocks and can sometimes be affected by a single transaction. However, data on FDI stocks were not available for the range of countries and the period under investigation.

influence FDI inflows, because factors related to the business cycles in home countries can be expected to also play an important role in the decision on acquiring a foreign firm or setting up a subsidiary abroad.[132] According to this hypothesis, a company's profits and, thus, available funds for FDI activities are likely to be higher in times of an economic upswing. Hence, economic activity in developed countries should affect FDI flows to emerging economies.[133] This leads us to control for the effect of the business cycle in industrial countries on FDI flows to emerging economies.

Our empirical study is based on the idea that FDI home and host country specificities together with gravity forces are important in determining FDI flows between individual countries. Therefore, we follow Brainard (1993, 1997), who provides a theoretical model for gravity-like forces in the context of FDI flow analyses.[134] The basic gravity model introduced by Tinbergen (1962) and modified by Brainard (1997) takes the form $F_{ij} = c\frac{M_i M_j}{D_i}$. The equation reflects that the flow (F) between two objects (i and j) is determined by the masses of the objects (M_i and M_j)[135] and the distance (D) between them; c is a constant. In log form the corresponding estimation equation reads as follows:

$$\log F_{ij} = c + \beta_1 \log M_i + \beta_2 \log M_j - \beta_3 \log D_i .$$

There are good reasons to include distance as a determinant of FDI flows. In particular, transaction costs of control and potential problems stemming from cultural differences and so forth are expected to increase with distance. Therefore, we use linear distances between the capitals of the home and the host countries as a proxy for the relative magnitude of these costs.

We begin our study by examining a crude form of a gravity model for FDI flows. In this specification, we include the logarithm (log) of home and host country GDP levels and the log of the distance between home and host countries

132 Levy-Yeyati, Panizza, and Stein (2003) follow a similar approach when examining the impact of business cycles in industrial countries on north-south FDI flows.

133 Sometimes, a firm may consider FDI particularly in times of economic downturn. This is the case if a firm is forced to respond to cost pressures that are higher during difficult economic times. One response can take the form of shifting a firm's production activities to countries with significantly lower wages.

134 Bergstrand (1985) offers a microeconomic foundation of gravity models in the context of international trade. His arguments can easily be applied to the case of FDI flows. However, to formally show this is beyond the scope of this study.

135 In the context of economic analysis the mass of a country is its GDP. Therefore, we replace mass (M) with GDP (Y).

as elementary variables. FDI_{ijt} represents the log of FDI flows from the home country i (i.e., a G-6 country) to the host country j (i.e., an emerging market) during period t. Denoting log GDP of the home country i (i.e., a G-6 country) and of the host country j (i.e., an emerging market) in year t by Y_{it} and Y_{jt}, respectively, and log distance between countries i and j by $DIST_{ij}$, the specification takes the form

$$FDI_{ijt} = \beta_0 + \beta_1 Y_{it} + \beta_2 Y_{jt} + \beta_3 DIST_{ij} + \varepsilon_{ijt}, \qquad (1)$$

where ε_{ijt} is a white noise error term.

In an extended gravity approach, we separate home- and host country-specific effects to capture individual characteristics of the different G-6 countries and the emerging markets.[136] We also introduce a time effect to reflect the influence of individual years on the FDI flows across countries. This leads to the following specification of the gravity model for the FDI flows between a home country i (i.e., a G-6 country) and host country j (i.e., an emerging market) in period t:

$$FDI_{ijt} = \beta_0 + \beta_1 Y_{it} + \beta_2 Y_{jt} + \beta_3 DIST_{ij} + \alpha_i + \gamma_j + \lambda_t + \varepsilon_{ijt}. \qquad (2)$$

In equation (2), α_i is the home country specific effect, γ_j is the host country specific effect, and λ_t is the time-specific effect.[137] We take the specific effects α_i, γ_j, and λ_t into account as fixed parameters.

We also modify the generic gravity model approach applied to FDI flows by examining whether more specific economic variables have explanatory power and can, therefore, replace the home and host country effects. Thus, we replace country dummy variables, i.e., the host and the home country specific effects, by explanatory variables that are characteristics for the home and the host countries' economic fundamentals, respectively, and can, therefore, be regarded as specifications of the push and pull factors of FDI.

Pull factors, i.e., factors that make a country an attractive location for investors are economic factors that positively impact the expected return on investment. For investors who look for a business location abroad, these factors are country characteristics that impact growth opportunities, production costs, and

136 We hereby apply arguments of Mátyás (1997, 1998), who emphasizes the importance of correctly specifying a gravity model to avoid false interpretation of the estimated coefficients and improper economic inference.

137 Home country specific effects, host country specific effects as well as time-specific effects are taken into consideration by including dummies for home countries, host countries, and the year of observation.

business risk. We, therefore, include the major macroeconomic variables that can be expected to have an impact on either of the three factors.

Economic growth and the openness of the host country are decisive macroeconomic factors that determine growth opportunities for the private sector and thus the potential return on an FDI project. GDP growth of the host countries, which measures recent dynamics of an economy, can serve as an indicator for expected developments, i.e., high economic growth in the past is often associated with high dynamics in the future. We, thus, include host country growth (g_{jt}) as one host country fundamental and expect the coefficient to be positive.

In theory, openness of an economy may be an important driver for FDI if a company aims at benefiting from low production costs in a potential host country. If the company wants to export its products from the host country of its FDI to other markets, it is interested in facing low trade barriers to be able to export at low costs. However, if a country offers a very attractive market and if trade barriers exist, foreign companies might invest in the country, i.e., undertaking FDI in the country, to serve the market from inside while circumventing trade barriers. Hence, the effect of a liberalized trade system on FDI flows is ambiguous and depends on the relative magnitude of the two effects. As it is convention to measure openness of a country ($OPEN_{jt}$) by the sum of exports and imports normalized by the country's GDP, an additional reason for the ambiguity of the effect on FDI is included. Specifically, as larger countries usually have lower shares of exports and imports relative to GDP, this measure is affected by the size of the country. The proxy will, thus, indicate higher trade barriers for a larger country than for a smaller country even if the two countries effectively have the same trade barriers in place.

FDI activities are associated with different types of risk in the host country. To capture both political and economic risk factors, we use the *Euromoney* country risk rating ($RISK_{jt}$). The rating index combines political risk with some aspects of economic risk.[138] As the index is constructed in such a way that it increases as risk declines, i.e., it can be considered a stability index, we expect a positive value of the risk coefficient in our regressions.

The high correlation between openness and risk that we find in our data (see Table A 3-3 in the Appendix)—the correlation coefficient is 0.58—suggests that the dominating effect on our openness variable is the degree of trade liberalization which, in turn, is associated with risk considerations. Therefore, we use the two variables OPEN and RISK as alternatives.

---

138 For a discussion of the interdependence of country risk and FDI, see Bevan and Estrin (2000).

Price stability is another macroeconomic indicator for economic stability and, thus, low business risk. Inflation is not taken into account in the *Euromoney* country risk index and inflation and the *Euromoney* country risk index are not correlated. We therefore use inflation ($INFL_{jt}$) as an additional indicator for economic stability and expect a negative coefficient.

Exchange rate volatility is an additional source of risk for foreign investors. One may, therefore, argue that investors prefer stable exchange rates. Whether they perceive more stability to be associated with fixed or flexible exchange rates is an empirical question. The Asian crisis and the Argentinean experience demonstrate that fixed exchange rates must not be confused with stable exchange rates. However, investors' perception in the 1990s may have been different. We also examine whether the exchange rate regime has an effect on the attractiveness of FDI. We use a dummy for a fixed exchange rate system in host countries (FIX_{jt}) as opposed to intermediate and floating exchange rate regimes.[139] The dummy takes a value of one in case of fixed exchange rates and zero otherwise. If investors preferred fixed regimes the coefficient should be positive and significant indicating that there is an additional stimulus of fixed exchange rates on FDI inflows.

High productivity and a low wage level are factors that make a country an attractive location for direct investors who seek to move production sites to low-cost locations. Productivity and wage developments are reflected in unit labor cost (ULC). We expect that ULC in host countries relative to ULC in the home country and other potential host countries can have an impact on the investment decision. Low relative ULC makes a country more competitive and thus an attractive place for investors, therefore, a negative coefficient is expected for relative ULC. Since consistent and reliable data on ULC are available for only few of the relevant countries[140] we run separate estimations including relative ULC (R_ULC_{jt}) as host country fundamental with a reduced host country sample.

---

139 While official data on the exchange rate system are regularly published by the International Monetary Fund, this data set represents only a de jure classification, which means that it is based on the regime the governments claim to have. However, it could well be that governments officially have a fixed exchange rate system but actually change the exchange rate regularly, while governments with officially flexible exchange rates subordinate their monetary policy to an exchange rate target. To address this problem Levy-Yegati and Sturzenegger (2002) construct a de facto classification by using a cluster analysis. We find this an appropriate approach and, therefore, use their data to classify exchange rate systems in the emerging markets included in our sample.

140 Data on ULC is available for Hong Kong, Singapore, South Korea, the Czech Republic, Hungary, Poland, Slovakia, Slovenia, Argentina, Brazil, Columbia, and Mexico.

We do not take into account host country population, since, for our sample, there is high multicollinearity between population and host country GDP.

As a home country characteristic or a push factor, we take into account the influence of economic development in the home countries on FDI flows to emerging economies. Specifically, we include GDP growth of the home countries (g_{it}) in the extended of the gravity model. Although one may argue that changes in GDP may only affect FDI flows with a lag, we do not include a lagged variable because one could also argue that investors pursue FDI projects in the future dependent on their expectations about future economic activity (i.e., future GDP) and that actual growth rates can serve as proxies for past expectations of investors.[141]

On the basis of these considerations, we estimate several additional specifications. When replacing the home country effects by home country fundamentals, i.e., GDP growth (g_{it}), the specification takes the following form:

$$FDI_{ijt} = \beta_0 + \beta_1 Y_{it} + \beta_2 Y_{jt} + \beta_3 DIST_{ij} + \beta_4 g_{it} + \gamma_j + \lambda_t + \varepsilon_{ijt}. \quad (3)$$

Starting again from specification (2), in the next step we replace the host country specific effects by host country fundamentals. As discussed above, we take either openness or risk into account, which leads to the two alternatively specifications (4a) and (4b):

$$\begin{aligned} FDI_{ijt} &= \beta_0 + \beta_1 Y_{it} + \beta_2 Y_{jt} + \beta_3 DIST_{ij} \\ &+ \beta_5 g_{jt} + \beta_6 OPEN_{jt} + \beta_7 INFL_{jt} + \beta_8 FIX_{jt} + \alpha_i + \lambda_t + \varepsilon_{ijt}, \end{aligned} \quad (4a)$$

$$\begin{aligned} FDI_{ijt} &= \beta_0 + \beta_1 Y_{it} + \beta_2 Y_{jt} + \beta_3 DIST_{ij} \\ &+ \beta_5 g_{jt} + \beta_6 RISK_{jt} + \beta_7 INFL_{jt} + \beta_8 FIX_{jt} + \alpha_i + \lambda_t + \varepsilon_{ijt}. \end{aligned} \quad (4b)$$

For the smaller host country sample for which ULC data are available, we estimate two specifications, including the same variables as given in (4a) and (4b) plus relative ULC (R_ULC_{jt}):

$$\begin{aligned} FDI_{ijt} &= \beta_0 + \beta_1 Y_{it} + \beta_2 Y_{jt} + \beta_3 DIST_{ij} + \beta_5 g_{jt} + \beta_6 OPEN_{jt} \\ &+ \beta_7 INFL_{jt} + \beta_8 FIX_{jt} + \beta_9 R\_ULC_{jt} + \alpha_i + \lambda_t + \varepsilon_{ijt}. \end{aligned} \quad (4c)$$

$$\begin{aligned} FDI_{ijt} &= \beta_0 + \beta_1 Y_{it} + \beta_2 Y_{jt} + \beta_3 DIST_{ij} + \beta_5 g_{jt} + \beta_6 RISK_{jt} \\ &+ \beta_7 INFL_{jt} + \beta_8 FIX_{jt} + \beta_9 R\_ULC_{jt} + \alpha_i + \lambda_t + \varepsilon_{ijt}. \end{aligned} \quad (4d)$$

141 More formally and using E as the expectation operator, one could write that $FDI_{ijt} = f(E_{t-1}[g_{it}], \ldots)$ with $E_{t-1}[g_{it}] = g_{it}$.

Finally, the complete form of our extended gravity model, where home country and host country specific effects are replaced by fundamentals, can be expressed as follows:

$$FDI_{ijt} = \beta_0 + \beta_1 Y_{it} + \beta_2 Y_{jt} + \beta_3 DIST_{ij} + \beta_4 g_{it} + \beta_5 g_{jt} + \beta_6 OPEN_{jt} + \beta_7 INFL_{jt} + \beta_8 FIX_{jt} + \lambda_t + \varepsilon_{ijt}, \quad (5a)$$

$$FDI_{ijt} = \beta_0 + \beta_1 Y_{it} + \beta_2 Y_{jt} + \beta_3 DIST_{ij} + \beta_4 g_{it} + \beta_5 g_{jt} + \beta_6 RISK_{jt} + \beta_7 INFL_{jt} + \beta_8 FIX_{jt} + \lambda_t + \varepsilon_{ijt}, \quad (5b)$$

$$FDI_{ijt} = \beta_0 + \beta_1 Y_{it} + \beta_2 Y_{jt} + \beta_3 DIST_{ij} + \beta_4 g_{it} + \beta_5 g_{jt} + \beta_6 OPEN_{jt} + \beta_7 INFL_{jt} + \beta_8 FIX_{jt} + \beta_9 R\_ULC_{jt} + \lambda_t + \varepsilon_{ijt}, \quad (5c)$$

$$FDI_{ijt} = \beta_0 + \beta_1 Y_{it} + \beta_2 Y_{jt} + \beta_3 DIST_{ij} + \beta_4 g_{it} + \beta_5 g_{jt} + \beta_6 RISK_{jt} + \beta_7 INFL_{jt} + \beta_8 FIX_{jt} + \beta_9 R\_ULC_{jt} + \lambda_t + \varepsilon_{ijt}. \quad (5d)$$

Equations (5a), (5b), (5c), and (5d) differ again by the use of openness and risk as alternative explanatory variables and in the case of (5c) and (5d) by extending host country fundamentals by taking relative ULC into account for the reduced host country sample.

As the dependent variable, we use the log of net annual FDI flows from each of the G-6 countries to an emerging economy. These flows include reinvested earnings[142] of the home country.[143] Regarding emerging economies included in our study as host countries of FDI, we focus on the three main regions of emerging markets mentioned above, i.e., Latin America, Asia, and central and eastern Europe.

We include all emerging markets of these regions provided that complete data on bilateral FDI flows and the explanatory variables used in the study are available. This condition is not met by, for example, Taiwan, Pakistan, Kazakhstan, Ukraine, and Peru. However, we are able to include a total of twenty-two emerging markets, of which nine are in Asia, seven are in Europe, and six are in Latin America. This sample group can be considered representative of the important emerging market regions. As Table 16 shows, FDI flows to this sample

142 Reinvested earnings on direct foreign investment consist of the retained earnings of a direct foreign investment enterprise that are treated as if they were distributed and remitted to the foreign investor and then reinvested in the foreign enterprise.

143 See OECD (1996).

of host countries represent nearly 80 percent of all FDI inflows to developing countries and the CEECs during the period under examination.

Table 16: FDI to emerging markets and importance of countries included in the study

		1992	1994	1996	1998	2000	2001	2002	2003
Total Inflows	Developing countries and central and eastern European countries (USD billions)	59.3	115.1	166.7	218.4	280.0	246.1	188.8	193.0
	Total FDI flows to Latin American host countries (USD billions)	13.2	25.7	37.8	60.9	71.7	61.8	36.9	28.7
	Total FDI flows to Asian host countries (USD billions)	27.8	61.6	83.3	87.8	134.7	95.1	80.7	90.5
	Total FDI flows to CEEC host countries (USD billions)	4.9	5.6	13.1	18.5	22.8	23.0	25.7	11.7
	Total FDI flows to all host countries (USD billions)	45.9	92.8	134.2	167.2	229.3	179.9	143.3	130.9
	... as % of developing countries and central and eastern European countries	77%	81%	81%	77%	82%	73%	76%	68%

Source: UNCTAD (2005) and own calculations.

3.2.2 Data sources

Data on bilateral FDI flows are taken from the 2005 electronic edition of the OECD's (2005a) *International Direct Investment Statistics Yearbook.* The time series available cover the period from 1992 through 2003 and are denominated in USD. OECD data for Japan are only partly available. However, complete data are available from the Japanese Ministry of Finance. A consistency check between the data provided by the Ministry of Finance and the OECD data for Japan reveals a correlation of 99.5 percent between the two data sets. We thus use the data of the Japanese Ministry of Finance. To take logs of all FDI flows we follow the method proposed by Eichengreen and Irwin (1995, 1997) and refined by Levy-Yeyati, Panizza, and Stein (2003). Both use a semi-log specification to cope with zeros and negative values. Instead of the log of the raw FDI data, we use sign(FDI) log (1 + |FDI|). By applying this transformation we are able to include all available data points including zeros and negative values[144] in our analysis. Furthermore, all data points that were zero before the transformation retain their value through the transformation. The advantage of this technique over the conventional log transformation is that no data points are lost. Additionally, this transformation does not impact the general outcome of the analysis. Adding one unit to the observed absolute amount of FDI flows allows the logarithm also of data points recording zero FDI flows to be calculated. Since the lowest amount of a nonzero observation is USD 0.6 million and is not significantly impacted by an increase by USD 1 this operation has a negligible impact on the log of FDI flows. Due to this fact the estimated coefficients based on the transformed FDI flows can still be interpreted as elasticities.

Data on nominal *GDP* in USD are taken from the World Development Indicators (World Bank, 2004b). GDP *growth* is calculated as the annual change of GDP. *Distance* between home country and host country is the great circle distance between the capitals of home and host country, which is obtained from www.koordinaten.de/online/dist_wel.shtml.

For *risk*, we applied the *Euromoney* country risk rating published in *Euromoney* magazine. The index ranges from zero to 100. A value of zero represents the highest and a value of 100 the lowest risk level. The index summarizes different influences on the overall risk of a country including economic performance, political risk, debt indicators, access to bank lending, access to short-term finance, access to capital markets, discount on forfeiting, credit ratings, and debt in default or rescheduled. Details on the methodology of the index construction are published regularly in the March and in the September issues of *Euromoney* magazine. *Inflation* is the annual change in the CPI. Data on the CPI are taken from the International Financial Statistics (IMF, 2005c) database. The categorization of *exchange rate systems* is taken from Levy-Yeyati and Sturzenegger (2002). The classification is based on the actual developments in exchange rates and the behavior of central banks. Based on the changes in foreign reserves, the tendency of central banks to intervene in the foreign exchange market is determined. The *de facto* exchange rate regime is derived from the change in nominal exchange rate, the volatility of the changes, and the volatility of foreign reserves. The regimes are categorized in three groups, float, intermedi-

---

144 Negative FDI inflows are recorded if the repatriation of returns on FDI from a host country to the home country exceeds the amount of new FDI undertaken by home country investors within the respective year.

ate, and fix. The data provided in the paper by Levy-Yeyati and Sturzenegger cover the time period 1992 through 2000. For 2001 through 2003 we assume that the exchange rate system from 2000 persisted. The *de facto* exchange rate classifications do not change frequently and while we did not conduct an empirical analysis on the exchange rate system for 2001 through 2003, qualitative evidence indicated that the exchange rate systems of the host countries that we consider in the analysis did not change over the period from 2000 through 2003. Furthermore, neither significance nor the sign of the exchange rate dummy changes when the empirical analysis is carried out on data covering the period 1992 through 2000 for which data on the *de facto* classification of the exchange rate are actually available.

Relative host country ULC is an index value calculated as the ratio of host country ULC and a common index of ULC for advanced economies countries. The index is based on data of ULC for the manufacturing sector. The data are taken from the World Economic Outlook (IMF, 2005h) database. ULC data are available for the Czech Republic, Hungary, Poland, Slovakia, Slovenia, Hong Kong, Singapore, South Korea, Argentina, Brazil, Columbia, and Mexico.

3.2.3 Results

3.2.3.1 Outcome for the panel including all host countries

Considering bilateral FDI flows from the G-6 to twenty-two emerging markets we apply OLS estimates[145] to the model specifications outlined in section 3.2 . The countries included in the sample are Czech Republic, Hungary, Poland, Slovakia, Slovenia, Russia, Turkey, China, Hong Kong, India, Indonesia, Malaysia, Philippines, Singapore, South Korea, Thailand, Argentina, Brazil, Chile, Columbia, Mexico, and Venezuela.[146] While the selection of the home countries considered in

145 We conduct panel unit root tests for all variables (for the results of the Levin, Lin, and Chu (2002) *t*-statistics see Table A 3-5 in the Appendix). Since the null of a unit root must be rejected for all panels, OLS is an appropriate estimation technique.

146 Regarding the group of the CEECs, no data on bilateral FDI flows are available for the Baltic countries. The estimations have been carried out with the whole panel of host countries as well as with a reduced panel excluding Russia and Turkey. These two countries are not part of the CEECs or one of the other two emerging market regions and they add significant volatility to the data sample.

the study is based on the size of the economies, the selection of the emerging markets is also based on data availability considerations.[147]

The estimation results of the basic gravity-specification as given in equation (1)—where the GDP of the home and the host countries and distance serves as the explanatory variable—show that size of home and host economy positively impact FDI flows while distance has an obstructive effect. The results of this benchmark specification (1) are provided in the first column of Table 17. All coefficients are significant and have the expected sign. The basic gravity model allows about 13 percent of the annual bilateral FDI flows from the G-6 countries to the twenty-two emerging economies included in the sample to be explained.

In a second step, we include country-specific effects for home and host countries as well as time-specific effects as outlined in section 3.2 and as given in equation (2). The results are shown in the second column of Table 17. Two of the gravity variables, i.e., distance and host country GDP, are still significant and show the expected sign. The coefficient of home country GDP, however, is significant but reveals the wrong sign while all home country fixed effects emerge as significant at conventional levels. An explanation for this result can be seen in the nonlinear relation between home country size and FDI outflows. FDI outflows do not increase proportionally with GDP; i.e., a large country like the United States in 2003 had more than six times the GDP of a country like France but less than three times the amount of FDI outflows. This is due to the fact that large countries offer more opportunities to diversify investment within the country itself and have a more diverse economic structure from which companies may benefit when choosing business locations. In the results generated by estimating equation (2), the coefficient of home country GDP reflects this nonlinear relation ship. The host country dummy coefficients are significantly negative and show that, compared to the flows coming from the United States, emerging markets received relatively smaller FDI flows from the smaller G-6 countries. This line of argumentation is supported by the results of an estimation of a specification that include the square of the log of home country GDP as an explanatory variable.[148] While the coefficient of this variable turns out to be negative, the home GDP coefficient turns positive again. The coefficients of the two variables, however,

147 Since no comprehensive data set on bilateral FDI flows from Canada is available, we had to exclude Canada. Emerging markets for which a complete data set for our estimations is not available include Taiwan, Pakistan, Kazakhstan, Ukraine, and Peru.

148 Dunning (1981) argues for a nonlinear relationship between FDI and country size and suggests including a quadratic term in the estimation. Dunning and Narula (1996) apply such a specification and find statistical support for the use of quadratic specifications.

reach significance levels of only about 15 percent and 30 percent, respectively.[149] We, therefore, apply the nonquadratic model while acknowledging that the estimation results of a specification including host country specific effects are affected by the nonlinear relationship between home country size and FDI outflows.

The time-specific effects are positive and significant for all years except 2002. Since 2003 is considered the benchmark year, the time effects reflect the sharp fall in FDI toward the end of the observation period. The insignificant coefficient of the 2002 time effect reflects that it does not differ significantly from the 2003 effect. We therefore conclude that in 2002 and 2003 there exist common cyclical factors that affected FDI flows for the countries included in our study as a whole. To cover these time-specific effects in specifications (3) through (5) of our analysis we include time dummies for the years 2002 and 2003.

Host country specific effects are significant in more than half of all cases. The benchmark country is Columbia and a significantly positive coefficient means that a country receives relatively more FDI inflows than Columbia and than can be explained by host country fundamentals. The fact that some countries, e.g., China, Korea, India, and Russia, reveal negative country-specific effects might be due to a nonlinear relationship between country size and FDI flows, equivalent to the relation discussed above. The economies of all four countries are relatively large compared to, for example, Singapore or the CEECs. FDI inflows to such large countries might be smaller relative to their country size than the flows received by a small country. Reasons for this might be that investors have an incentive to invest in different countries to diversify the country risk of their investments. At the same time a minimum investment might be necessary in each location to reach the critical mass for a profitable investment.[150] In the case of small countries this leads to investments that are relatively large compared to the countries' size. The R^2 value is now nearly twice as high as in the benchmark case.

---

149 Table A 3-6 in the Appendix presents the results of an estimation of specification (1) including the square of *Yit*. The estimation reveals the nonlinear relation between home country GDP and FDI flows and thus supports our line of argumentation.

150 In some emerging countries as well as other developing countries, minimum investment requirements are imposed of foreign investors. India for example requires a minimum of USD 10 million capital investment for wholly owned subsidiaries or a minimum of USD 5 million capital investment for joint ventures (Consulate General of India, 2005). The amount of foreign investment in Korea is required to be at least Korean wong 50 million per case (Invest Korea, 2005). See OECD (2005c) for an overview on such requirements in African countries.

In a third step, we replace the home country specific effect (i.e., the variable α_i) by GDP growth of the individual home countries while keeping the host country specific effects. The results are shown as specification (3) in Table 17. All three gravity factors reveal the expected sign and are significant at conventional levels. The coefficient of the push factor of FDI included in our study, i.e., the home GDP growth rate, is positive and significant as well. This indicates that the business cycle of the home country has a significant impact on the decision to invest abroad. The positive sign of the estimated coefficient indicates that the propensity to conduct FDI will increase during an economic upswing. The results also indicate that the number of significant host country effects as well as the impact of host country effects on FDI remains basically the same. The coefficients of the time dummies for 2002 and 2003 are significantly negative and, thus, reflect the observed slowdown in FDI flows. The adjusted R^2 declines slightly from about 23 percent for specification (2) to 21 percent for specification (3).

In a fourth step, we keep the home country effects from specification (2), but replace the host country effect by host country fundamentals that present specific pull factors for FDI. These factors comprise GDP growth, openness, inflation, and the fixed exchange rate dummy. As a modification of this specification (4a), we use the risk variable as an alternative to openness and show this result as specification (4b) in Table 17. The results from the two specifications differ slightly. Two of the coefficients of the gravity variables, namely the host country size and distance coefficient, are significant and reveal the expected sign. Home country GDP, however, is insignificant in both specifications. As for specification (2) above, all home country specific effects are significantly negative. An interpretation of these results is that the home country specific effects replace home country GDP and since the United States is the benchmark home country the negative sign of the coefficient reflects the impact of the home country size. A negative coefficient for home country GDP captures the nonlinear relationship between home country size and FDI flows. While the coefficient for home country GDP is negative it is significant at a level of 25 percent and below only.

The openness variable as well as the variable indicating the absence of risk are significant and both reveal the expected sign. However, while inflation is found to have a significantly negative impact on FDI in case of openness being considered instead of risk, it turns out to be insignificant in specification (4b). In turn the fixed exchange rate dummy changes from insignificant to significant when openness is replaced by risk. As shown in Table A 3-3 in the Appendix, on the one hand $OPEN_j$ is weakly positively correlated with the fixed exchange rate dummy but almost not with inflation, and $RISK_j$ on the other hand is weakly negatively correlated with inflation but not with the fixed exchange rate dummy.

These results suggest that a fixed exchange rate regime might have a positive impact on FDI inflows as well as on a country's international trade. Additionally, inflation is suggested to have a negative impact on FDI inflows. To some extent the destabilizing effect of inflation might go together with other country risks and is, to some extent, also reflected in the indicator for country risk.

The economic development in the host country, i.e., host country growth, has a significantly positive coefficient when applying specification (4a). Since host country growth reveals a higher degree of co-movement with the $RISK_j$ variable than with the $OPEN_j$ variable, namely a correlation of about 48 percent compared to 7 percent, we do not find a significant impact of host country growth on FDI when including $RISK_j$ as an explanatory variable. As in the previous specifications, the time dummies for 2002 and 2003 are significant and negative. The R^2 value is about the same as for the estimates of specifications (2) and (3).

Turning to specification (5a) and (5b) we replace home country and host country dummies with country-specific fundamentals, i.e., home country GDP growth, host country GDP growth, inflation, and the fixed exchange rate dummy, as well as openness or risk in the two alternative specifications. The estimation results are presented in the last two columns of Table 17. The coefficients of all three gravity factors, home country GDP growth as well as of the openness or risk variable are significant and reveal the expected sign. As in specifications (4a) and (4b), the coefficient of host country GDP growth is only significantly positive when openness is considered as an explanatory variable while the fixed exchange rate dummy is only significantly positive when risk is considered instead of openness. We find, however, no significant impact of host country inflation on the magnitude of FDI flows. Again, the time dummies for 2002 and 2003 are significant and reflect the drop in FDI flows toward the end of the observation period.

The adjusted R^2 value is 19 percent and 20 percent for specifications (5a) and (5b), respectively. While these specifications do not include country-specific effects, the explanatory power is almost as high as for specifications (3), (4a), and (4b), which include such effects. This finding shows that the macroeconomic factors we consider as push and pull factors carry most of the information necessary to explain the differences among bilateral FDI flows between G-6 home countries and the twenty-two emerging market economies considered in this part of the analysis. The overall result from the analysis covering the broad panel of host countries can be interpreted as support for applying the gravity model as suggested by Mátyás (1997) to FDI flows.

Regarding the magnitude of the impact that the different explanatory variables have on bilateral FDI flows from the G-6 countries to emerging markets, depending on the specification we find that an increase of host country GDP of 1 percent leads, ceteris paribus, to an increase in FDI inflows of between 0.9 percent and 2.5 percent. According to our results an increase in the home country GDP by 1 percent leads, ceteris paribus, to an increase in FDI outflows of about 1.2 percent. Increasing the distance between home country and host country by 1 percent—all other factors being equal—causes FDI flows between the two countries to decline by 0.8 percent to 1.4 percent. The coefficients of the remaining variables cannot be interpreted as elasticities. The fact that the size of these coefficients is stable across specifications shows the robustness of the estimations.

While almost all of the emerging economies considered in the analysis above belong either to the group of CEECs or to the Asian or Latin American region, neither Russia nor Turkey fit any of these three regional clusters. Additionally, the economic developments as well as the evolution of FDI flows to these two countries have been quiet volatile over the past decade. We therefore consider a reduced panel of 20 emerging markets excluding Russia and Turkey and undertake the same empirical analysis as for the whole panel. The results of the estimations are presented in Table 18. Compared to the outcome from the full panel, the results change only slightly. In particular, no specification reveals a significant impact of host country GDP growth on FDI flows. In specification (3) the coefficient of home country GDP growth is insignificant. Other than these, the exclusion of the two host countries from the panel had no notable impact on the magnitude or the sign of the estimated coefficients.

Table 17: Regression results based on a panel including all home and host countries

Specification 1)	(1)	(2)	(3)	(4a)	(4b)	(5a)	(5b)
C 2)	-3.095***	17.480**	-4.783***	13.953**	10.208*	-3.940***	-5.213***
	(-2.961)	(2.284)	(-2.447)	(2.186)	(1.609)	(-3.823)	(-4.906)
Y_j	0.913***	2.456***	2.025***	1.175***	1.068***	1.137***	1.047***
	(-10.708)	(-5.754)	(5.911)	(12.473)	(12.453)	(12.071)	(12.174)
Y_i	1.174***	-1.477**	1.291***	-0.736	-0.454	1.206***	1.207***
	(10.565)	(-1.874)	(11.655)	(-1.043)	(-0.649)	(10.925)	(10.992)
$DIST_{ij}$	-0.788***	-1.365***	-1.312***	-0.962***	-0.952***	-0.924***	-0.921***
	(-8.527)	(-10.606)	(-10.283)	(-10.564)	(-10.568)	(-10.193)	(-10.268)
g_i			0.146***			0.143***	0.159***
g_j				0.028*	-0.02	0.031**	-0.018
OPEN / RISK				0.572***	0.038***	0.537***	0.038***
INFL				-0.067**	-0.032	-0.046	-0.014
FIX				0.158	0.267*	0.209	0.298**
D_FR		-4.636***		-3.122***	-2.618**		
D_DE		-4.165***		-2.859***	-2.461***		
D_JP		-1.448***		-0.805*	-0.603		
D_UK		-4.684***		-3.092**	-2.553**		
D_IT		-6.351***		-4.636***	-4.074***		
D_CN		-2.812**	-1.790**				
D_HK		0.496	0.747*				
D_IN		-2.234***	-1.551**				
D_ID		-0.551	-0.268				
D_MY		0.604	0.6				
D_PH		0.834*	0.762*				
D_SG		2.796***	2.770***				
D_KR		-2.621***	-1.867***				
D_TH		0.459	0.661				

Table 17: Regression results based on a panel including all home and host countries (concluded)

D_CZ		0.238	0.146				
D_HU		1.236**	1.083**				
D_PL		-1.334**	-1.024**				
D_RU		-3.458***	-2.904***				
D_SK		1.589**	0.98				
D_SI		0.831	0.199				
D_TR		-1.329**	-0.941*				
D_AR		-0.753	-0.328				
D_BR		-1.964**	-1.140*				
D_CL		1.301***	1.191**				
D_MX		-1.989**	-1.258*				
D_VE		0.458	0.485				
D_1992		1.305***					
D_1993		1.607***					
D_1994		1.809***					
D_1995		1.598***					
D_1996		1.921***					
D_1997		1.587***					
D_1998		1.368***					
D_1999		1.956***					
D_2000		1.418***					
D_2001		1.333***					
D_2002		0.089	-1.478***	-1.468***	-1.372***	-1.418***	-1.288**
D_2003			-2.000***	-1.587***	-1.455***	-1.896***	-1.700***
R-squared	0.13	0.252	0.226	0.21	0.218	0.192	0.201
Adjusted *R*-squared	0.128	0.232	0.212	0.203	0.21	0.186	0.195
F-test 3)		6.073***	6.915***	11.032***	12.150***		
Cross-sections	132	132	132	132	132	132	132
Observations	1,534	1,534	1,534	1,534	1,534	1,534	1,534

*, **, *** denotes significance at a 10%, 5%, or 1% level, respectively. *t*-statistics are shown in parentheses.

1) Pooled least squares estimation; Sample: 1992–2003.
2) When home country, host country, and/or time specific effects are included in the specifications, the estimated constant reflects the United States, Columbia, and the year 2003.
3) The *F*-test tests the joint significance of the included dummy variables by comparing the explanatory power of each specification to that of specification (1).

Table 18: Regression results based on a panel including all home countries and all host countries but Russia and Turkey

Specification 1)	(1)	(2)	(3)	(4a)	(4b)	(5a)	(5b)
C 2)	-3.526***	15.448**	-7.112***	13.813**	10.085*	-4.475***	-5.658***
	(-3.187)	-1.898	(-3.400)	-2.054	-1.502	(-4.118)	(-4.970)
Yj	1.006***	2.710***	2.318***	1.285***	1.102***	1.249***	1.083***
	-11.356	-5.699	-6.171	-12.937	-12.298	-12.594	-12.072
Yi	1.277***	-1.430**	1.405***	-0.686	-0.411	1.306***	1.297***
	-11.009	(-1.710)	-12.403	(-0.923)	(-0.555)	-11.333	-11.266
DISTij	-0.871***	-1.320***	-1.266***	-1.026***	-0.958***	-0.994***	-0.934***
	(-8.963)	(-9.863)	(-9.551)	(-10.743)	(-10.158)	(-10.432)	(-9.927)
gi			0.022			0.134**	0.146**
			-1.009			-2.161	-2.354
gj				0.01	-0.026	0.016	-0.021
				-0.52	(-1.160)	-0.796	(-0.955)
OPEN / RISK				0.609***	0.035***	0.575***	0.035***
				-5.662	-5.535	-5.31	-5.413
INFL				-0.054*	-0.031	-0.039	-0.017
				(-1.358)	(-0.762)	(-0.963)	(-0.405)
FIX				0.013	0.218	0.069	0.254*
				-0.071	-1.254	-0.376	-1.449
D_FR		-4.723***		-3.278***	-2.762**		
D_DE		-4.143***		-2.935***	-2.511**		
D_JP		-1.438**		-0.811*	-0.59		
D_UK		-4.655***		-3.123**	-2.577**		
D_IT		-6.325***		-4.692***	-4.113***		
D_CN		-3.398***	-2.634***				
D_HK		0.35	0.545				
D_IN		-2.622***	-2.079***				
D_ID		-0.736	-0.514				
D_MY		0.595	0.507				
D_PH		0.872**	0.783*				
D_SG		2.799***	2.691***				

Table 18: Regression results based on a panel including all home countries and all host countries but Russia and Turkey (concluded)

D_KR		-3.047***	-2.428***				
D_TH		0.336	0.475				
D_CZ		0.414	0.347				
D_HU		1.438***	1.297**				
D_PL		-1.414**	-1.168**				
D_SK		2.032**	1.463**				
D_SI		1.284*	0.695				
D_AR		-1.030*	-0.642				
D_BR		-2.460**	-1.713**				
D_CL		1.338***	1.166**				
D_MX		-2.419***	-1.762**				
D_VE		0.461	0.542				
D_1992		1.445***					
D_1993		1.800***					
D_1994		1.963***					
D_1995		1.696***					
D_1996		2.065***					
D_1997		1.691***					
D_1998		1.625***					
D_1999		2.011***					
D_2000		1.576***					
D_2001		1.507***					
D_2002		0.253	-1.615***	-1.451***	-1.345***	-1.415***	-1.283**
D_2003			-2.274***	-1.716***	-1.566***	-2.046***	-1.837***
R-squared	0.154	0.264	0.238	0.234	0.233	0.216	0.216
Adjusted *R*-squared	0.152	0.243	0.224	0.226	0.225	0.21	0.211
F-test 3)		5.283***	5.961***	10.198***	10.089***		
Cross-sections	120	120	120	120	120	120	120
Observations	1,390	1,390	1,390	1,390	1,390	1,390	1,390

*, **, *** denotes significance at a 10%, 5%, or 1% level, respectively. *t*-statistics are shown in parentheses.

1) Pooled least squares estimation; Sample: 1992–2003.
2) When home country, host country, and/or time-specific effects are included in the specifications, the estimated constant reflects the United States, Columbia, and the year 2003.
3) The F-test tests the joint significance of the included dummy variables by comparing the explanatory power of each specification to that of specification (1).

3.2.3.2 *Outcome for the regional host country panels*

The three emerging market regions included in the full panel covered by the analyses above are in different economic situations and experienced different regional paths of economic development. Over the period under examination the CEECs were going through the process of economic transition while the major concern of the Asian and the Latin American countries was to cope with the effects of different financial crises.

To examine how regional differences impact bilateral FDI flows we first include regional dummies into the analysis while keeping the sample of 20 emerging economies. The results are given in Table 19. In a next step we split the panel into three regional subpanels, i.e., a panel including the five CEECs, an Asian panel of nine host countries, and a Latin American panel covering six host countries.

Including regional dummies in the analysis reveals that significant interregional differences exist with respect to bilateral FDI from the G-6 to the twenty emerging markets. The results presented in Table 19 shows significantly positive coefficients for the regional dummies of Asia and Latin America. This indicates that the benchmark region, i.e., the CEECs, ceteris paribus, received less FDI inflows than the other two emerging market regions. The gravity factors have coefficients of the same sign, about the same magnitude, and comparable level of significance as in the estimations excluding regional dummies. Home country GDP growth reveals a significantly positive impact whenever included as an explanatory variable. Furthermore, the coefficient of country risk or openness has the expected sign and continues to be highly significant.

As regional-specific effects have an effect on FDI flows, we split the sample into regional samples to see whether the macroeconomic factors considered as push and pull factors for FDI have a different impact on FDI flows, depending on the region a country is located in. We estimate specifications (1) through (5b) for the three regional panels separately and present the results for the three regions in Table 20 through Table 22.

Regarding FDI flows to the CEECs, host country size as in the previous estimations has a significantly positive impact on FDI flows to this region. Home country GDP coefficients are significantly positive in all cases except when home country specific effects are included in the estimation. These two results are inline with the outcome of the estimations based on the entire set of host countries. Results differ slightly from previous estimations for the third gravity factor, i.e., distance. The distance between home and host country becomes insignificant in specifications (2), (4a), and (4b) for the panel of the CEECs. This particularity in the outcome for the regional panel of the CEECs could be due to the geographical proximity of the countries in the region. Compared to the distance between the countries and for example the United States or Japan the intraregional distances are relatively small. Therefore, the perceived difference in distance to each of the five CEECs for investors coming from one of the G-6 countries might be negligible. Furthermore, specifications (4a) and (4b) take home country specific effects into account, which in the case of the CEECs partly capture the specific impact of the distance between the home country and the host country.

In the case of the CEECs our results show that for the period under review home country GDP growth has no significant impact on FDI flows to the five European transition countries under consideration. This finding suggests that FDI inflows to the CEECs did not depend on the economic development in the home countries. The impact of the privatization process in the transition economies can be seen as one explanation for this observation. Investors had to invest according to the one-off opportunities resulting from the privatization of state-owned assets. In this context the timing of the investment decision was not in the hand of the investors but was driven by the progress of the transition process.

According to our analysis, host country GDP growth as well as inflation have no significant impact on FDI flows to the CEECs. Openness and risk, however, have a significant effect on the expected direction. Compared to the estimation results for the full panel of host countries, the coefficient of openness in the case of the CEEC panel is found to be significantly larger[151] while the impact of country risk is slightly smaller than for the full panel. The parallel occurrence of economic transition and EU integration might be part of the driving forces behind this finding. The transition process, or more specifically the privatization of public assets during this process, attracted FDI. The integration into the EU on the one hand allowed the CEECs to integrate into the European market and thus to extend their external trade; on the other hand the orientation of the CEECs toward the EU and the declaration of willingness to adhere to EU rules with respect to policies and governance standards might have reduced the perception of country risk for this region. Therefore, in the case of the CEECs investors might be less influenced by risk assessments than in the case of countries where they see no external standard to which a country commits to comply with.

The coefficient of the fixed exchange rate dummy is found to be significantly positive. Slovakia is the only country among the CEECs that follows a

151 The coefficient for openness in specifications (4a) and (5a) in the case of the CEEC panel is more than two times the coefficient estimated for the full panel of host countries. The deviation is statistically significant at a probability level of 95 percent.

fixed exchange rate system over most of the observation period.[152] The results for specifications (2) and (3) that include country dummies show a significantly positive country specific effect for Slovakia. Specifications (4a) through (5b) do not take into account country-specific effects. The fixed exchange rate dummy might, therefore, partly assume the function of a country specific effect for Slovakia.

The overall results for the CEEC panel indicate that FDI flows to the transition countries were to a lesser extent driven by economic fundamentals or country-specific effects. Compared to the results generated for the full host country panel, the explanatory power[153] of the estimation for the CEEC panel is lower for all specifications except for specification (1), which reveals about the same explanatory power for both panels. Furthermore, the F-test is insignificant for all of the four specifications including country dummy variables, i.e., specifications (2) through (4b). The relatively better performance of the basic gravity model suggests that in the case of the CEECs the gravity factors contribute most of the explanatory power and that country-specific effects cannot significantly improve the model's performance. Time dummies for 2002 and 2003 are significantly negative when included in the estimation. This shows that FDI flows to the CEECs were affected by the general downturn in global FDI flows.

Turning to the Asian host country panel, Table 21 shows that FDI flows from the G-6 to the Asian host countries are mostly driven by the gravity factors as well as by the countries' openness or country risk. The home country GDP coefficient and the distance coefficient become insignificant if home country specific effects are included in the specification. As discussed above, the nonlinear relationship between FDI and home country size and the geographical closeness of the host countries, respectively, are the probable causes for this outcome. Home country GDP growth has a positive impact on FDI inflows to the Asian countries and the coefficient is found to be significant at conventional levels for two out of three specifications. With regard to host country fundamentals openness or country risk play a dominant role. The coefficients of these two variables are significant at a 1 percent significance level and reveal the expected sign. No other host country fundamentals are found to have a significant impact on FDI inflows.

Compared to the benchmark home country, i.e., the United States, Italy and to a lesser extent also Germany provide relatively less FDI to the Asian coun-

152 Slovakia, according to the definition of Levy-Yeyati and Sturzenegger (2002), follows a fixed exchange rate system for eight out of twelve observations. For the Czech Republic, Hungary, and Slovenia a fixed exchange rate system is only observed for three out of twelve years.

153 Explanatory power is measured by the adjusted R-squared.

tries. Compared to the benchmark host country, i.e., Thailand, Singapore receives relatively more while India or Korea receives relatively smaller FDI inflows. The time dummy for 2003 is significantly negative whenever it is included in the estimation and the size of the coefficient is about the same as for the full panel and the CEEC's panel estimations. The 2002 dummy is smaller than in the case of the other panels and insignificant in two out of the five specifications, including a dummy for 2002 and 2003. Furthermore, in specification (2) the 2002 dummy is significantly positive. This indicates that the Asian countries in 2002 as in all the years before received relatively more FDI inflows than in 2003. The major effect of the downturn in global FDI flows occurred in the Asian host countries only in 2003, about one year later than in the CEECs.

The explanatory power for all specifications is higher for the Asian panel than for the full panel and for the CEEC panel. The *F*-test shows that the inclusion of country-specific effects and time dummies in specifications (2) through (4b) adds to the performance of the model.

The main factors determining FDI flows to the Latin American host countries are gravity factors, home country GDP growth, and host country inflation. The results for the Latin American panel are provided in Table 22. Among the gravity factors, host country size has a prominent role for the determination of FDI flows. The coefficient of home country GDP is positive and significant at a 1 percent significance level for all seven specifications. The home country GDP coefficient, across specifications, shows the same pattern as in the case of the full panel and the Asian panel; i.e., it turns negative when home country specific effects are included in the estimation. Again, the nonlinear relation between FDI outflows and country size is the likely reason for this outcome. Distance has a negative coefficient that is significant if no host country fundamentals are included in the estimation.

Regarding the economic fundamentals, home country GDP growth reveals a significantly positive coefficient. The impact of home country GDP growth is more significant than for the other two regional panels. This might be due to the dominant role of the United States as a source of FDI for the Latin American countries and to the relatively high growth rate of the U.S. economy in comparison to the other home countries.[154]

154 GDP in the United States between 1992 and 2003 grew by over 3.2 percent per year while the GDP of the other five home countries over the same period grew on average by less than 1.7 percent per year.

Table 19: Regression results including regional dummies based on a panel including all home countries and all host countries except Russia and Turkey

Specification 1)	(1)	(2)	(3)	(4a)	(4b)	(5a)	(5b)
C 2)	-1.882*	21.919***	-1.859*	15.160***	11.181*	-3.578***	-4.219***
	(-1.495)	(2.755)	(-1.499)	(2.256)	(1.663)	(-2.837)	(-3.250)
Yj	0.878***	0.906***	0.925***	1.281***	1.003***	1.225***	0.976***
	(8.851)	(9.312)	(9.516)	(11.082)	(10.067)	(10.581)	(9.756)
Yi	1.329***	-1.394*	1.337***	-0.71	-0.334	1.343***	1.341***
	(11.330)	(-1.635)	(11.385)	(-0.956)	(-0.451)	(11.572)	(11.542)
DISTij	-1.115***	-1.175***	-1.158***	-1.211***	-1.174***	-1.187***	-1.159***
	(-8.383)	(-8.948)	(-8.877)	(-9.320)	(-9.030)	(-9.195)	(-8.981)
gi			0.161***			0.137**	0.157***
			(2.568)			(2.211)	(2.527)
gj				0.024	-0.021	0.029*	-0.017
				(1.180)	(-0.946)	(1.400)	(-0.753)
OPEN / RISK				0.767***	0.036***	0.710***	0.036***
				(5.964)	(5.465)	(5.492)	(5.325)
INFL				-0.072**	-0.034	-0.054	-0.019
				(-1.772)	(-0.836)	(-1.323)	(-0.468)
FIX				-0.034	0.219	0.029	0.254*
				(-0.188)	(1.259)	(0.160)	(1.451)
D_FR		-4.598***		-3.400***	-2.717**		
D_DE		-4.005***		-3.082***	-2.538***		
D_JP		-1.303**		-0.888**	-0.613		
D_UK		-4.510***		-3.245***	-2.522**		
D_IT		-6.177***		-4.829***	-4.065**		

Table 19: Regression results including regional dummies based on a panel including all home countries and all host countries except Russia and Turkey (concluded)

Asia	1.012***	1.042***	3.099***	0.242	0.653**	0.327	0.704**
Latin America	0.766**	0.795**	2.211**	0.897***	0.880***	0.924***	0.921**
D_1992		0.519					
D_1993		1.016**					
D_1994		1.363***					
D_1995		1.363***					
D_1996		1.879***					
D_1997		1.561***					
D_1998		1.296***					
D_1999		1.750***					
D_2000		1.416***					
D_2001		1.323***					
D_2002		0.07	-1.293***	-1.443***	-1.329***	-1.404***	-1.250***
D_2003			-1.851***	-1.726***	-1.553***	-2.059***	-1.807***
R-squared	0.16	0.224	0.2	0.24	0.237	0.221	0.22
Adjusted *R*-squared	0.157	0.212	0.195	0.231	0.228	0.214	0.213
F-test 3)		5.357***	9.986***	6.974***	7.108***		
Cross-sections	120	120	120	120	120	120	120
Observations	1,390	1,390	1,390	1,390	1,390	1,390	1,390

*, **, *** denotes significance at a 10%, 5%, or 1% level, respectively. *t*-statistics are shown in parentheses.

1) Pooled least squares estimation; Sample: 1992–2003.
2) When home country, host region, and/or time-specific effects are included in the specifications, the estimated constant reflects the United States, central and eastern Europe, and the year 2003.
3) The *F*-test tests the joint significance of the included dummy variables by comparing the explanatory power of each specification to that of specification (1).

Table 20: Regression results based on a panel including all home countries and central and eastern European host countries

Specification 1)	(1)	(2)	(3)	(4a)	(4b)	(5a)	(5b)
C 2)	-0.73	-7.07	-3.636**	-10.52	-13.93	-5.548***	-4.454**
	(-0.452)	(-0.475)	(-2.006)	(-0.786)	(-1.027)	(-2.466)	(-2.116)
Y_j	1.169***	2.357***	1.975***	1.906***	1.529***	1.926***	1.553***
	(6.37)	(4.61)	(4.98)	(6.36)	(6.97)	(6.55)	(7.29)
Y_i	0.804***	1.39	0.958***	1.24	1.61	0.936***	0.956***
	(2.48)	(0.93)	(2.92)	(0.91)	(1.19)	(2.86)	(2.91)
$DIST_{ij}$	-0.870***	-1.424*	-1.035***	-0.72	-0.58	-0.969***	-0.962***
	(-3.902)	(-1.575)	(-4.608)	(-1.177)	(-0.945)	(-4.335)	(-4.289)
g_i			0.01			0.01	0.03
			(0.08)			(0.13)	(0.25)
g_j				0.02	0.01	0.01	0.00
				(0.27)	(0.11)	(0.23)	(0.07)
OPEN / RISK				1.398**	0.028*	1.402**	0.026*
				(2.04)	(1.66)	(2.04)	(1.54)
INFL				0.27	0.09	0.29	0.05
				(0.32)	(0.10)	(0.36)	(0.06)
FIX				1.206***	1.164***	1.193***	1.122***
				(3.01)	(2.91)	(3.03)	(2.86)
D_FR		0.64		1.56	2.46		
D_DE		-0.14		1.36	2.22		
D_JP		0.74		0.48	0.71		
D_UK		0.31		1.11	2.02		
D_IT		-0.27		0.82	1.83		

Table 20: Regression results based on a panel including all home countries and central and eastern European host countries (concluded)

D_CZ		-0.50	-0.06				
D_HU		0.49	0.795*				
D_PL		-1.977**	-1.267*				
D_SK		0.784*	0.729*				
D_1992		2.012**					
D_1993		2.217**					
D_1994		2.027**					
D_1995		1.389**					
D_1996		1.232*					
D_1997		1.378**					
D_1998		1.333**					
D_1999		1.711**					
D_2000		2.165***					
D_2001		1.899***					
D_2002		0.42	-1.143**	-1.223**	-1.117**	-1.196**	-1.042**
D_2003			-1.427***	-1.619***	-1.436***	-1.552***	-1.278**
R-squared	0.13	0.21	0.19	0.19	0.19	0.18	0.18
Adjusted *R*-squared	0.12	0.15	0.16	0.16	0.15	0.15	0.15
F-test 3)		1.29	2.13	1.62	1.51		
Cross-sections	31	31	31	31	31	31	31
Observations	332	332	332	332	332	332	332

*, **, *** denotes significance at a 10%, 5%, or 1% level, respectively. *t*-statistics are shown in parentheses.

1) Pooled least squares estimation; Sample: 1992–2003
2) When home country, host country, and/or time-specific effects are included in the specifications, the estimated constant reflects the United States, Slovenia, and the year 2003.
3) The *F*-test tests the joint significance of the included dummy variables by comparing the explanatory power of each specification to that of specification (1).

Table 21: Regression results based on a panel including all home countries and Asian host countries

Specification 1)	(1)	(2)	(3)	(4a)	(4b)	(5a)	(5b)
C 2)	-0.441	0.549	-1.243	1.275	-4.072	-2.86	-2.786
	(-0.142)	(0.041)	(-0.276)	(0.116)	(-0.370)	(-0.838)	(-0.830)
Y_j	0.477***	1.348*	0.977*	1.177***	0.858***	0.905***	0.592***
	(3.154)	(1.476)	(1.511)	(5.253)	(4.749)	(4.208)	(3.591)
Y_i	1.692***	-0.217	1.690***	-0.179	0.288	1.699***	1.696***
	(9.982)	(-0.178)	(9.946)	(-0.164)	(0.266)	(9.935)	(9.951)
$DIST_{ij}$	-1.244***	-0.141	-1.410***	-0.11	0.025	-1.343***	-1.346***
	(-4.631)	(-0.235)	(-4.891)	(-0.203)	(0.045)	(-4.738)	(-4.768)
g_{ji}			0.136*			0.118	0.152*
			(1.349)			(1.186)	(1.534)
g_{ij}				0.006	-0.043	0.019	-0.031
				(0.200)	(-1.302)	(0.639)	(-0.975)
OPEN / RISK				0.617***	0.037***	0.588***	0.037***
				(3.646)	(4.115)	(3.412)	(4.040)
INFL				0.743	0.744	1.336	1.396
				(0.441)	(0.447)	(0.784)	(0.830)
FIX				0.116	0.315	0.149	0.322
				(0.390)	(1.175)	(0.495)	(1.179)
D_FR		-2.575		-2.496	-1.62		
D_DE		-2.579*		-2.512*	-1.805		
D_JP		0.622		0.689	1.175		
D_UK		-2.459		-2.377	-1.456		
D_IT		-4.265**		-4.176**	-3.194*		

Table 21: Regression results based on a panel including all home countries and Asian host countries (concluded)

D_CN		-0.881	-0.518				
D_HK		0.245	0.189				
D_IN		-1.198	-1.098				
D_ID		-1.022**	-0.687				
D_MY		-0.5	-0.538				
D_PH		-0.346	-0.562				
D_SG		1.611**	1.582***				
D_KR		-1.337	-1.252*				
D_1992		1.121*					
D_1993		2.137***					
D_1994		2.311***					
D_1995		1.852***					
D_1996		2.439***					
D_1997		1.238**					
D_1998		1.703***					
D_1999		2.189***					
D_2000		1.293**					
D_2001		1.722***					
D_2002		1.034**	-0.667*	-0.803**	-0.58	-0.708*	-0.407
D_2003			-2.024*	-1.877*	-1.657*	-2.102*	-1.760*
R-squared	0.188	0.3	0.256	0.273	0.277	0.241	0.247
Adjusted *R*-squared	0.185	0.27	0.24	0.257	0.261	0.229	0.235
F-test 3)		3.655***	4.101***	5.212***	5.492***		
Cross-sections	54	54	54	54	54	54	54
Observations	648	648	648	648	648	648	648

*, **, *** denotes significance at a 10%, 5%, or 1% level, respectively. *t*-statistics are shown in parentheses.

1) Pooled least squares estimation; Sample: 1992–2003
2) When home country, host country, and/or time-specific effects are included in the specifications, the estimated constant reflects the United States, Thailand, and the year 2003.
3) The *F*-test tests the joint significance of the included dummy variables by comparing the explanatory power of each specification to that of specification (1).

Table 22: Regression results based on a panel including all home countries and Latin American host countries

Specification 1)	(1)	(2)	(3)	(4a)	(4b)	(5a)	(5b)
C 2)	-1.767	60.397***	-10.549**	27.789**	28.682**	-7.649*	-7.372*
	(-0.342)	(3.303)	(-1.689)	(1.946)	(2.007)	(-1.433)	(-1.412)
Y_j	1.261***	2.724***	2.677***	1.590***	1.488***	1.423***	1.385***
	(6.682)	(3.452)	(4.012)	(6.426)	(7.347)	(5.827)	(6.985)
Y_i	1.010***	-5.356***	0.992***	-2.676**	-2.576**	1.029***	1.023***
	(4.205)	(-3.272)	(4.299)	(-1.819)	(-1.755)	(4.522)	(4.492)
$DIST_{ij}$	-0.991**	-2.451**	-0.760*	-0.713	-0.924	-0.5	-0.56
	(-2.182)	(-2.104)	(-1.405)	(-0.933)	(-1.147)	(-1.065)	(-1.170)
g_i			0.317**			0.366***	0.534***
			(2.367)			(2.835)	(2.784)
g_j				0.055*	0.04	0.070**	0.057
				(1.362)	(0.909)	(1.801)	(1.303)
OPEN / RISK				1.036	0.017	0.378	0.012
				(0.582)	(0.861)	(0.212)	(0.658)
INFL				-0.116***	-0.109**	-0.086**	-0.078*
				(-2.405)	(-2.181)	(-1.792)	(-1.607)
FIX				-0.605*	-0.54	-0.525	-0.454
				(-1.391)	(-1.220)	(-1.239)	(-1.092)
D_FR		-10.791***		-7.087***	-6.779***		
D_DE		-8.107***		-5.593***	-5.311**		
D_JP		-2.541*		-2.669**	-2.370*		
D_UK		-10.472***		-6.501**	-6.186**		
D_IT		-12.641***		-8.424***	-8.089***		

Table 22: Regression results based on a panel including all home countries and Latin American host countries (concluded)

D_AR		-0.64	-1.173*				
D_BR		-2.302*	-2.465**				
D_CL		1.767***	1.143**				
D_MX		-2.451**	-2.336**				
D_VE		0.37	0.528				
D_1992		0.482					
D_1993		0.075					
D_1994		0.876					
D_1995		1.562**					
D_1996		2.256***					
D_1997		2.394***					
D_1998		1.322*					
D_1999		1.765**					
D_2000		1.505**					
D_2001		0.777					
D_2002		-0.932	-2.334***	-2.464***	-2.349***	-2.156***	-2.108***
D_2003			-2.527***	-2.119***	-1.942***	-2.596***	-2.489***
R-squared	0.156	0.313	0.269	0.281	0.282	0.27	0.271
Adjusted *R*-squared	0.15	0.272	0.249	0.256	0.257	0.253	0.253
F-test 3)		3.758***	5.706***	4.970***	5.004***		
Cross-sections	36	36	36	36	36	36	36
Observations	422	422	422	422	422	422	422

*, **, *** denotes significance at a 10%, 5%, or 1% level, respectively. *t*-statistics are shown in parentheses.

1) Pooled least squares estimation; Sample: 1992–2003.
2) When home country, host country, and/or time-specific effects are included in the specifications, the estimated constant reflects the United States, Columbia, and the year 2003.
3) The *F*-test tests the joint significance of the included dummy variables by comparing the explanatory power of each specification to that of specification (1).

Among the host country fundamentals, inflation and host country GDP growth are the only variables that come out as significant. The coefficient of inflation is significantly negative for all relevant specifications. Inflation is found to be a specific concern for direct investors in the Latin American countries. The average annual inflation rate in the Latin American countries from 1992 to 2003 amounted to 88 percent. That is notably higher than the rate of inflation in the CEECs and the Asian host countries, which reached an average annual inflation rate of 16 percent and 5 percent, respectively, for the same time period. Inflation being one factor driving business risk might also serve as an indicator for institutional weaknesses and political instability. This explains why according to our results country risk as such has no significant impact on FDI inflows to the Latin American host countries. Host country inflation might not have a significant impact on FDI as long as it does not increase above a threshold level. Beyond the threshold it might have a signaling role for investors and in such cases FDI flows do react to inflation.[155]

The dominant role of the United States as a source of FDI for the Latin American countries is reflected in the coefficients for home country specific effects that are significantly negative for all home countries across the relevant specifications. The size of the coefficients shows that FDI flows to the Latin American countries especially from the European home countries are lower than suggested by gravity factors and host country fundamentals. Compared to the benchmark country, i.e., Columbia, three host countries, i.e., Argentina, Brazil, and Mexico, received relatively smaller FDI inflows while Chile recorded more FDI inflows than expected according to gravity factors and home country fundamentals.

Time-specific patterns in Latin America are to some extent different from the other two regional panels. Compared to the benchmark year, i.e., 2003—as in the other panels—FDI inflows were not significantly impacted by time-specific developments in 2002. In contrast to the results of the other panels, time dummies for 2001 as well as for 1992 through 1994 are also insignificant. This outcome suggests that the Latin American host countries in contrast to the CEECs and the Asian host countries experienced already one drop in FDI inflows in the beginning of the observation period and that the decline in inflows in the early 2000s occurred one year earlier than in the CEECs and two years earlier than in the Asian host countries. Despite these observations in specification (2), we preserve specifications (3) and (5b) as shown above and include time dummies for 2002

155 We do not analyze the threshold level that inflation has to cross to have an impact on FDI.

and 2003 only.[156] The time dummies for 2002 and 2003 included in specifications (3) through (5b) are significantly negative and they are large compared to the outcomes for the other regional panels and the full panel. This indicates that the decline in global FDI flows had a larger impact on Latin American countries than on the other two regions.

The *F*-test is significant for specifications (2) through (4b), which include country-specific effects. The estimations for the Latin American panel for all specifications reveal a higher explanatory power than for the full panel or the CEEC panel. The results based on the Asian panel, however, outperform all alternative estimations.

Overall the results from the regional panels show that regional-specific differences exist regarding the determinants of FDI inflows. The specifications applied to the three regional panels perform better in explaining FDI flows to the Asian and Latin American host economies than in explaining FDI flows to the CEECs. The results for the regional panels as in the case of the full panel show that gravity factors are important for bilateral FDI. The impact of the different home and host country fundamentals differs, however, across regional panels. Home country GDP growth and host country inflation are found to play a major role for Latin American FDI inflows. Openness or country risk is the driving factor for FDI inflows in the case of the Asian host countries. The same variables have some impact on FDI flows to the CEECs.

In general, direct investors seem to pay special attention to those economic fundamentals that reveal the most vulnerable part of an economy, i.e., high inflation in the case of Latin America and overall country risk and openness in the Asian countries. These factors vary from region to region.

In the case of the CEECs the relatively smaller explanatory power and the limited impact on FDI assigned to economic fundamentals shows that over the period under consideration other aspects must have been important for FDI flows to the CEECs. The transition process and the privatization of state-owned assets are probably the most important factors.

3.2.3.3 Unit labor cost and FDI

One important aspect in the context of FDI is the cost advantage a potential host country might have over the home country and other potential host countries. In

156 The purpose of this analysis is to compare the factors that determine FDI flows to the CEECs and different emerging market regions. For reasons of comparability we do not change specifications (3) through (5b) but include time dummies for 2002 and 2003 only.

the next step we extend specifications (4a) through (5b) by including relative ULC as a host country fundamental. The sample considered for this part of the analysis comprises a limited group of host countries for which ULC data are available. Table 23 shows the estimation results for the sample including all available host countries as well as for regional panels for the CEECs and Latin American countries.[157]

The overall results of the estimations for the panel including all regions and for the regional panels are close to the outcome of the estimations of the respective specifications excluding relative ULC. The coefficient for relative ULC is insignificant for the panel including all host country regions and for the Latin American panel. In the case of the CEECs, relative ULCs are found to have a significantly negative impact on FDI inflows in specifications (4d) and (5d) where country risk is considered as an explanatory variable. When openness is considered instead of country risk [specification (4c) and (5c)] the relative ULC coefficient remains negative but its significance falls to a level of 28 percent and 25 percent, respectively. These results suggest that among the CEECs a country with relatively high relative ULC receives less FDI than a country with low relative ULC. At the same time we find no significant impact of relative ULC on FDI flows to Latin American host countries.

157 Out of the sample of Asian host countries ULC data were available for Hong Kong, Singapore, and South Korea only. Since Hong Kong and Singapore are not typical cases of emerging market economies we do not run the estimations for the Asian regional panel.

Table 23: Regression results based on panels including all home countries and different groups of host countries

(a) Panel including all host countries [1)]

	(4c)	(4d)	(5c)	(5d)
C [2)]	11.833	7.6	-4.425***	-5.292***
	(1.284)	(0.823)	(-3.071)	(-3.568)
Y_j	1.362***	1.108***	1.305***	1.070***
	(10.334)	(9.286)	(10.000)	(9.025)
Y_i	-0.521	-0.162	1.228***	1.210***
	(-0.508)	(-0.157)	(7.802)	(7.673)
$DIST_{ij}$	-1.011***	-0.932***	-0.966***	-0.898***
	(-7.733)	(-7.234)	(-7.529)	(-7.104)
g_i			0.230***	0.241***
			(2.746)	(2.868)
g_j	0.008	-0.006	0.006	-0.011
	(0.257)	(-0.194)	(0.195)	(-0.339)
OPEN / RISK	0.674***	0.038***	0.647***	0.038***
	(5.447)	(4.750)	(5.235)	(4.747)
INFL	-0.054	-0.035	-0.046	-0.028
	(-1.201)	(-0.764)	(-1.035)	(-0.607)
FIX	0.188	0.411**	0.202	0.411**
	(0.777)	(1.733)	(0.835)	(1.730)
R_ULC	-0.072	-0.277	-0.305	-0.488
	(-0.181)	(-0.698)	(-0.774)	(-1.235)
D_FR	-2.717*	-2.032		
D_DE	-2.808**	-2.239*		
D_JP	-1.172*	-0.893		
D_UK	-3.245*	-2.517		
D_IT	-4.418**	-3.644**		
D_2002	-1.322***	-1.220***	-1.096***	-0.967**
D_2003	-1.352***	-1.200***	-1.492***	-1.264***
R-squared	0.208	0.201	0.198	0.193
*A*djusted R-squared	0.192	0.185	0.186	0.181
F-test [3)]	5.730***	5.158***		
Cross-sections incl.	72	72	72	72
Observations incl.	778	778	778	778

(b) Panel including CEECs as home countries [1)]

	(4c)	(4d)	(5c)	(5d)
C [2)]	-10.798	-13.444	-5.227**	-5.425**
	(-0.732)	(-0.910)	(-2.140)	(-2.289)
Y_j	1.967***	1.646***	1.979***	1.675***
	(6.265)	(6.987)	(6.384)	(7.336)
Y_i	1.084	1.474	0.958***	0.982***
	(0.727)	(0.997)	(2.786)	(2.865)
$DIST_{ij}$	-0.414	-0.515	-0.929***	-0.941***
	(-0.532)	(-0.665)	(-3.860)	(-3.921)
g_i			0.127	0.134
			(1.110)	(1.178)
g_j	-0.054	-0.028	-0.066	-0.042
	(-0.752)	(-0.392)	(-0.908)	(-0.576)
OPEN / RISK	1.712***	0.060***	1.615**	0.058***
	(2.427)	(2.736)	(2.309)	(2.662)
INFL	-0.404	-0.31	-0.373	-0.306
	(-0.449)	(-0.346)	(-0.422)	(-0.349)
FIX	1.072***	1.184***	1.070***	1.164***
	(2.537)	(2.761)	(2.565)	(2.760)
R_ULC	-0.835	-1.468**	-0.867	-1.468**
	(-1.079)	(-1.765)	(-1.147)	(-1.808)
D_FR	1.572	2.09		
D_DE	1.599	1.906		
D_JP	0.06	0.398		
D_UK	1.017	1.576		
D_IT	0.943	1.513		
D_2002	-1.366***	-1.304**	-1.187**	-1.112**
D_2003	-1.189**	-1.044**	-1.039**	-0.837*
R-squared	0.205	0.21	0.199	0.204
Adjusted R-squared	0.161	0.166	0.167	0.172
F-test [3)]	1.884	2.012		
Cross-sections incl.	30	30	30	30
Observations incl.	285	285	285	285

(c) Panel including Latin America as home countries [1)]

	(4c)	(4d)	(5c)	(5d)
C 2)	24.789*	19.499	-10.050*	-14.548**
	(1.338)	(1.039)	(-1.379)	(-2.039)
Y_j	1.645***	1.778***	1.494***	1.596***
	(5.593)	(6.154)	(5.312)	(5.685)
Y_i	-2.123	-2.401	0.907***	0.936***
	(-1.136)	(-1.280)	(3.226)	(3.313)
$DIST_{ij}$	-0.84	-0.224	-0.033	0.142
	(-0.700)	(-0.193)	(-0.053)	(0.232)
g_i			0.529***	0.534***
			(3.345)	(3.358)
g_j	0.116**	0.115**	0.126**	0.122**
	(2.116)	(1.991)	(2.346)	(2.137)
OPEN / RISK	-5.097*	0	-5.175**	0.005
	(-1.625)	(0.009)	(-1.738)	(0.191)
INFL	-0.159***	-0.118**	-0.135***	-0.086*
	(-2.783)	(-2.113)	(-2.401)	(-1.581)
FIX	-0.728*	-0.438	-0.746*	-0.319
	(-1.400)	(-0.859)	(-1.520)	(-0.690)
R_ULC	-0.001	0.205	-0.213	-0.051
	(-0.001)	(0.374)	(-0.396)	(-0.096)
D_FR	-5.258*	-6.134**		
D_DE	-4.570*	-5.387**		
D_JP	-1.665	-2.515		
D_UK	-5.037*	-5.934*		
D_IT	-6.960**	-7.937**		
D_2002	-1.672**	-2.081***	-1.100*	-1.500**
D_2003	-1.856**	-2.327***	-2.075***	-2.569***
R-squared	0.305	0.298	0.31	0.302
Adjusted R-squared	0.265	0.257	0.281	0.273
F-test 3)	4.186***	3.948***		
Cross-sections incl.	24	24	24	24
Observations incl.	277	277	277	277

*, **, *** denotes significance at a 10%, 5%, or 1% level, respectively. *t*-statistics are shown in parentheses.

1) Pooled least squares estimation; Sample: 1992–2003.

2) When home country specific effects are included in the specifications, the estimated constant reflects the United States.

3) The *F*-test tests the joint significance of the included dummy variables by comparing the explanatory power of each specification to that of specification (1).

3.3 Conclusions

The empirical study presented in this chapter analyzes the determinants of bilateral FDI flows between six major industrial countries and twenty-two emerging economies in central and eastern Europe, Asia, and Latin America. We use a panel analysis and apply different specifications of a gravity-type model adopted from the empirical work on international trade flows. The results suggest that the classical gravity factors, i.e., distance, home country size, and host country size, as well as other home and host country characteristics play a significant role in determining the amount of FDI flows. We find that FDI flows are inversely related to the distance between the home and the host country, supporting the view that distance implies costs associated with FDI activities. FDI flows to a country increase with the market size of the host country. While FDI outflows increase with home country size, the relationship between home country size and FDI flows is found to be nonlinear. Larger countries, relative to their size, record smaller FDI outflows than small countries.

In addition to the gravity factors, economic developments in the home country and host country have an impact on FDI flows. More specifically, cyclical factors in the economies of the home countries seem to be an important factor for the magnitude of the FDI flows from these countries to emerging economies. In addition, on the side of the host countries, our results suggest that important pull factors are economic fundamentals such as the openness of the host country, the extent of country risk, inflation, and in some cases economic growth. The impact of the different factors for FDI inflows differs across regions. We find less support for the influence of the type of exchange rate system implemented by the host countries.

The differentiation between three host country regions allows us to highlight some regional differences as well as regional similarities. The results for the regional analyses show that economic factors in home and host countries have been more important for FDI flows to Asia and Latin America. Economic growth, openness, and low country risk are host country characteristics that attracted FDI to Asia and Latin America. High inflation in Latin America had a discouraging effect on foreign investors. FDI flows to the CEECs depend to a lesser extent on such economic fundamentals. Due to the transition process FDI flows into the region over the past fifteen years were possibly more driven by the privatization of publicly owned assets and by the integration into the European market and the EU.

For a smaller host country sample for which ULC data are available we also examine the impact of relative host country ULC on FDI inflows. Our results show that low relative ULCs have a positive impact on FDI inflows to the CEECs. For the overall host country panel as well as for the Latin American panel we find no significant effect of relative ULC on FDI flows.

Regarding FDI inflows to the CEECs we can conclude that besides the impact of the transition process and integration into the European market—over the past fifteen years—openness or the absence of country risk and cost efficiency were the most important economic factors that helped to pull FDI into the region. These results are in line with the general findings presented by Lansbury, Pain, and Smidkova (1996) and Bevan and Estrin (2000), who analyze FDI flows to the CEECs. These two studies, like many others, concentrate on the analysis of FDI flows to a specific region and adjust the empirical model to the regional specificities. To assess regional similarities and differences we apply the same model to three different emerging market regions that compete for FDI inflows.

To finance their current account deficits without incurring an unsustainable foreign debt situation, the CEECs need to preserve the level of FDI inflows recorded over the past decade. Our regional analysis of bilateral FDI flows allows us to draw some conclusions not only regarding the determinants of past FDI inflows to the CEECs but also regarding the factors that will be important for the countries' future attractiveness for foreign direct investors. The CEECs are about to complete and partly have already completed the privatization process, which has been a driving force for past FDI inflows to the region. If the countries want to maintain the level of FDI inflows as recorded over the past fifteen years they will have to attract more and more greenfield investment. Competition for greenfield investment comes mainly from other emerging economies, e.g., those economies in Asia and Latin America covered by our analysis. In light of the competition from the other emerging market regions the CEECs will have to demonstrate their relative attractiveness to foreign investors.

According to our analysis, the characteristics that allow the CEECs to maintain their status of attractive FDI host countries are mainly a positive economic development and a stable economic and political environment, strong integration into the international trade system, and cost efficiency. The integration into the EU is likely to support a positive economic development and stable political environment as well as the required trade integration. The way in which this integration process affects wages and productivity and thus relative cost efficiency is not foreseeable. Whether the CEECs will be able to maintain their relative cost advantage over the EU-15 and other emerging markets will be a decisive factor for the countries' relative attractiveness to foreign investors. Our findings, however, also suggest that economic development in home countries have an impact on FDI flows to nontransition emerging economies. For the

CEECs the development in home countries will gain in importance when the transition process is completed and foreign investors are able to base their decision solely on their own needs and capacities instead of reacting to one-time investment opportunities occurring in the process of mass privatization.

Some caveats apply to our analysis. An inevitable shortcoming of an empirical analysis that mainly concentrates on macroeconomic factors as explanatory variables for FDI is that it does not account for the impact of regional policies, e.g., designated preferred investment areas, and individually negotiated investment incentives, e.g., subsidies or tax exemptions for foreign-owned entities, or any company-specific factors that have an impact on investment decisions. Since we are interested in the relation between economic fundamentals and FDI flows with a special focus on regional differences and since we look at a longer time span, it appears to be justified to focus on macroeconomic characteristics. Furthermore, we apply the same specification to all host country panels and do not accommodate for regional differences for instance with respect to time-specific effects. Especially in the case of the CEECs we do not account for the impact of the transition process, privatization, or EU accession. Again, our focus is a comparable regional analysis that allows us to determine the differences in the impact of some general economic fundamentals on FDI inflows to the three emerging market regions. We therefore concentrate on the most important economic factors that are relevant across regions. Region-specific studies for the CEECs that take into account the impact of transition and privatization aim to assess the specific relation between economic transition and FDI flows, which is not the focus of this analysis.

3.4 Appendix to Chapter 3

Table A 3-1: Summary statistics by host country regions

	FDI_{ij}	Y_j	$DIST_{ij}$	g_j	OPEN	RISK	INFL	ULC
CEEC								
Mean	3.49	3.76	3,338	2.86	1.02	59.72	0.16	1.2
Min	-7.53	2.47	285	-6.70	0.44	34.22	0.01	0.5
Max	8.36	5.34	9,413	6.82	1.56	76.14	2.08	1.7
Stdv. 1)	2.68	0.79	3,424	2.79	0.31	9.96	0.27	0.3
Obs. 2)	320	60	30	60	60	60	60	53
Asian								
Mean	3.95	5.21	9,131	5.38	1.35	66.86	0.05	1.0
Min	-8.54	3.90	1,158	-13.13	0.18	27.20	-0.06	0.8
Max	8.65	7.25	16,374	14.20	3.79	97.36	0.75	1.2
Stdv. 1)	3.50	0.86	3,196	4.41	1.08	16.17	0.08	0.1
Obs. 2)	648	108	54	108	108	108	108	36
LA								
Mean	3.54	5.16	10,049	2.56	0.37	53.53	0.88	1.0
Min	-7.33	3.83	3,040	-10.89	0.15	25.78	-0.02	0.00
Max	9.56	6.69	18,378	12.28	0.69	78.01	22.40	2.2
Stdv. 1)	3.73	0.89	3,410	4.36	0.14	11.04	3.62	0.5
Obs. 2)	35	72	36	72	72	72	72	47
All								
Mean	3.71	4.89	7,621	3.66	0.94	59.22	0.44	1.1
Min	-8.54	2.47	285	-14.50	0.15	17.67	-0.06	0.00
Max	9.56	7.25	18,378	14.20	3.79	97.36	22.40	2.2
Stdv. 1)	3.36	1.02	4,301	4.67	0.83	15.59	2.20	0.3
Obs. 2)	1534	264	132	264	264	264	264	136
All but Russia and								
Mean	3.72	4.83	7,959	3.90	0.98	61.07	0.33	1.1
Min	-8.54	2.47	285	-13.13	0.15	25.78	-0.06	0.00
Max	9.56	7.25	18,378	14.20	3.79	97.36	22.40	2.2
Stdv. 1)	3.41	1.05	4,275	4.27	0.86	14.55	2.02	0.3
Obs. 2)	1390	240	120	240	240	240	240	136

Source: Own calculations.

1) Stdv. = Standard deviation

2) Obs. = Number of observations

Table A 3-2: Summary statistics for home countries

		FDI	Yi	DISTij	gi
Home	Mean	3.71	7.76	7,621	1.92
	Min	-8.54	6.87	285	-1.19
	Max	9.56	9.31	18,378	4.50
	Stdv. 1)	3.36	0.73	4,301	1.40
	Obs. 2)	1,534	1,584	132	1,584
FR	Mean	3.42	7.27	7,002	1.81
	Min	-6.40	7.15	886	-0.94
	Max	8.36	7.47	11,662	4.21
	Stdv. 1)	3.11	0.09	3,944	1.34
	Obs. 2)	263	264	22	264
DE	Mean	3.60	7.65	6,685	1.25
	Min	-6.87	7.53	285	-1.09
	Max	7.66	7.81	12,533	2.86
	Stdv. 1)	3.64	0.09	4,173	1.13
	Obs. 2)	263	264	22	264
IT	Mean	2.17	7.05	6,835	1.42
	Min	-4.37	6.90	497	-0.88
	Max	6.98	7.29	11,906	3.03
	Stdv. 1)	1.98	0.10	4,028	1.10
	Obs. 2)	259	264	22	264
JP	Mean	4.83	8.39	8,671	1.16
	Min	0.24	8.24	1,158	-1.19
	Max	8.34	8.57	18,378	3.54
	Stdv. 1)	1.96	0.09	4,959	1.33
	Obs. 2)	240	264	22	264
UK	Mean	3.52	7.17	7,054	2.67
	Min	-8.54	6.87	1,034	0.20
	Max	8.35	7.49	11,723	4.43
	Stdv. 1)	4.03	0.18	3,883	1.02
	Obs. 2)	248	264	22	264
USA	Mean	4.76	9.04	9,481	3.22
	Min	-7.53	8.75	3,040	0.75
	Max	9.56	9.31	16,374	4.50
	Stdv. 1)	3.94	0.18	3,918	1.08
	Obs. 2)	261	264	22	264

Source: Own calculations.

1) Stdv. = Standard deviation

2) Obs. = Number of observations

Table A 3-3: Correlation matrix

	FDI_{ij}	Y_j	Y_i	$DIST_{ij}$	g_i	g_j	OPEN	RISK	INFL	FIX
FDI_{ij}	1.00	0.21	0.22	-0.08	0.15	0.09	0.01	0.13	-0.02	0.08
Y_j	0.21	1.00	0.02	0.21	0.03	0.17	-0.35	-0.08	0.10	0.10
Y_i	0.22	0.02	1.00	0.23	0.19	-0.01	0.01	0.00	-0.02	0.00
$DIST_{ij}$	-0.08	0.21	0.23	1.00	0.06	0.09	0.05	0.12	-0.01	0.10
g_i	0.15	0.03	0.19	0.06	1.00	0.06	0.01	0.02	-0.04	-0.03
g_j	0.09	0.17	-0.01	0.09	0.06	1.00	0.07	0.48	-0.17	0.07
OPEN	0.01	-0.35	0.01	0.05	0.01	0.07	1.00	0.58	-0.10	0.25
RISK	0.13	-0.08	0.00	0.12	0.02	0.48	0.58	1.00	-0.23	0.16
INFL	-0.02	0.10	-0.02	-0.01	-0.04	-0.17	-0.10	-0.23	1.00	-0.12
FIX	0.08	0.10	0.00	0.10	-0.03	0.07	0.25	0.16	-0.12	1.00

Source: Own calculations.

Table A 3-4: FDI inflows to host countries as percentage of GDP (1992-2003)

	Min	Mean	Max	Standard deviation
Czech Republic	1.7%	5.4%	11.5%	3.5%
Hungary	2.7%	6.4%	11.4%	2.5%
Poland	0.8%	2.9%	5.6%	1.2%
Slovakia	0.8%	4.1%	17.0%	4.7%
Slovenia	0.5%	1.5%	7.3%	1.8%
Russia	0.2%	0.8%	1.7%	0.4%
Turkey	0.2%	0.6%	2.1%	0.5%
China	2.3%	4.4%	6.2%	1.0%
Hong Kong	3.8%	10.3%	37.5%	8.9%
India	0.1%	0.5%	0.9%	0.2%
Indonesia	-3.0%	0.3%	2.7%	1.7%
Korea	0.1%	0.7%	2.1%	0.6%
Malaysia	0.6%	5.2%	8.7%	2.4%
Philippines	0.4%	1.9%	3.3%	0.7%
Singapore	4.4%	12.2%	19.5%	4.6%
Thailand	0.8%	2.4%	6.7%	1.7%
Argentina	0.4%	2.4%	8.5%	2.1%
Brazil	0.3%	2.5%	5.5%	1.9%
Chile	2.0%	5.2%	12.0%	2.6%
Columbia	1.0%	2.4%	5.2%	1.1%
Venezuela	0.6%	2.8%	7.0%	1.8%
Mexico	1.1%	2.7%	4.3%	0.9%

Source: UNCTAD (2005) and own calculations.

Table A 3-5: Results for Levin, Lin, and Chu panel unit root test

	t-statistic	Probability [1)]
FDI_{ij}	-31.319	0.000
Y_j	-10.349	0.000
Y_i	-6.487	0.000
g_i	-26.923	0.000
g_j	-27.324	0.000
OPEN	-6.639	0.000
RISK	-14.406	0.000
INFL	-80.559	0.000
R_ULC	-18.788	0.000

1) As the null hypothesis, the test assumes that a common unit root process exists.

Table A 3-6: Panel including all home and host countries

	Specification (1) [1)]
C[2)]	-30.896***
	(-2.528)
Y_j	0.902***
	(10.570)
Y_i	8.138***
	(2.666)
$DIST_{ij}$	-0.768***
	(-8.279)
Y_i^2	-0.434***
	-2.283
R-squared	0.132
Adjusted *R*-squared	0.130
Cross-sections included	132
Observations included	1534

*, **, *** denotes significance at a 10%, 5%, or 1% level, respectively. *t*-statistics are shown in parentheses.
1) Pooled least squares estimation; Sample: 1992–2003

The negative coefficient of Y_i^2 reflects the nonlinear relationship between FDI flows and country size. This result supports the argument that large countries relative to the size of their GDP undertake less FDI than smaller countries.

4 Fiscal policies and the trade account[158]

4.1 Introduction

Some of the CEECs face the challenge of correcting simultaneously large fiscal and current account deficits. To comply with the convergence criteria, these countries have to undertake fiscal consolidation while at the same time ensuring external balance and preserving a stable exchange rate that fluctuates only within the margins of ERM II. The usual fiscal policy advice from European institutions is that expenditure-based consolidations are preferable over revenue-based ones as they tend to be more durable and conducive to growth.[159] This raises the question whether the choice of policy measures adopted to achieve fiscal consolidation has an impact on the external balance and, thus, affects the exchange rate stability.

Little is known about the effects a lasting change in government expenditures could have on a country's external balance. There seems to be consensus that lower expenditures and the concomitant improvement in the fiscal balance lead to an improvement in the current account. Empirical research so far, however, led to ambiguous results: Some empirical studies find that higher budget deficits lead to higher current account deficits; others prove the opposite or show no significant impact at all. A flaw of the models applied in this field of research seems to be that they estimate reduced form equations, in which different effects might counteract each other without showing the underlying causalities. The latter can only be revealed in a structural model of the current account. Furthermore, earlier studies suffer from the fact that econometric techniques that allow studying long-run equilibrium relationships between time series data were not yet developed.

Trade account deficits are at the heart of the current account problems of most of the CEECs. A structural model of the trade account is, therefore, an important step when modeling the impact of fiscal policies on the external balance of the CEECs in a structural form. Trade equations are the building pillars of trade account models and the incorporation of fiscal variables into trade equations would therefore allow the direct impact of expenditure cuts on trade flows to be analyzed. In their general specification trade equations describe the relationship between import or export volumes on the one hand and relative prices and overall demand on the other. However, specifying demand by overall demand, i.e., GDP, does not take into account that the composition of demand might have an impact

158 The analysis presented here is an extended and revised version of Funke and Nickel (2005).
159 See for example von Hagen, Hallett, and Strauch (2001).

on trade flows. Furthermore, this kind of specification does not allow to analyse the direct impact of changes in government expenditure on the trade account.

This chapter takes a new look at the long-run empirical relationship between fiscal policy and the trade account and analyzes the relationship between government expenditures and imports.[160] To pin down the effects of fiscal policy we estimate goods and service import equations on the basis of disaggregate demand variables. This implies that in contrast to the conventional form of trade equations, which takes total demand as an explanatory variable, our model allows for all components of demand, i.e., private consumption, private sector investment, government expenditure, and exports, to exhibit different elasticities. For trade equations the differentiation between elasticities of the demand components is essential because the import content differs across components; hence, the level of aggregate demand and its composition matters for import demand. In particular, government expenditure might be expected to have lower import content than other demand components.

Earlier empirical studies that estimate disaggregated trade equations do not provide any insights regarding the impact of fiscal policy measures on trade flows. They take into account the effect of different import contents of the components of demand, i.e., consumption, investment, and exports, but they do not discriminate between private and public demand. We extend this approach by differentiating between public and private demand components. This allows us to examine the direct impact of changes in government expenditure on imports.

Our empirical analysis is based on annual panel data of the G-7 countries for the years 1970 through 2002. Due to data limitations, we are not able to extend the empirical analysis to the CEECs. Under the assumption that the import demand structure of the CEECs resembles the import demand structure of the G-7, the general conclusions that we draw from our results could well be applied to the CEECs. We determine the cointegration relationship by pooled mean group estimation. This technique allows the intercepts, short-run coefficients, and error variances to differ freely across countries, while the long-run coefficients are constrained to be the same for all cross sections. We are, thus, able to account for cross-country differences without losing the general message about the long-run relationships between the variables determining the demand for imports and exports. Previous research on trade equations showed that it is reasonable to assume that long-run coefficients are similar across countries.

160 Given that export and import prices as well as the level of export demand are determined by the world market, we concentrate on imports because fiscal policy can be expected to have an impact on imports, which are determined by domestic demand factors.

The analysis shows that government expenditure has a significant positive impact on both goods and service imports; i.e., an increase in government expenditures by one percent leads ceteris paribus to an increase in goods imports by about 0.4 percent and to an increase in service imports by almost 0.5 percent. This implies that an increase in government expenditure would ceteris paribus lead to a deterioration of the trade account. The policy implication of this result would be that an expenditure-based consolidation should lead to an improvement of the trade account.

This assessment would change fundamentally if we considered that a variation in government expenditures is likely to lead to a shift in the composition of aggregate demand and, thus, to an indirect effect on import demand. This indirect effect is based on the different import content of government expenditure versus private consumption and private investment. Our analysis shows that a 1 percent change in either private consumption or investment demand has a stronger impact on import demand than a 1 percent change in government expenditures. Thus, if private demand was crowded-in as government expenditures were cut, the decline in import demand due to lower government expenditure would be overcompensated by the increase in import demand stemming from the increase in private demand components. In sum, this indirect effect implies that a decrease in government expenditure leads to a deterioration of the current account.

The remainder of the chapter is structured as follows. Section 4.2 provides some stylized facts on government expenditure and imports in our data sample and the CEECs. The most relevant literature related to our topic is reviewed in section 4.3. Section 4.4 presents the model and the estimation technique. In section 4.5, we report the results of our empirical analysis and discuss the implications of our findings for an expenditure based consolidation strategy. Section 4.6 concludes.

4.2 The trade account and government expenditure

Looking at the import content of the different demand components reveals that notable differences exist with respect to the import content of private consumption, government expenditure, investment, and exports, respectively. Table 24 reports the import content of the different demand components for Germany, France, Italy, and the United Kingdom. Despite some cross-country variation in the general level of import contents, it becomes obvious that compared to other demand components, government expenditure reveals the lowest import content across countries.

Table 24: Total import content of demand components

	Germany	France 1980	Italy	UK 1979	UK 2001*
Aggregate expenditure	0.243	0.198	0.216	0.235	0.200
Private consumption	0.264	0.208	0.229	0.249	0.200
Government expenditure	0.134	0.060	0.064	0.097	0.132
Gross investment	0.244	0.267	0.261	0.372	0.318
Exports	0.272	0.201	0.241	0.235	0.224

Source: Giovannetti (1989), * Bank of England (2002).

Due to the low import content of government expenditure, one would expect that the import-to-GDP ratio is relatively larger for countries with a relatively small government sector—measured as government expenditures in percent of GDP. A change in the composition of aggregate demand that causes a shift from public demand to private demand should, therefore, also impact import demand and thus the trade account.

To validate this idea we plotted government expenditure-to-GDP ratios against the import-to-GDP ratios for the G-7 countries for annual data covering 1990-2004 (see Figure 1). The two panels show our findings for general government expenditure (panel a) and central government expenditure (panel b), respectively.

Figure 21 illustrates that an increase in the public expenditure ratio generally goes together with a decrease of the import ratio. This relation is independent of government sector size; it holds for the United States with a 1990-2004 average government expenditure-to-GDP ratio of 35 percent as well as for the EU countries and Canada with a 1990-2004 average government expenditure-to-GDP ratio of 49 percent and 48 percent, respectively. The only exception from this finding is Japan, but this could be related to the exceptional, decade-long stagnation of the economy. Figure 21 also reveals that the negative relation between government expenditures and imports generally holds regardless of the degree of openness; it holds for the United States with a 1990-2004 average export and import-to-GDP ratio of 23 percent as well as for the EU countries and Canada with a 1990-2004 average export and import-to-GDP ratio of 52 percent and 71 percent, respectively.

Figure 21: Import ratio and government expenditure ratio for G-7 countries (1990-2004)

(a) General government expenditure

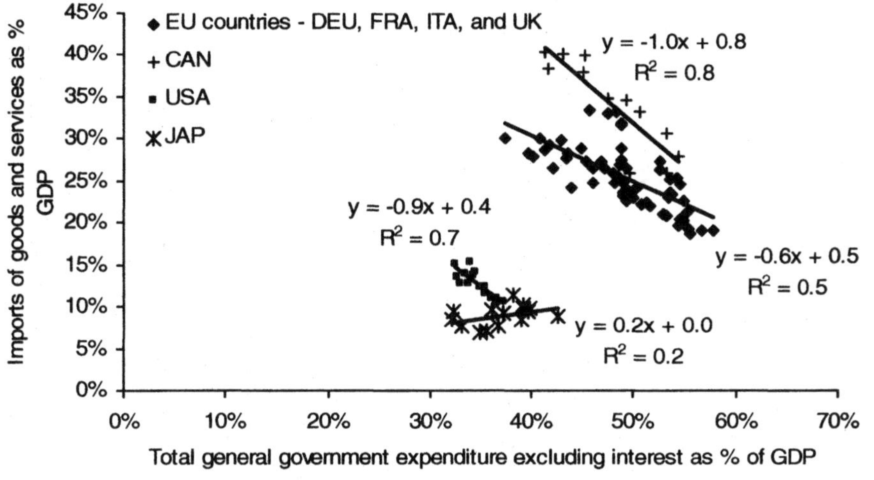

(b) Central government expenditure

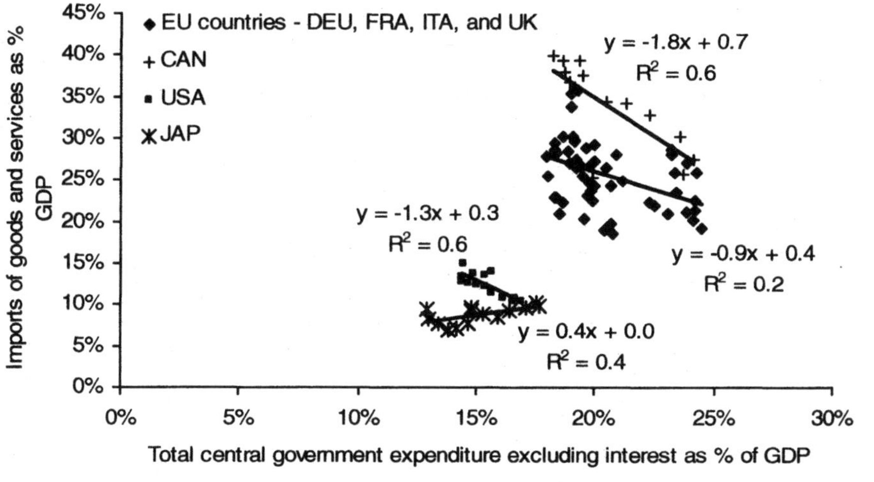

Source: IMF (2005c), ECB (2005a), and own calculations.

This observation would not change if we extended our sample for other countries, i.e., other EU countries, European Free Trade Association (EFTA) countries and the new EU member states. Table 25 shows that—with few exceptions—the negative correlation between imports and public expenditure holds. Though the correlation coefficients differ across countries, the behavioral relationship seems to be relatively similar. This finding suggests that it might not be too far fetched to apply conclusions drawn from trade account estimates of the G-7 countries to other countries.

Table 25: Correlations of government expenditure ratio and import to GDP ratio

Countries	Correlation	Countries	Correlation
G-7 Countries		**EFTA Countries**	
Canada	-0.88	Switzerland	**0.06**
Germany	-0.57	Norway	0.43
France	-0.35	**New EU Member States**	
Great Britain	-0.59	Cyprus	-0.98
Italy	-0.94	Czech Republic	-0.34
Japan	**0.42**	Estonia	-0.28
USA	-0.84	Hungary	-0.73
Other EU Countries		Lithuania	-0.47
Austria	-0.81	Latvia	**0.17**
Belgium	-0.89	Malta	-0.68
Denmark	-0.89	Poland	-0.41
Finland	-0.40	Slovakia	-0.62
Ireland	-0.91	Slovenia	-0.43
Luxembourg	-0.76		
Portugal	-0.44		
Netherlands	-0.91		
Sweden	-0.96		

Note: Calculations are based on annual data from 1990 through 2004.
Source: IMF (2005c) and own calculations.

Regarding the relevance of the trade account for the overall current account balance in the CEECs, Figure 22 shows that the current account balance of most of the CEECs, namely Estonia, Latvia, Lithuania, Poland, and the Slovak Republic, is dominated by a deficit in the trade account. Only the Czech Republic and Hungary accumulate the major part of their current account deficits through negative net income and transfers.

Figure 22: The trade balance and the current account (2004)

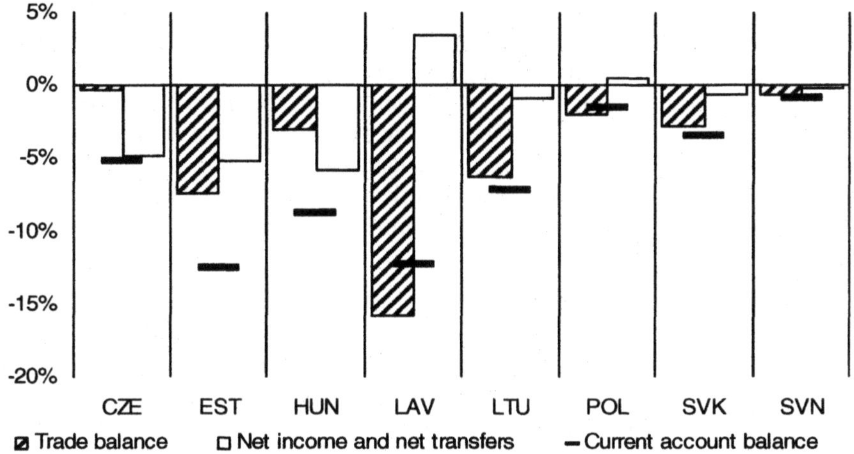

Source: IMF (2005a), ECB (2005a), and own calculations.

High trade account deficits prevailing in some of the CEECs together with the EU institutions' recommendation to consolidate fiscal deficits make the linkage between fiscal policy and the trade account a relevant topic in economic and political discussions regarding euro area accession of the CEECs and the framework of the EMU in general. The relevance of this topic is also reflected in the notable body of literature that studies these links from different angles.

4.3 Literature overview

In the following we briefly review three different stands of literature that all feed into our analysis: (i) research on the relation between fiscal policies and the current account or trade account, (ii) publications on the formulation and estimation of trade equations, and (iii) literature devoted to the relation between fiscal policies and domestic demand.

The simultaneous occurrence of high fiscal deficits and large current account deficits in the United States under the Reagan administration in the 1980s received considerable attention in the political discussion as well as in academic research. Diverse empirical papers study the relation between fiscal deficits and the current account balance. However, the findings presented in the empirical literature are inconclusive; depending on the empirical model, the country under examination, and the time period considered, the estimation results reveal a positive, a negative, or no significant relation between fiscal deficits and the current account. For example Berenheim (1988) finds that current account deficits in Canada, Germany, the United Kingdom, and the United States can partly be explained by fiscal deficits. Bussière, Müller, and Fratzscher (2004), Normandin (1999), and Piersanti (2000) also find evidence that an increase in the fiscal deficit induces a deterioration of the current account. However, Enders and Lee (1990) and Dewald and Ulan (1990) find no significant link between the two deficits and Kim and Roubini (2004) find even a significant negative relation between the fiscal and the current account balance.

Regarding the relation between fiscal policies and the trade account, results of empirical studies are as ambiguous as for the current account. Erceg, Guerrieri, and Gust (2005) use an open economy dynamic general equilibrium (DGE) model to assess the impact of fiscal shocks on the trade balance for the United States and find that the fiscal deficit has only a relatively small effect on the trade balance. Baxter (1995) also finds a positive relation between the two deficits. Lane and Perotti (1998) take a different approach and investigate the impact of fiscal policy on the production of traded goods. They find that an expansion in government consumption expenditure affects exports negatively and thus leads to a deterioration of the trade account.

A common feature of the studies that look for linkages between fiscal policies and the current account is that they are based on the estimation of reduced form equations where different variables are taken together to explain the current account. However, fiscal policies might impact the current account through different channels, e.g., by affecting private demand, local production, or interest rates. The results generated by a reduced form model reflect overlapping and may be counteracting effects of fiscal measures on the current account balance. Depending on the magnitude and dominance of the diverse effects, the findings might show different and contradicting results. The estimation of a structural model allows the impact fiscal policy reveals to be analyzed through different channels.

The building blocks of a structural trade account model are trade equations. As Marquez (2002, p.13) states, "one can not exaggerate the usefulness of knowing how changes in income and prices affect trade". Economic theory and the empirical literature concentrate on the traditional form of trade equations in which import and export demand depend only on two factors, namely the level of final expenditure and prices of traded goods relative to the prices of local substitutes. Structural trade equations thus explain the volume of imports and exports by GDP and relative prices. Marquez (2002) provides an overview of the literature on trade equations and discusses the proper formulation of trade equations. He points out that a trade-off exists between the predictive accuracy and the theoretical consistency when constructing trade equations. In the empirical literature, the method with higher predictive accuracy, i.e., log linear formulations following Houthakker and Magee (1969) are employed. Empirical estimates of trade elasticities for the G-7 countries are provided by, e.g., Houthakker and Magee (1969), Cline (1989), Caporale and Chui (1999), and Hooper, Johnson, and Marquez (2000). All four studies apply log linear formulations. In line with economic theory they all report a positive impact of demand on imports and exports and a negative impact of relative prices on either of the two trade flows. The size of the estimated coefficients varies across countries and between the different studies. Marquez (2002) shows that—according to theoretical considerations—the elasticity of total demand should be equal to one if elasticities are assumed to be constant. However, the estimated elasticities in many cases deviate considerably from this theoretical value.[161] Driver and Wren-Lewis (1998) apply cointegration techniques to estimate log linear trade equations for the G-7 and in most cases obtain coefficients that have signs in line with economic theory but that deviate in terms of size from the expected value of one.

Trade equations and elasticities derived through the empirical estimation of trade equations are a building block of structural current account and general equilibrium models. Williamson (1994) and Driver and Wren-Lewis (1998), for example, estimate equilibrium exchange rates based on structural current account models that are mainly determined by the trade account. To be more precise regarding the estimated elasticities, Driver and Wren-Lewis (1998) separate between the goods account and the service account. A further refinement of trade equations and their estimates feeds into the modeling of different economic questions and topics.[162]

Standard import equations as presented by Marquez (2002) consider domestic output, i.e., GDP, as the relevant measure for domestic demand. In this setting imports are assumed to be affected by changes in the level of demand but not by changes in the composition of aggregate demand. As we discussed above, demand components reveal significant differences in their import content and the

---

161 The results of Houthakker and Magee (1969), Cline (1989), Caporale and Chui (1999), and Hooper, Johnson, and Marquez (2000) are reported in the chapter's appendix.

162 The variance of the size of coefficients across countries and studies shows that trade elasticities are not the same for all countries and that they are likely to vary over time.

structure of demand might, therefore, have an impact on trade flows. Since the overall demand for a country's exports is equivalent to the overall demand of the rest of the world, disaggregating the demand in the export equation is not possible. In the case of import demand, Abbott and Seddighi (1996), Giovannetti (1989), Alias and Cheong (2000), and Tang (2003) address this issue and estimate import equations by taking disaggregated demand components into account. They divide total demand into consumptive expenditure, investment expenditure, and exports. The results of their estimations are provided in Table 26. In line with theory they find that import volumes decrease as relative prices of import goods increase and that import volumes increase when demand increases. The results also show that the elasticities of the different demand components differ significantly.[163]

Table 26: Import elasticities of disaggregated expenditure components

Author	Abbott and Seddighi	Alias and Cheong	Giovannetti	Tang
Estimation technique	Johansen Cointegration	Johansen Cointegration	OLS	Error Correction Model
Country	UK	Malaysia	Italy	Thailand
Relative price	-0.11	-0.69	-0.21	-0.68
Consumption expenditure	1.30	0.73	0.72	0.53
Investment expenditure	0.26	0.78	0.91	-0.04
Exports	0.10	0.38		0.65

Source: Abbott and Seddighi (1996), Alias and Cheong (2000), Giovannetti (1989), and Tang (2003).

Since the disaggregated expenditure components reveal different elasticities, the composition of aggregate demand matters for the trade account. The impact that a change in fiscal policy has on the trade balance, therefore, depends on how the private sector reacts to such a change.

A growing body of literature is devoted to this question, and more recently the assessment of non-Keynesian effects of fiscal policies gained special attention. Empirical studies by Giavazzi and Pagano (1990, 1996), Perotti (1999) and Giavazzi, Jappelli, and Pagano (2000) find that under special circumstances

163 Abbott and Seddighi (1996) apply a likelihood ratio test to see whether the long-run elasticities estimated by a Johansen procedure could be restricted to be the same for all demand components. They had to reject the restriction.

contractionary fiscal policy may have expansionary effects on consumption, investment, and/or output. The non-Keynesian hypothesis has, however, been rejected by Hjelm (2002a, 2002b), Hogan (2004), van Aarle and Garretsen (2003) and Schclarek (2003).

Considering the impact of government expenditure on consumption and investment separately, Blanchard and Perotti (2002) reveal that fiscal expansion has a positive impact on consumption and a negative impact on investment. Fatás and Mihov (2001), however, find that consumption increases as a response to a positive expenditure shock while investment is not affected significantly. Karras (1994) finds evidence that private consumption and government spending are rather complementary; private consumption decreases as government expenditures are cut.

Overall, the outcome of empirical studies regarding the relation of fiscal policies and the level and structure of overall demand is mixed.

4.4 The empirical model

As discussed above, our analysis concentrates on the impact of fiscal policy on the trade account. The trade account is quantitatively the most important of the three parts of the current account (foreign trade, factor income, and net transfers). Additionally, the trade account allows for a direct impact of fiscal policy measures. Since public expenditure is partly spent on imports, changes in public expenditure affect import demand directly. Furthermore, fiscal policy has an impact on private demand and thus affects the trade account indirectly through its effect on other demand components.[164]

164 Both factor income and net transfers are, however, not directly affected by fiscal policy measures. Because governments generally purchase or sell assets from or to foreign investors only to a limited amount, we do not consider factor income in our analysis. However, the structure of the government's assets and liabilities might have an impact on the factor income via the interest rate. If investors feel that the level of public debt might have a destabilizing effect on the economy they might require a risk premium when holding securities from the country. Through this channel fiscal policy would have an impact on factor income even in the case of constant net foreign assets holdings. Furthermore, transfers involving the government as a counterpart, e.g., technical assistance, grants, and membership fees to international organizations, should not be subject to fiscal policy considerations, either.

4.4.1 Standard formulations of trade equations

We base our analysis on an extension of the traditional model of the trade account. The basic trade model consists of an import and an export equation that relate import (*M*) and export (*X*) volumes to domestic (*Y*) and foreign (*Y**) real income and relative prices (*RP*). Equations (1) and (2) show the export and import equations as given in the literature in their general and their log form:

Exports: $X_t = \gamma_0 Y_t^{*\gamma_1} RPX_t^{\gamma_2}$ in logs $x_t = \gamma_0 + \gamma_1 y_t^* + \gamma_2 rpx_t$ (1)

Imports: $M_t = \delta_0 Y_t^{\delta_1} RPM_t^{\delta_2}$ in logs $m_t = \delta_0 + \delta_1 y_t + \delta_2 rpm_t$. (2)

RPX and *RPM* are the relative prices; γ_1 and δ_1 represent the income elasticities and γ_2 and δ_2 the price elasticities of exports and imports, respectively. Domestic real income (*Y*) is equivalent to real GDP, which equals the sum of final demand components, i.e., final private consumption, final public expenditure, final private investment, and net exports. Foreign real income (*Y**) represents the total income of the rest of the world and cannot easily be decomposed into demand components. Relating import volumes to total real income implicitly assumes that the import content and the import elasticity are the same for all demand components. However, as shown above this assumption does not hold. We address this issue by constructing modified import equations that take a decomposition of demand components into account.

4.4.2 Import equations and expenditure components

Earlier research has shown that import demand is not only determined by the level of income or final expenditure but also by the composition of expenditure and the import content of the different components. For example, Abbott and Seddighi (1996), Alias and Cheong (2000), Giovannetti (1989), and Alias and Cheong (2000) find that the elasticities of the different demand components differ significantly. They divide total demand into consumptive expenditure, investment expenditure, and exports but do not differentiate between private and public demand. Therefore, these studies are not able to analyze the impact of fiscal policy measures on import volumes.

To our knowledge, fiscal measures have not been considered when estimating trade equations in the existing literature. It is usually assumed that at least private consumption and government expenditure reveal the same elasticities.

To gauge the impact of public spending on imports we extend the empirical models used by Abbott and Seddighi (1996), Alias and Cheong (2000),

Giovannetti (1989), and Alias and Cheong (2000). We therefore disaggregate domestic real income into its demand components and consider private and public expenditure separately. The extended import equation thus takes private consumption (C), private investment (I), government expenditure (G) and exports (X) into account:

$$M_t = \partial_0 C_t^{\partial_1} I_t^{\partial_2} G_t^{\partial_3} X_t^{\partial_4} RPM_t^{\partial_5} \quad \text{in logs}$$

$$m_t = \partial_0 + \partial_1 c_t + \partial_2 i_t + \partial_3 g_t + \partial_4 x_t + \partial_5 rpm_t. \qquad (3)$$

Equation (3) permits divergent elasticities for private consumption and government expenditure. This is important since the import content of government expenditure is generally lower than that of private consumption (see Table 24). The major parts of government expenditures are public wages and social expenditures, which have low or marginal import content.[165] Equation (3) already shows that the impact of fiscal policy on the trade account depends on the direct effect of government expenditure on imports. Furthermore, fiscal policy measures might have indirect effects on the trade account by impacting the other demand components, i.e., private consumption and private sector investment.

A more detailed analysis could consider public consumption and public investment demand separately. These two components of public expenditure can be expected to reveal major differences in terms of import content. However, due to limitations in the availability of consistent data for the empirical analysis, disaggregating public expenditure is not possible.

4.4.3 Specification of the empirical model

In our empirical analysis, we estimate both conventional trade equations and extended import equations. Our conventional trade volume equations are based on export and import equations (1) and (2) that are separated into trade volume equations for goods (equations (4) and (6)) and services (equation (5) and (7)).[166]

---

165 Data from the OECD 1990 input-output table for Germany reveals that about 50% of government expenditure is spent on inputs from producers of government services, which in turn have human labor as their only input. Without having a thorough look at the components of government consumption, it seems reasonable to conclude that a major portion of government demand is satisfied by domestic output.

166 When estimating the trade volume equations we follow the approach taken by Driver and Wren-Lewis (1998). For simpler reference, we also follow their notation.

First, the following conventional trade volume equations given in their log form are estimated:[167]

Goods exports: $$xg_t = \gamma_0 + \gamma_1 yg_t^* - \gamma_2 rpxg_t,^{168} \tag{4}$$

Service exports: $$xs_t = \theta_0 + \theta_1 ys_t^* - \theta_2 rps_t, \tag{5}$$

where xg_t and xs_t are export volumes of goods and services in period t. Overall demand for goods exports (yg_t*)[169] and service export (ys_t*) are proxied by the sum of world export volumes and world real GDP, respectively. Relative prices of export goods ($rpxg_t$) and services (rps_t) are world export prices relative to domestic export price and world consumer prices relative to domestic consumer prices, respectively.

Goods imports: $$mg_t = \delta_0 + \delta_1 y_t + \delta_2 rpmg_t, \tag{6}$$

Service imports: $$ms_t = \psi_0 + \psi_1 y_t + \psi_2 rps_t, \tag{7}$$

where mg_t and ms_t are import volumes of goods and services in period t. Overall demand for goods and service imports (y) is given by real domestic GDP. Relative prices of import goods ($rpmg_t$) are proxied by world export prices relative to domestic wholesale prices. Prices for service imports ($rpxg_t$) are the same as for service exports.

To capture the impact of changes in government expenditure on import volumes, import volume equations for goods (equation 6) and services (equation 7) are extended along the lines described before:

Extended form of goods imports: $$mg_t = \partial_0 + \partial_1 c_t + \partial_2 i_t + \partial_3 g_t + \partial_4 x_t + \partial_5 rpmg_t, \tag{8}$$

Extended form of service imports: $$ms_t = \vartheta_0 + \vartheta_1 c_t + \vartheta_2 i_t + \vartheta_3 g_t + \vartheta_4 x_t + \vartheta_5 rps_t. \tag{9}$$

---

167 In contrast to Driver and Wren-Lewis (1998), a time trend is not included. This, however, does not change the estimation results. In a first step, Driver and Wren-Lewis also estimated the elasticities without considering the time trend and in a second step estimated the time trend while applying the coefficients as derived in the first step (Driver and Wren-Lewis, 1998).

168 The construction of our relative price variables implies a negative relation between export volumes and relative prices. This negative relation is taken into account by the minus sign in front of the coefficients $\gamma 2$ and $\theta 2$ while the coefficients themselves are expected to reveal a positive sign.

169 The world demand for goods exports (yg*) is proxied by world merchandise trade, which only includes goods trade. Similar data are not available for services. Hence, the world demand for service imports (ys*) is proxied by world real GDP.

For the conventional trade equations (4) to (7), domestic income (*y*) is expected to have a positive impact on import volumes (*ms*) or (*mg*). Likewise, export volumes (*xg*) or (*xm*) are expected to increase with foreign income (*yg**) or (*ys**). Since demand decreases as prices increase, the coefficients of relative prices are expected to be negative in all six equations.

As discussed by Marquez (2002), economic theory postulates the income elasticity to be equal to one provided it is assumed to be constant. However, various empirical studies show that the estimated coefficients for major industrialized countries deviates from one but remain close to one.[170] In the present analysis income elasticities are therefore also expected to be close to one across all sample countries. Likewise, it is assumed that the sum of the demand elasticities (i.e. for consumption, investment, government expenditure, and exports) should also be equal or close to one in the extended trade equations (8) and (9).

The estimation considers annual data for the G-7 countries from 1970[171] through 2002. A full description of the variables is given in the chapter's appendix.

4.5 Estimations and results

Since we employ time series data to estimate the trade elasticities, the specific properties of the data have to be tested in order to choose the appropriate econometric approach for the estimation. We therefore apply panel unit root tests to test for stationarity of the time series. Almost all variables turn out to be integrated of order one. Based on this result, panel cointegration techniques are applied to a panel of G-7 countries to estimate the elasticities of the export and import volume equations in the conventional form as well as in the extended form in the case of import volumes.[172]

---

170 See, for example, Cline (1989), Caporale and Chui (1999), Hooper, Johnson, and Marquez, (2000) and Marquez (2002).

171 Due to missing data points, equations (5), (7), and (9) are estimated using data from 1977 through 2002.

172 We also used Johansen cointegration estimates for each country individually to verify whether the common coefficients derived from the panel analysis appropriately reflect the individual country data. Comparing the country by country estimation with the results of the panel cointegration only provides an eyeball test for the adequacy of the common coefficient from the pooled estimation. As shown by existing empirical studies, the elasticities vary across countries. However, the general tendency is consistent across countries and rectifies the application of a panel approach.

4.5.1 Panel unit root test

Multiple methods for unit root tests as well as cointegration analyses have been developed for panel data in the recent past. The proposed panel unit root tests are mostly based on estimating some version of a standard dynamic model for a panel, such as

$$y_{it} = \rho y_{it-1} + \delta_0 + \delta_1 t + \eta_i + v_t + \varepsilon_{it}, \tag{10}$$

and testing whether the coefficient ρ is equal to one. The subscript $i = (1, 2, ..., N)$ distinguishes the N countries included in the panel. Examples for such tests are Levin, Lin, and Chu (2002; hereafter referred to as LLC) and Breitung (2000). Other procedures, for example, Im, Pesaran, and Shin (2003), are based on averages of the individual unit root test statistics. They recommend, for example, applying the Dickey-Fuller (DF) and the augmented Dickey-Fuller (ADF) tests to the individual time series and calculating one common test statistic from the individual t-tests.

By determining their test statistics based on the full information contained in the data panel, the techniques proposed by LLC and Breitung (2000) best offer the most suitable asymptotic properties in the case of medium size panels, i.e., an equivalent extension of the cross section and the time series dimension. We, therefore, apply both methods to test the relevant time series for stationarity. LLC and Breitung test the null hypothesis that each individual time series in the panel is integrated versus the alternative hypothesis that all individual time series are stationary. Both tests are based on the following pooled ADF equation

$$\Delta y_{it} = \delta y_{it-1} + \sum_{L=1}^{p_i} \theta_{it} \Delta y_{it-L} + \alpha_{0i} + \alpha_{1i} t + \varepsilon_{it}, \tag{11}$$

where a common $\delta = \rho - 1$ is assumed. The null of H_0: $\delta = 0$ under the assumption that $\delta_i = \delta$ for all i is tested against the alternative hypothesis, H_a: $\delta < 0$ for $\delta_i = \delta$ for all i. The tests allow for country-specific intercepts (α_{0i}) and the trend coefficients (α_{1i}). However, while the LLC test is based on a technique that removes autocorrelation as well as the deterministic components, i.e., individual intercept and individual trend, when making the relevant standardizations the test statistic proposed by Breitung is calculated by removing the autoregressive component but not the deterministic portion of the ADF equation. The results of the LLC and the Breitung tests are given in Table 27.

Table 27: Results of the Levin, Lin, and Chu and Breitung unit root tests

		LLC H$_0$: $\delta = 0$ Critical probability	Breitung H$_0$: $\delta = 0$ Critical probability
Relative price of exported goods	*Rpxg*	0.0579	0.0584
Relative price of imported goods	*Rpmg*	0.8771	0.4112
Relative price of services	*Rps*	0.3403	0.9864
Export goods	*Xg*	0.0117	0.9861
Export services	*Xs*	0.0059	0.9992
Import goods	*Mg*	0.7915	0.7326
Import services	*Ms*	0.0473	0.8527
World trade volume	*yg**	0.9836	0.2974
World real GDP	*ys**	0.0001	0.9760
Real GDP	*Y*	0.0076	0.6657
Private consumption	*C*	0.0000	0.8933
Government consumption	*G*	0.0001	0.2520
Private investment	*I*	0.3343	0.6828
Export	X	0.0113	0.8442

Note: The ADF specification takes individual intercepts but no trend term into account.

According to the Breitung's test statistic, the null of nonstationarity cannot be rejected for all data series but can be rejected for the relative price for exported goods (*rpxg*). The results generated by the LLC are somewhat weaker. Alternative test procedures, e.g., the unit root test by Im, Pesaran, and Shin (2003), confirm that all but the *rpxg* series possess a unit root and thus support the outcome of the Breitung test. Cointegration techniques are, therefore, the appropriate tool to estimate the trade volume equations.

4.5.2 Panel cointegration test

The available techniques for panel cointegration tests are Engle-Granger-like residual based tests. Similar to single time series, these approaches test the residuals from the estimation for stationarity. If the estimated residuals are stationary, a linear combination of the time series included in the estimation exists so that the resulting time series is a stationary process. The time series are, thus, cointegrated. As in the case of single time series, this form of cointegration test does not allow the number of cointegrating relations among the variables to be tested for. In cases where more than one cointegration relation exists and/or not all variables are part of the cointegration space, these tests only show that some combination of the included variables reveals stationary residuals, which means that some of the variables but not necessarily all of them are cointegrated. Therefore, the trace and the maximum eigenvalue statistics suggested by Johansen (1988) are applied on a country by country basis for all G-7 countries. Since these tests reveal in almost all cases of the trade volume equations that all relevant variables are part of a single cointegration equation, it is reasonable to apply the available residual-based panel cointegration tests.[173]

For the following estimations, residual-based panel cointegration tests as suggested by Pedroni (1999) and Kao (1999) are employed. Both assume homogenous slope coefficients across countries. This is in line with the purpose of our analysis, namely deriving a general relationship between government expenditure and import volumes. Pedroni as well as Kao apply the null hypothesis of no cointegration.

Kao (1999) tests the residuals $\hat{\varepsilon}_{it}$ of the OLS panel estimation by applying DF- (equation (12)) and ADF- (equation (13)) like tests.

$$\hat{\varepsilon}_{it} = \rho\hat{\varepsilon}_{it-1} + v_{it} \tag{12}$$

$$\hat{\varepsilon}_{it} = \rho\hat{\varepsilon}_{it-1} + \sum_{j=1}^{p} \varphi_j \Delta\hat{\varepsilon}_{it-j} + v_{itp} \tag{13}$$

The null hypothesis of no cointegration, i.e., H_0: $\rho = 1$, is tested against the alternative hypothesis of stationary residuals, i.e., H_a: $\rho < 1$. Pedroni (1995) suggests a Phillips-Perron-type test, which implies less strict assumptions with respect to the distribution of the error terms than the DF and ADF tests do.

The results of the cointegration tests are presented in Table 28. They show that the null hypothesis of no cointegration can be rejected at conventional significance levels in all cases. These results combined with the outcome of the Johansen procedure indicate that the variables included in the different trade volume equations are cointegrated. Due to the results of the Johansen test, we are

173 The fact that the relative price does not appear as a separate cointegration relationship might indicate that the time series is in fact not stationary. This supports the decision to apply cointegration analysis despite the fact that the panel unit root test does not support the null of a unit root for these variables.

also confident in assuming that one cointegration relationship exists that includes all relevant variables.

Table 28: Panel cointegration tests

	Goods exports	Service exports	Goods imports	Service imports	Extended goods imports	Extended service imports
Kao (1999) 1)						
DF-rho	-2.14	-3.5994	-0.9768	-2.6577	-3.5242	-5.4910
	(0.0162)	(0.0002)	(0.1643)	(0.0039)	(0.0002)	(0.000)
DF-t	-1.421	-2.2892	-0.6161	-1.7807	-2.1827	-3.4352
	(0.0777)	(0.0110)	(0.2689)	(0.0375)	(0.0145)	(0.0003)
DF-rho*	-6.4188	-8.8235	-4.8909	-7.2725	-8.6555	-10.5543
	(0.000)	(0.000)	(0.000)	(0.000)	(0.000)	(0.000)
DF-t*	-1.9633	-2.6689	-1.5068	-2.3184	-2.6025	-3.6898
	(0.0248)	(0.038)	(0.0659)	(0.0102)	(0.0046)	(0.0001)
Kao (1999) 2)						
ADF	-1.5318	-2.0591	-1.1518	-2.0725	-2.3835	-3.1681
	(0.0628)	(0.0197)	(0.1247)	(0.0191)	(0.0086)	(0.0008)
Pedroni (1995) 3)						
PC_1	-11.0199	-14.1563	-8.7730	-12.4306	-13.1817	-17.6491
	(0.000)	(0.000)	(0.000)	(0.000)	(0.000)	(0.000)
PC_2	-10.8347	-13.8814	-8.6391	-12.1892	-12.9805	-17.3063
	(0.000)	(0.000)	(0.000)	(0.000)	(0.000)	(0.000)

Note: *p*-values are given in parentheses.

1) The DF test statistics given above are analogous to the parametric Dickey-Fuller test for nonstationary time series. The DF-rho and DF-t statistics assume strict exogeneity of the regressors with respect to errors and no autocorrelation. DF-rho* and DF-t* statistics are based upon endogenous regressors. Note that these tests depend on consistent estimates of the long-run variance-covariance matrix to correct for nuisance parameters once the limiting distribution has been found.
2) The ADF test is analogous to the parametric augmented Dickey-Fuller test for nonstationary time series.
3) PC1 and PC2 are the nonparametric Phillips-Perron tests.

Since the results of the cointegration test support the assumption that a cointegration relation exists between the variables considered in the different trade equations, we proceed in our analysis by estimating the trade equations with panel cointegration techniques.

4.5.3 Estimation of trade volume equations

Trade elasticities are estimated by applying the pooled mean group (PMG) estimator proposed by Pesaran, Shin, and Smith (1999). The long-run relationships are estimated in a pooled as well as in a country-by-country setting. The cross-country average of the coefficients from the latter is the mean group (MG) estimator. A Hausman test allows one to assess whether slope homogeneity exists among cross sections and thereby reveals whether the PMG estimator provides a consistent and efficient estimation for the coefficients across all countries.

The estimation is based on the following reparameterization of the standard autoregressive distributed lag (ARDL) model

$$\Delta y_{it} = \phi_i y_{i,t-1} + \beta_i' x_{it} + \sum_{j=1}^{p-1} \lambda_{ij}^{*} \Delta y_{i,t-j} + \sum_{j=0}^{p-1} \delta_{ij}^{*'} \Delta x_{i,t-j} + \mu_i + \gamma_i t + \varepsilon_{it}, \quad (14)$$

where y_i and x_i are a vector of observations on the dependent variable, i.e., trade volume, and a vector of explanatory variables, i.e., relative price and income, for country i, respectively. μ_i represents the country-specific fixed effect, γ_i is the individual time trend coefficient, and ε_i stands for the country-specific error term. The long-run relationship between y_i and x_i is given by

$$y_{it} = -\left(\beta_i' / \phi_i\right) x_{it} + \eta_{it}, \quad (15)$$

where $-\left(\beta_i' / \phi_i\right)$ is the long-run coefficient, i.e., the respective elasticity, η_{it} is the error term, and all other variables are defined as given above.

To address the problem of cross-sectional correlation, demeaned data[174] are used in the case of all import equations. In the case of export equations, a time trend is considered instead. This is due to the fact that world income is common for all cross sections and can, therefore, not be demeaned. Table 29 shows the estimation results, which take the log of the respective trade volume as the dependent variable.

The country sample included in the estimation is adjusted where necessary to include only those countries for which the data allow a long-run relationship to

---

174 Demeaned data are constructed by subtracting the cross-sectional average of a respective variable from each data point of the respective cross section: $\bar{y}_i = T^{-1}\sum_{t=1}^{T} y_{i,t}$.

be determined.[175] The results show that income elasticities and price elasticities for both export and import equations reveal the expected sign. Income elasticities of goods and service export volumes are close to unity and are, therefore, in line with theoretical considerations. In the case of imports, income elasticities exceed unity.

Table 29: Cointegration estimation of conventional trade volume equations

	Goods export (equation 4) PMGE 1) 2)	Service exports (equation 5) PMGE 1) 2) 3)	Goods imports (equation 6) PMGE 4)	Service imports (equation 7) PMGE 2) 4)
Price elasticity	-0.849* (-8.647)	-0.726* (-3.500)	-0.313* (-3.076)	-1.263* (-15.921)
Income elasticity	0.906* (36.395)	1.018* (3.572)	1.953* (9.896)	1.316* (56.190)
Joint Hausman test	0.66	0.89	0.31	0.94

Source: Own estimations.
* denotes statistical significance at a 1% level. *t*-statistics are given in parentheses.
1) Estimation equation includes time trend.
2) Japan is excluded from the estimation.
3) France is excluded from the estimation.
4) The estimation is based on demeaned data.

Comparing the results of the estimation above with those generated by Hooper, Johnson, and Marquez (2000) and Driver and Wren-Lewis (1998)[176] shows that the estimated coefficients are in the range of those estimated by single time series analysis. The results of Hooper, Johnson, and Marquez and Driver and Wren-Lewis reflect that empirically determined income elasticities usually deviate from unity and that price elasticities vary significantly among countries.

175 The fact that no reasonable cointegration relationship can be established, for example, for France in the case of service export might be a country-specific problem that, for example, forced Driver and Wren-Lewis (1998) to assign values for the elasticities in such cases. Our analysis does not intend to determine country-specific elasticities but general results and the number of cross sections is large enough so that the exclusion of one or two countries from the parts of the analysis does not harm the general propositions drawn from the estimation results.

176 The findings of Hooper, Johnson, and Marquez (2000) and Driver and Wren-Lewis (1998) are provided in the chapter's appendix.

We employ a joint Hausman test to assess the null hypothesis of slope homogeneity against the alternative hypothesis of heterogeneous slope coefficients across countries. The *p*-values of the joint Hausman test reveal that for the countries included in the estimations the null of slope homogeneity cannot be rejected. While the elasticity estimates of former empirical studies differed across countries, those studies did not test whether the difference was significant.

In the next step, the extended form of the import volume equations (8) and (9) are estimated to analyze the effects of government expenditure on foreign trade. While total demand (GDP) is the sum of final private consumption, final private investment expenditure, final government expenditure, and net trade, due to data availability and consistency we replace total demand with total private consumption, total private investment expenditure, total government expenditure, and exports. The sum of the domestic demand components considered in our estimation, therefore, exceeds final domestic absorption. However, the validity and the interpretation of our results are not affected since the estimated elasticities reflect the impact of a percentage change in the respective demand components and elasticities are not affected by the demand component's level.

Table 30: Cointegration estimation of extended import volume equations

	Goods imports (equation 8) PMGE 1) 2) 3)	Service imports (equation 9) PMGE 1) 2) 4)
Price elasticity	-0.665** (-5.015)	-1.592** (-6.747)
Private consumption (ln C)	1.102** (3.481)	1.433** (1.916)
Government expenditure (ln G)	0.392* (1.762)	0.491** (2.485)
Private sector investments (ln I)	0.427** (5.152)	0.030 (0.076)
Exports (ln X)	0.435** (4.156)	0.503** (1.972)
Joint Hausman test	0.12	0.22

Source: Own estimations.

* and ** denote statistical significance at a 5% and 1% level, respectively. *t*-statistics are given in parentheses.

1) The estimation is based on demeaned data.
2) Japan is excluded from the estimation.
3) France is excluded from the estimation.
4) The coefficients of private consumption and private sector investment are not restricted to being homogenous across countries.

The results of the PMG estimation for the disaggregated trade equations are summarized in Table 30. The dependent variable in the estimation is the log of the respective trade volume.

As in the case of conventional trade equations, the relative price variable is significant and has the expected sign. All demand variables, except private sector investment in the service import equation, are significant. They show a positive effect on goods and service imports. The magnitude of the elasticities differs across the demand components. This confirms that the composition of demand matters for import volumes and that using a single aggregate demand variable might distort the result. For both goods and service imports, private consumption reveals the highest elasticity and government expenditure the lowest. In the case of services, private investment does not have a significant impact on import volumes and government expenditure reveals the smallest elasticity among the remaining demand components. More precisely, our results show that a one percent increase in private consumption increases goods and service import volumes by 1.1 and 1.4 percent, respectively. However, a one percent increase of government expenditure increases goods and service import volumes by only 0.4 and 0.5 percent, respectively.

As in the case of the conventional trade equations, the p-values of the joint Hausman test suggest that for the countries included in the estimations the null of slope homogeneity cannot be rejected. This result indicate that trade elasticities even for the disaggregated demand components are somewhat similar across the G-7. We are aware that elasticities might still differ across countries, and elasticities, for example for transition countries, might deviate from those determined for the G-7. However, we are confident that the general finding of our analysis—a notable divergence of elasticities across demand components and a relatively low size of the elasticity of government expenditure—holds for other countries as well. The interpretation of our results, therefore, discusses the general implications for the impact of fiscal policy on import volumes and thus the trade account.

4.5.4 Implications of the empirical results

The impact of a change in public expenditure on the trade account is twofold. (i) An increase (decrease) in government expenditure, ceteris paribus, causes a(n) decrease (increase) in import volumes. (ii) A change in government expenditure is expected also to impact private consumption and private investment demand, and a change in either of the two demand components, ceteris paribus, affects import volumes. The overall impact of a change in government expenditure depends on both effects, the direct impact of the change in public spending and the indirect effect through the change in the private demand components, i.e., private consumption and private investment. Depending on the assumptions made regarding the effect an increase of government expenditure has on these two demand components, different conclusions could be drawn from our empirical results. At the opposite ends of the spectrum, two different assumptions could be made:

(i) An increase (decrease) in government expenditures has no effect on other demand components but translates one on one into an increase (decrease) of total demand.

(ii) An increase (decrease) in government expenditures fully crowds out (in) private demand and therefore has only a composition effect but no impact on the level of total demand.

Under the first assumption a lasting increase in government expenditure of 1 percent will lead to an increase of demand for goods and service imports of 0.4 and 0.5 percent, respectively. An increase in public spending will thus, ceteris paribus, cause the trade account to deteriorate and as a consequence also affect the current account balance negatively.

Under the second assumption the total effect of an increase in government expenditure on import demand depends on which of the components of private demand, i.e., consumption or investment, is crowded out. If an increase in government expenditure is assumed to crowd out private investment one to one and, thus, that total demand is unchanged, goods imports will decrease. This is due to the lower elasticity of government expenditure compared to investment demand. In the case of service imports the impact of the shift from private investment demand to public demand is less clear. While, according to our results, an increase in public expenditure increases service imports, a decline in private investment is expected to have no significant impact. Service imports could, therefore, increase. The reaction of the overall trade balance depends on the relative size of the service and the goods account.

Empirical studies have, however, shown that an increase in public spending might crowd out private sector investment while private consumption is likely to increase as public expenditure rises.[177] If an increase in government expenditure crowds out private investment but positively impacts private consumption, the impact on import volumes becomes even less predictable. If public expenditure and private consumption replace private investment—due to the combination of a high elasticity of private consumption and the low elasticity of public expenditure—the decline in import demand due to the slowdown in private investment

177 See, for example, Karras (1994) and Blanchard and Perotti (2002).

might or might not be compensated by the surge in import demand caused by the increase in public expenditure and private consumption. The overall effect of such a demand shift on goods imports depends on the relative size of the change in public expenditure and private consumption. In the case of service imports the effects are more predictable. According to our results the increase in government expenditure and the related rise in private consumption cause an increase in service imports while the decrease in private investment does not impact the service account. An increase in government expenditure would thus lead to a deterioration of the service account.

Because the goods account is more sizeable than the service account,[178] it can be expected that the effect coming from the goods account overrides the effect stemming from the service account. If this is the case, the overall impact of an increase in government expenditure of the trade account depends on the reaction of private consumption and private investment on the expansion of the government sector.

Overall the results of our estimation provide unambiguous insights regarding the direct effect of a change in government expenditure on import demand. Government expenditure reveals a positive elasticity with respect to goods imports and service imports. An increase in government expenditure, ceteris paribus, causes an increase in import volumes. However, the indirect effects of fiscal policy measures caused by the reaction of private consumption and private investment to a change in public expenditure are less clear-cut. Since the empirical literature does not provide unanimous evidence regarding the impact that fiscal policy measures have on private demand, the interpretation of our results depends on the assumptions one makes regarding this interaction between the public and the private sector.

4.6 Conclusions

This chapter analyzes the empirical relationship between fiscal policy and the current account. Research prior to this paper did not take into account that the components of private and public demand in the import equation exhibit different elasticities. Using pooled mean group estimation for annual panel data of the G-7 countries for the years 1970 through 2002, we find that an increase in government expenditures has a significant positive impact on both goods and service imports.

178 In the case of the G-7 countries, the service imports have less than one third of the size of goods imports.

An increase in government expenditures by 1 percent leads to an increase in goods imports by about 0.4 percent and to an increase in service imports by almost 0.5 percent. This implies that ceteris paribus an increase in government expenditure would also lead to a deterioration of the current account.

We also find that the elasticities of all private demand components are larger than the one of government expenditure. Therefore, it would be possible to derive the opposite result if an increase in expenditure crowded out private investment. In this case the current account could be expected to improve as government expenditure increases. However, the implications of our results become unpredictable if an increase in government expenditure affects private consumption and private investment in opposite directions, as is also suggested by the empirical literature.

Looking back at the literature on the effects of fiscal deficits on the current account, the ambiguous effect of government expenditures on import demand might in part be explained by the compositional effect that an increase in government expenditures has on aggregate demand. The nature of this effect would not have been revealed when using a reduced-form equation. We saw that higher government expenditures, ceteris paribus, lead to higher imports simply because the government consumes more from abroad in line with its import content. However, when considering the compositional effect that fiscal policy measures have on overall demand—depending on the reaction of private demand—the opposite conclusion can also be derived.

Turning to the implications that an expenditure-based consolidation might have on the external balance of the CEECs, our findings do not allow any unanimous projections to be made. In line with our argumentation above, the reaction of the trade account to a cut in public expenditure depends on how private demand reacts to the fiscal policy measure. If overall demand is constant and public demand is fully replaced by private investment demand, the higher elasticity of investment demand compared to public expenditure would cause a net increase in imports of goods; consequently, the goods account would deteriorate. If a decrease in public demand causes private consumption to decline, while the increase in private investment keeps total demand unchanged, the overall impact on import demand will depend on the relative change of public expenditure and private consumption.

Overall, we conclude that a change in government expenditures has an impact on import demand and thus on the trade and current account. However, it is not clear at the outset in which direction the effect will push. In this sense our results are in line with the findings provided in the existing literature on the relation between fiscal policy and the trade account balance. Our results do, however, also show that the accuracy of trade account models and any model that incorporates the trade account might be improved by taking into account that demand components reveal different trade elasticities and that the composition of demand matters for the determination of the trade account.

4.7 Appendix to Chapter 4

Table A 4-1: Trade elasticities for the G-7 countries

	Caporale and Chui (1999)	Cline (1989)	Hooper, Johnson, and Marquez (2000)	Houthakker and Magree (1969)
		Income elasticities for exports		
Canada	1.8	1.6	1.1	1.4
France	2.2	1.8	1.5	1.5
Germany	2.0	2.0	1.4	2.1
Italy	2.0	2.6	1.6	3.0
Japan	1.6	2.2	1.1	3.6
United Kingdom	1.3	1.8	1.1	0.9
United States	1.5	1.7	0.8	1.0
Average	1.7	1.9	1.2	1.7
		Income elasticities for imports		
Canada	1.3	2.0	1.4	1.2
France	2.1	2.7	1.6	1.7
Germany	2.1	2.3	1.5	1.8
Italy	1.7	2.5	1.4	2.2
Japan	1.3	1.2	0.9	1.2
United Kingdom	2.3	2.4	2.2	1.7
United States	1.8	2.4	1.8	1.5
Average	1.8	2.2	1.6	1.6
		Price elasticities for exports		
Canada	-0.2	-1.0	-0.9	-0.6
France	-0.04	-0.4	-0.2	-2.3
Germany	-0.1	-0.5	-0.3	+1.7
Italy	-0.5	-1.1	-0.9	-0.03
Japan	-0.2	-0.9	-1.0	-0.7
United Kingdom	-0.3	-0.7	-1.6	-0.4
United States	-1.4	-1.1	-1.5	-1.5
		Price elasticities for imports		
Canada	-1.1	-2.4	-0.9	-1.5
France	-0.2	-0.6	-0.4	+0.2
Germany	-0.6	-0.5	-0.06	-0.2
Italy	-0.7	-0.5	-0.4	-0.1
Japan	-0.6	-0.7	-0.3	-0.8
United Kingdom	-0.6	-1.0	-0.6	+0.2
United States	-0.2	-1.4	-0.3	-0.5

Source: Caporale and Chui (1999), Cline (1989), Hooper, Johnson, and Marquez (2000), and Houthakker and Magree (1969).

Table A 4-2: Trade elasticities for the G-7 countries

	Income				Price			
	Exports		Imports		Exports		Imports	
	ECM	Johansen	ECM	Johansen	ECM	Johansen	ECM	Johansen
Canada	1.32	-	0.51	0.62	0.44	-	-0.80	-0.68
France	0.74	0.77	-1.79	0.63	-0.02	-0.03	-3.45	0.01
Germany	0.74	0.58	-0.70	-0.65	-0.22	-1.15	-1.33	-1.28
Italy	1.00	0.96	0.85	0.67	-0.34	-0.27	-0.72	-0.98
Japan	0.81	0.91	0.49	-	-1.22	-1.36	-0.31	-
United Kingdom	0.91	0.93	-0.57	-0.80	-1.26	-1.52	-0.71	-0.85
United States	1.12	1.21	1.71	1.95	-0.96	-0.65	-0.32	-0.21

Source: Driver and Wren-Lewis (1998).

Data and sources

All estimations are carried out with annual data for the G-7 countries (Japan, the United States, Canada, the United Kingdom, France, Italy, and Germany). Data series are taken from the IMF's international financial statistic (IFS; IMF, 2005c), the OECD's main economic indicators (MEI) databases (OECD, 2005b) and the IMF's Direction of Trade Statistics (IMF, 2005b).

For this part of the analysis data series for the G-7 countries and world aggregates or OECD data for world variables covering the period from 1970 through 2002 are considered.

The trade equations (equations (4) through (9)) include the following variables:[179]

Data sources for goods export volumes (*XG*), service export volumes (*XS*), goods import volumes (*MG*), and service import volumes (*MS*) are given below. World income relevant for goods export demand (*YG**) and for service export demand (*YS**) are world trade volume and world (OECD) real GDP, respectively. Domestic income (*Y*) is measured by domestic real GDP. The demand components in the extended version of the import equations are real private consumption (*C*), real private sector investment (*I*), real government expenditure (*G*), and real exports (*X*). Competitiveness is measured by three different variables reflecting relative prices: first, the relative price for goods exports (*RPXG*) given by (*WPXG*r*)/*PXG*; second, the relative price for goods imports (*RMPG*), the real exchange rate, given by (*WPXG*r*)/*PD*; and third, the relative price for service exports and service imports (*RPS*), given by *PCW*/(*PC*EFEX*).

Trade volumes:

XG is domestic goods-exports volume. Export volumes (IFS line 72) are turned from an index into a constant price series using the 1995 average for merchandise exports in USD (IFS line 78aa) converted into domestic currency using the 1995 average for the exchange rate (*r*). *XS* denotes domestic export services volume. Service credits in USD (IFS line 78ad) are converted into domestic currency using the actual exchange rate (*r*).

The series are then turned into a volume series by deflating by *PC*. *MG* is domestic goods import volume. The import volume FOB series (IFS line 73) is turned from an index into a constant price series using the 1995 average by multiplica-

179 The uppercase abbreviations for the variables correspond to the lowercase equivalents in the equations as given in the text. However the uppercase stands for absolute values while the equations are given in logs.

tion with merchandise exports in USD (IFS line 78ab) and is converted into domestic currency using the 1995 average for the USD exchange rate (*r*). *MS* denotes service import volume. Service debits in USD (IFS line 78ae) are converted into domestic currency using the actual USD exchange rate (*r*) and into a volume series by deflating by *PCW* after converting *PCW* into domestic currency terms using *EFEX*.

Demand and demand components:

*YG** as world trade volume is proxied by total world exports in USD at current prices (IFS line 70), deflated using *WPXG*. *YS** is world (OECD) real GDP: Total OECD GDP at constant market prices in USD. *Y* is domestic real GDP taken from the IFS (line 99b) and deflated by *PY*. *I* is real private sector investment (IFS line 93i plus IFS line 93e), *G* denotes real government expenditure (IFS line 91f), and *X* stands for real exports (IFS line 90c); all three are deflated by *PY*. *C* denotes private consumption (IFS line 96f) and is deflated by *CP*.

Price variables:

WPXG are world export prices in USD and are given as unit value of world exports in USD (IFS line 74). *PXG* denotes domestic export prices. For Canada, France, Germany, and Italy this is an export unit value index (IFS line 74). Export prices index (IFS line 76) are used in the case of Japan, the United Kingdom, and the United States. *PD* as the domestic prices index in domestic currency is given by wholesale prices (IFS line 63). *PCW*, the world consumer price index, is taken from the MEI of the OECD. *PC* is the domestic consumer price index in domestic currency (IFS line 64). *PY* is the domestic GDP deflator (IFS line 99bi).

Exchange rate:

The nominal USD exchange rate (*r*) is the average exchange rate in national currency units per USD (IFS line rf). *EFEX* is the nominal effective exchange rate calculated from the exchange rates (*r*) and the bilateral trade weights [exports plus imports (lines 70 and 71 of the direction of trade statistics)] of the G-7 countries and their thirty-nine largest trading partners (including the G-7 countries themselves).

5 Lessons learned

5.1 Summary of the findings

In 2004, eight countries from central and eastern Europe entered the EU; all eight countries intend to access the euro area within three to six years after entering the EU. To be eligible for full EMU membership the CEECs must have reached a certain level of economic convergence with the EU-12. In this context, the body of EU laws requires the new member states to comply with the conditions described in the Maastricht treaty before they can adopt the euro. These conditions include quantitative criteria regarding stable prices, sound public finances, and monetary conditions—measured by exchange rate stability and long-term interest rate—and the nonquantified requirement of a sustainable balance of payments and current account.

Many of the CEECs in the late 1990s and the early 2000s ran sizable current account deficits and, as a consequence, face a high and increasing burden of external debt. Current account deficits in transition economies might reflect the effects of consumption smoothing since consumers expect their lifetime income to increase due to economic convergence. Furthermore, growth expectations related to the convergence process might rectify high capital inflows in light of an efficient allocation of resources. However, in most of the CEECs current account deficits in recent years exceeded estimated equilibrium levels. Additionally, the financing structure of the CEECs' current account deficits changed from long-term equity flows, e.g., FDI, to short-term debt financing. This development is also reflected in the rapid increase of the countries' external debt burden—the stock of the CEECs' external debt increased by between 100 and 380 percent between 1997 and 2004. Due to the high and persistent current account deficits and the growing external debt burden the CEECs' external sustainability might be at risk. Measures against these external imbalances might, therefore, become a critical aspect for the CEECs' euro area accession. The three analytical chapters presented in this study focus on selected aspects related to the CEECs' balance of payments, prevailing external imbalances, and related issues that are of interest in the countries' run-up to full EMU membership.

The first study, which is presented in the second chapter, focuses on assessing the external sustainability of the CEECs. When comparing the CEECs' current account balances with equilibrium current account estimates, which are taken from the existing body of empirical literature on the CEECs' current account, it is shown that 2004 deficits and 2001-2004 average current account deficits of more than half of the CEECs exceed equilibrium levels. Applying two of the most commonly used approaches to assess the sustainability of external debt, we find that external debt levels in some countries breached critical levels.

As a first approach to assessing debt sustainability, we determine debt stabilizing current account balances and compare them to actual balances. More precisely, we calculate minimum current account-FDI balances, i.e., current account balances plus FDI inflows, that would be required to stabilize the countries' debt-to-GDP ratio. Given the actual level of current account deficits, FDI inflows, growth, and interest rates, according to our calculations the debt-to-GDP ratio would not stabilize but increase further in six of the eight CEECs. To stabilize their debt-to-GDP ratio in 2005, these countries—assuming all other economic factors remain unchanged—would either have to reduce current account deficits or to increase FDI inflows by between 0.5 and 7.3 percent of GDP compared to actual 2004 levels. However, compared to 2004, economic conditions, e.g., economic growth, are expected to deteriorate rather than to improve in 2005 and over the medium-term future. As a consequence, the current account deficit or FDI inflow corrections needed to prevent the debt-to-GDP ratio from increasing will have to be even more substantial. Such corrections are not expected to occur in the near future.

As a second approach to assessing the sustainability of the CEECs' external debt, we construct and calculate debt indicators that put the external debt in relation to some economic variable reflecting a country's debt repayment capacity. We provide both indicators reflecting a country's solvency and indicators allow a country's liquidity situation to be assessed. Calculated indicator values are assessed against threshold levels that are provided in the empirical literature on the debt sustainability of developing countries and emerging economies. We apply those thresholds that were determined for countries whose political and institutional environment has a quality similar to that of the CEECs. Depending on the measure used for the repayment capacity, a solvency-oriented indicator suggests that the stock of external debt of some of the CEECs might challenge or even exceed their repayment capacity. In particular, Estonia and Latvia record a rapid increase in their debt-to-GDP ratio while Hungary faces a continuously high debt-to-GDP ratio. According to this indicator the solvency of Estonia, Hungary, and Latvia might be at risk. Liquidity-oriented indicators, i.e., debt-service-based indicators, reveal that Latvia and Lithuania have to make debt service payments that are large compared to the available source for these payments, namely exports, government revenues, and reserve assets. These two countries might, therefore, be threatened by liquidity problems.

We point out that a pure indicator-based assessment cannot provide a comprehensive picture of a country's debt sustainability. The political situation and the stability of the institutional framework of countries with debt indicators that exceed critical levels need to be analyzed in depth. Finally, those countries that face critically high debt burdens and reveal weaknesses in the political and institutional environment are vulnerable to financial distress and need to be monitored closely. We limit ourselves to determining possible weaknesses in the external balance due to the CEECs' current external imbalance and the current debt burden they face. However, we do not assess the stability of the CEECs' political and institutional environment. The results of our assessment suggest that the current account and the debt level of some of the CEECs might be excessive. In these cases an assessment of the stability of the political and institutional environment would be necessary to determine the risk of financial distortion for these countries.

Given that current account deficits might be desirable in the catching-up process and that capital inflows to the CEECs might be reasonable in light of efficient allocation of resources, the CEECs could attempt to attract more long-term equity inflows, i.e., FDI, to prevent the stock of external debt from increasing. In the third chapter we address the question of how to attract these FDI inflows by analyzing the factors that determine FDI flows from industrialized countries to emerging economies. We apply different specifications of a gravity-type model to bilateral FDI flows from six industrialized countries to twenty-two emerging economies. Our results show that FDI inflows are inversely related to the distance between the home and the host country, probably due to control costs that rise with distance. While FDI inflows increase with host country market size, the relationship between home country GDP and FDI outflows is nonlinear. We find that FDI outflows from large economies are small relative to their size. Besides these gravity factors, further host and home characteristics have an impact on FDI flows. Some of the specifications that we apply reveal a positive relation between cyclical developments in host and home countries and FDI flows. Furthermore, our results suggest that some host country characteristics, such as openness, low country risk, price stability, and low unit labor costs relative to industrialized countries, increase an economy's attractiveness for foreign investors.

By dividing our host country sample into three regional subsamples, namely an Asian, a central and eastern European, and a Latin American subsample, we are able to show that the importance of the different factors for FDI flows differs across regions. Economic fundamentals, i.e., economic growth, openness, and low country risk, were of importance for countries in Asia and Latin America. Because the region experienced periods of high inflation, Latin American countries were able to attract more FDI flows if they maintained price stability. FDI flows to transition countries from central and eastern Europe in general were less dependent on economic fundamentals. While FDI flows to these countries were significantly affected by openness and the level of country risk, the privatization of publicly owned assets and the process of European integration might also have been important factors. When unit labor costs are included in the analysis, we find that FDI flows to CEECs are significantly affected by this factor, while no significant effect is seen for FDI flows to other regions or the overall panel.

Our results suggest that among other factors, host country characteristics have a significant impact on FDI inflows. Competing with other emerging economies for FDI flows from industrialized countries, policy makers could try to implement measures that make their country an attractive location for foreign investors. However, depending on the economic and political situation, the importance of the different country characteristics for foreign investors can vary. Investors seem to look at those factors that are most critical in a specific country or region, e.g., inflation in Latin America, and stability, i.e., low country risk, in the transition economies. Policy makers, therefore, need to determine the relevant factors for their country or region before looking for policy measures that could improve these factors in their country.

Most of the CEECs face both high current account deficits and public deficits in excess of the level allowed according to the Maastricht criteria. These countries would therefore need to consolidate their public households while not aggravating their current account positions. For these countries European institutions in general recommend expenditure-based consolidation strategies. In the fourth chapter we analyze the impact of such a strategy on the trade account. We focus on the trade account since the deficit in the trade account in most of the CEECs is at the center of their current account problem.

Calculating correlations between government expenditure and the trade account balance reveals an inverse relationship between these two factors for most countries, independent of country characteristics such as country size, size of the government sector, or state of development. From this observation we derive the hypothesis that imports have a lower elasticity with respect to government expenditure than with respect to private sector demand. To assess this hypothesis we estimate import volume equations by replacing GDP with the different components of demand, namely private consumption, private sector investment, government expenditure, and exports. Pooled mean group estimation is applied to determine the long-term relation between trade volumes, demand components, and relative prices for a panel of the G-7 countries. The estimation results reveal—in line with theory—that price elasticities are negative and demand elasticities for all demand components are positive for both goods imports and service imports. The elasticity of private sector investment, however, is insignificant in the case of service imports. In line with our hypothesis, government expenditure reveals the lowest elasticity among all demand components with significant elasticities for both goods and service imports.

We consider two different cases when using the results from our estimations to project the possible impact of expenditure-based consolidation on the trade account. In the first case we assume that the private sector does not react to expenditure cuts, i.e., no crowding in is observed, and total demand decreases by the amount of public expenditure cuts. In the second case we assume that the private sector is crowded in and, therefore, the lack in government expenditure will be replaced by private sector demand. Under this assumption only the composition of demand changes and total demand stays constant.

If private sector demand does not react to cuts in government expenditure, total demand and thus import volumes would decrease and, ceteris paribus, the trade account would improve. If total demand stays constant and government expenditure is replaced by private sector investment—given that relative import prices are kept constant—according to our findings import volumes would increase. Given that all other factors, e.g., foreign import demand and relative prices, remain unchanged, this implies that the trade account deteriorates as the government cuts expenditures in a world with pure crowding in. The empirical literature, however, suggests that a decline in government expenditure might cause a decrease in private consumption while private investment increases. If this was the case, the impact of cuts in public expenditure depends on the relative reaction of private demand and investment. If the shift from private consumption to private investment is strong, import demand could decrease and the trade account could improve. This is due to the high elasticity of private consumption relative to private investment.

Due to limitations in the availability of data on the CEECs, the estimations of the trade volume equations have been done for the G-7 countries. We are confident, however, that the general finding that a change in government expenditure has a smaller elasticity than any other demand component can be transferred to other countries. In the case of the CEECs, this would imply that the effect of an expenditure-based consolidation on the trade account—and thus also on the current account—depends on how private sector demand reacts to cuts in government expenditure, i.e., whether crowding in takes place and whether demand shifts between private investment and private consumption. The empirical literature that analyzes the impact of fiscal policy on private demand and overall output gives mixed results. From our analysis it can be inferred how the trade account reacts to a change in the structure and level of domestic demand. The impact of fiscal policy on the trade account, however, depends on how the structure of domestic demand is affected by a change in fiscal policy. Therefore, conclusions from our findings can only be drawn by making assumptions regarding the link between fiscal measures and the structure and level of domestic demand.

5.2 Implications for the CEECs

The CEECs aim at entering the euro area within the next several years. To be admitted to become a full member of the currency union, the countries have to fulfill the conditions specified in the Maastricht treaty. The CEECs have to follow policies that allow them to comply with these criteria. As discussed above, the Treaty requires a sustainable external balance and quantifies indicators to assess sound public finances, price stability, and sound monetary conditions. While the assessment of the quantified criteria is straightforward, the assessment of the sustainability of the external balance is more difficult. To know whether it is necessary to take action to achieve a sustainable external balance, the CEECs first have to determine whether their current economic situation and the economic developments projected under current policies will allow them to reach a sustainable external balance by the expected time of euro area accession.

The current account deficits of most of the CEECs exceed equilibrium levels. Our analysis shows that the financing of these deficits is a major issue for the external sustainability of some countries. Over recent years capital inflows covering the current account deficit shifted from long-term equity financing to short-term debt financing. The increasing debt burden and short maturities of external debt aggravate the possible impact of a sudden change in investor sentiments on the economy. As a debt sustainability assessment shows, some of the CEECs face debt burdens that are high compared to their potential repayment capacity. This could render them vulnerable to financial distress.

To address possible imbalances in the external sector the CEECs have mainly two options. (i) If the external deficit exceeds levels that could be rectified by consumption smoothing or efficient allocation of resources, policy makers might aim at improving net national savings through restrictive economic policies, which in turn would be expected to help control net import demand. Such a policy is especially reasonable when the current account deficit is caused by a deficit in the trade account, i.e., through high import demand, and restrictive policies can be expected to lower overall demand. (ii) If the current account deficit is in line with considerations of intertemporal optimization, policy measures should not aim at changing the current account balance but at affecting the structure of the deficit's financing. The sustainability of a country's external position depends on the debt burden rather than overall external liabilities. If capital inflows come in the form of long-term equity, i.e., mainly FDI inflows, the country has no contractual repayment obligation and the possibility for investors to withdraw their capital in the short run is very limited. This makes the country less vulnerable to changes in financial market sentiments; and a financial crisis occurring in a neighboring country or related region cannot translate into a sudden flight of these financial sources.

EU law prohibits all restrictions on movement of capital between member states and between member states and third-party countries. Affecting the structure of external financing by putting restrictions on certain types of capital flows is, therefore, not an option. The CEECs are, however, free to implement policies that make them attractive locations for certain types of investments. As a consequence, the countries might look for measures that increase their attractiveness for foreign direct investors. The actual data on FDI show that the major part of foreign investment flows originates from industrialized countries. Furthermore, the results of our analysis reflect that FDI flows are negatively affected by the distance between the host and the home country. This indicates that the major sources for FDI inflows to a country are geographically close, industrialized countries. In the case of the CEECs, this suggests that the neighboring EU countries would be the home country of the majority of their FDI inflows. Our results also show that home and host country size have a positive impact on FDI flows from industrialized countries to the CEECs while cyclical factors play no significant role. With respect to country-specific characteristics we find that openness, low country risk, and low unit labor costs relative to industrialized economies have a positive impact on FDI to countries in central and eastern Europe.

While some of the factors that determine FDI inflows to the CEECs, e.g., country size and geographic location, are not under the countries' control, some country-specific characteristics that impact the attractiveness of the CEECs for foreign investors can be affected by policy measures. Policy makers in the CEECs should concentrate on relevant country-specific factors that they can influence when trying to implement measures that affect FDI inflows positively. As the results of our analysis suggest, for the CEECs these factors were openness, country risk, and unit labor costs. While the transition process might have been a period of substantial political instability and uncertainty, the EU accession was only possible after the countries reached a certain minimum level of stability and EU membership can also be expected to support political and economic stability in the region. According to our results, investors tend to take those factors into account that are of special relevance for a country or region. It can, therefore, be expected that country risk considerations have lost already and will further decrease in importance for foreign investors when considering the CEECs as an investment location. Unit labor costs might remain one of the driving forces for FDI in the CEECs. In particular, investors from EU countries with high local labor costs might consider the relocation of production capacities to the CEECs. Retaining cost advantage over industrialized countries and other emerging market regions could be an important factor in the competition for FDI. The cost advantage of the CEECs over competing emerging market regions can be a combination of relatively low unit labor costs and the geographical proximity to potential host countries, e.g., the large western European countries.

The empirical analysis of the driving factors behind FDI flows from industrialized countries to the CEECs is backward looking. Since the situation of the CEECs changed over the transition process and continues to change during the process of European integration, the importance of the factors might change and new factors might come into play in the future. Policy makers, therefore, have to assess continuously whether the countries' position, the investors' preferences, and/or the relevant competitors for FDI have changed, and policy measures have to be adjusted according to these developments.

Besides prevailing external imbalances, half of the CEECs do not fulfill the Maastricht criteria for stable public finances; i.e., they are subject to an excessive deficit procedure. In these cases European institutions recommend an expenditure-based consolidation of the public deficit. Having to handle both the external and the public deficit at the same time, the countries might wonder whether the cuts in expenditures recommended to heal the public deficit affect the external balance. The current account balances of the CEECs with the most extensive current account deficits are dominated by large trade account deficits. Our findings regarding the linkage between the trade account and government expenditure show that import volumes are, ceteris paribus, less affected by a change in government expenditure than by a change in any other demand component.

If the CEECs implement expenditure-based consolidation strategies—depending on the reaction of private sector demand to public expenditures cuts—the trade account might react in different ways. The impact such a policy has on the current account is, therefore, uncertain. If the fiscal policy measures have no impact on overall demand and the decrease in government expenditure crowds in an equal amount of private demand, the trade account will deteriorate if the cut in public expenditure affects private demand components only positively. This is due to higher import content in private demand compared to government expenditure; spending a certain amount through the private sector will lead to higher import demand than spending the same amount through the public sector. However, if cuts in public expenditure are not compensated by increases in private sector demand, the trade account will improve. This is due to the government expenditure that is cut and that would partly have gone into import demand. For any situation between total crowding in and no crowding in at all, the impact on import volumes and thus on the trade account depends on the relative magnitude of the two effects.

Turning to the concrete situation of the CEECs, among the eight countries the Czech Republic, Hungary, Poland, and the Slovak Republic face excessive public deficits. Current account deficits of the Slovak Republic and Poland, however, have been within the range or close to estimated equilibrium levels. Current account deficits of the Czech Republic and Hungary exceeded equilibrium levels but deficits in both countries were mainly due to a deficit in the income account. Hence, the possible negative impact of an expenditure-based consolidation of the public household on the trade account might not cause significant problems in the concerned countries. Solving the public deficit problem by cutting government expenditure will most likely not cause any conflicts with a correction of external imbalances, no matter whether fiscal policy is neutral to total demand or not.

This assessment focuses on the linkage between government expenditure and the trade account. While the trade account plays an important role for the current account balance of most of the CEECs, changes in fiscal policies might affect the current account through channels other than trade, i.e., other subaccounts. These effects would also need to be assessed and have to be taken into account when considering the impact of fiscal policy on the overall external balance.

5.3 Outlook and concluding remarks

Whether and when the CEECs enter the EMU is a political decision that is based on the rules given by the legal framework of the EU that takes economic considerations into account. This study focuses on some specific aspects of the economic developments relevant for the CEECs' euro area accession. We do not show a comprehensive picture of the CEECs' economic and political situation and this study is not meant to assess economic convergence against the full range of Maastricht criteria or other aspects regarding the CEECs' ability to participate in the EMU. We rather focus on some selected questions regarding BOP issues that the CEECs might face in their run-up to full EMU membership and that are of interest for economic research.

We show that most of the CEECs face high current account deficits, which in many cases exceed equilibrium levels. These deficits result in a large and growing burden of external debt, which for some countries is high compared to their repayment capacity. While the sustainability of the CEECs' current account deficits has been the subject of recent research, the sustainability of the CEECs' external indebtedness has not been analyzed. We provide an assessment of the sustainability of the external debt and provide an overall evaluation of the CEECs' external balance by bringing together the results of previous research on the current account and our findings regarding the stock of external debt. We find that according to the technical analysis of macroeconomic variables, some of the CEECs might be vulnerable to financial distress. Whether these countries have a political and institutional environment that allows them to handle the prevailing external imbalances safely has, however, not been assessed in this study. Such an assessment would require an in-depth analysis of financial sector stability, governance regulations, the quality of the countries' external assets, and so forth, which is beyond the scope of our analysis.

To address problems regarding the structure of external financing, we analyze the determinants of FDI flows from industrialized countries to emerging economies and discuss possible ways for the CEECs to become more attractive for foreign direct investors. Financing current account deficits to a larger extent through FDI would allow the countries' dependence on external debt financing to be reduced. Since we wanted to derive policy implications on a country-wide level, we concentrate on the macroeconomic factors that impact FDI flows. Applying a gravity-type model to a panel of emerging economies from different regions allows us to investigate the impact of gravity factors and region-specific characteristics on FDI. This allows us to determine those macroeconomic factors that are most important for FDI flows to the CEECs. While microeconomic aspects also play an important role in the location decision of foreign investors, this would be a different topic, which is left open for further research.

Some of the CEECs face excessive fiscal deficit and are encouraged to address this problem following expenditure-based consolidation strategies. We investigate the impact that such a policy would have on the trade account. By estimating the import trade equation with disaggregated demand components, we show that import has a different elasticity with respect to the different demand components. Therefore, import demand depends not only on the level of total demand but also on the structure of demand. Depending on how cuts in public expenditure affect other demand components and total demand, the trade account might deteriorate or improve as a reaction to the consolidation. Former research on the relation between the external balance and fiscal policies showed equally inconclusive outcomes. However, the results that we derive from a structural model of the trade account reveal the underlying source of the uncertainty regarding the impact. Trade equations are an important pillar of structural open macroeconomic models. To improve the results derived from such models, the trade account should be modeled in a way that takes into account that the composition of demand has an impact on import demand. We do not incorporate our findings into a full-fledged trade account model or a general equilibrium model; this remains an issue that is open for future research.

Overall, this study analyzes specific aspects regarding BOP issues that the CEECs face in the context of euro area accession. We provide a comprehensive assessment of the CEECs' external sustainability, present new findings regarding the factors that determine FDI flows to the CEECs, and show how expenditure-based consolidation of public households might impact the trade account. While the interpretation of our analyses focuses on the specific situation of the CEECs, the general results can well be applied to other countries and regions. Our findings extend and supplement different strands of the recent economic literature and can be the base for further research in the respective area.

References

Aarle, B. and Garretsen, H. "Keynesian, Non-Keynesian or no Effects of Fiscal Policy Changes? The EMU Case." *Journal of Macroeconomics*, 2003, 25, pp. 213-240.

Abbott, A.J. and Seddighi, H.R. "Aggregate Imports and Expenditure Components in the UK: An Empirical Analysis." *Applied Economics*, 1996, *28*, pp. 1119–1125.

Agénor, P.R., Aizenman, J., and Hoffmaister, A. "Contagion, Bank Lending Spreads, and Output Fluctuations." NBER Working Paper 6850, Cambridge, MA, 1998.

Alias, M.H. and Cheong, T.T. "Aggregate Imports and Expenditure Components in Malaysia." *ASEAN Bulletin*, 2000, *17*, pp. 257–269.

Aliber, R.Z. "A Theory of Foreign Direct Investment," in C.P. Kindleberger, eds., *The international corporation: A symposium.* Cambridge, MA: MIT Press, 1970, pp. 17–34.

Ancharaz, V.D. "The Determinants of Foreign Direct Investment in a Comparative Perspective: Is There a Bias against Sub-Saharan Africa?". *University of Mauritius Research Journal - Law, Management and Social Sciences*, 2002, *4*.

Bank of England. *Quarterly Bulletin*, Spring 2002.

Barro, R.J. "Economic Growth in East Asia Before and After the Financial Crisis." NBER Working Paper 8330, Cambridge, MA, 2001.

Baxter, M. "International Trade and Business Cycles," in Grossman, G.M. and Rogoff K., eds. *Handbook of International Economics* Vol. 3. Amsterdam: North-Holland, 1995, pp. 1801-1864.

Beguna, A. "Competitiveness and Equilibrium Exchange rates in Latvia." EuroFaculty Working Papers in Economics 13, 2002.

Bénassy-Quéré, A., Coupet, M. and Mayer, T. "Institutional Determinants of Foreign Direct Investment." Centre d'Etudes Prospectives et d'Informations Internationales, Working Paper 5, 2005.

Berg, A. "The Asian Crisis: Causes, Responses, and Outcomes." Mimeo, IMF, Washington, DC, 1999.

Berenheim, B.D. "Budget Deficits and the Balance of Trade," *Swedish Economic Policy Review*, 1988, *3*, pp. 113–134.

Bergstrand, J.H. "The Gravity Equation in International Trade: Some Microeconomic Foundation and Empirical Evidence." *Review of Economics and Statistics,* 1985, *7*, pp. 474–481.

Bevan, A.A. and Estrin, S. "The Determinants of Foreign Direct Investment in Transition Economies." CEPR Discussion Paper 2638, 2000.

Bisignano, J.R., Hunter, W.C., and Kaufman, G.G., eds. *Global financial crises: Lessons from recent events*. Boston: Kluwer Academic, 2000.

Blanchard, O. and Perotti, R. "An Empirical Characterization of the Dynamic Effects of Changes in Government Spending and Taxes on Output." *Quarterly Journal of Economics*, 2002, *117*, pp. 1329–1368.

Borensztein, E., De Gregorio, J., and Lee, J-W. "How Does Foreign Direct Investment Affect Economic Growth? *Journal of International Economics, 45*, 1998, pp. 115–135.

Bos, J. and von de Laar, M. "Explaining Foreign Direct Investment in Central and Eastern Europe, an Extended Gravity Approach." DNB Working Paper 8, De Nederlandsche Bank, Amsterdam, 2004.

Brada, J.C., Kutan, A.M., and Yigit, T.M. "The Effects of Transition and Political Instability on Foreign Direct Investment: Central Europe and the Balkans." ZEI Working Paper B28, Center for European Integration Studies, Bonn, 2003.

Brainard, S.L. "An Empirical Assessment of the Proximity-Concentration Trade-Off Between Multinational Sales and Trade." *American Economic Review,* 1997, *87*, pp. 520–544.

Brainard, S.L. "A Simple Theory of Multinational Corporations and Trade within a Trade-off between Proximity and Concentration." NBER Working Paper 4269, Cambridge, MA, 1993.

Branson, W.H. "Monetary Policy and the New View of International Capital Movements." *Brookings Papers in Economic Activity,* 1970, 2, pp. 235–262.

Breitung, J. "The Local Power of Some Unit Root Tests for Panel Data." *Advances in Econometrics*, 2000, *15*, pp. 161–178.

Brentón, P. and DiMauro, F. "The Potential Magnitude and Impact of FDI Flows to CEECs." *Journal of Economic Integration*, 1999, *14*, pp. 59–74.

Buch, C.M., Kotka, R. M., and Piazolo, D. "Foreign Direct Investment in Europe: Is There Redirection from the South to the East? *Journal of Comparative Economics,* 2003, *31*, pp. 94–109.

Buch, C.M., Kotka, R. M., and Piazolo, D. "Does the East Get What Would Otherwise Flow to the South? FDI Diversion in Europe, Kiel Institute of World Economics." Kiel Working Paper No. 1061, 2001.

Burges, T., Fabrizio, S., and Xiao, Y. "Competitiveness in the Baltics in the Run-Up to EU Accession." IMF Country report 114, Washington, DC, 2003.

Burglund, S. and Aarebrot, F. *The political history of Eastern Europe in the 20th century.* Cheltenham: Edward Elgar, 1997.

Bussière, M., Müller, G., and Fratzscher, M. "Current Account Dynamics in OECD and EU Acceding Countries: An Inter-temporal Approach." ECB Working Paper 311, Frankfurt, 2004.

Caporale, G.M. and Chui, M.K.F. "Estimating Income and Price Elasticities of Trade in a Cointegration Framework." *Review of International Economics*, 1999, *7*, pp. 254–264.

Cerra, V. and Saxena, S.C. "Did Output Recover from the Asian Crisis?" *IMF Staff Papers*, 2005, *52*, pp. 1–23.

Clausing, K.A. and Dorobantu, C.L. "Re-entering Europe: Does European Union Candidacy Boost Foreign Direct Investment?" *Economics of Transition,* 2005, *13*, pp. 77–103.

Cline, W. *United States external adjustment and the world economy.* Washington, DC: Institute for International Economics, 1989.

Cohen, D. "The Sustainability of African Debt." World Bank Policy Research Department Working Paper 1691, World Bank, Washington, DC, 1996.

Consulate General of India. http://gx1.esol-group.com/100/17/main.asp, downloaded on June 15, 2005, Consulate General of India, Hong Kong, 2005.

Copeland, T.E., Weston, J.F., and Shastri, K. *Financial theory and corporate policy*, 4th ed. New York: Addison-Wesley, 2003.

Corden, W.M. "The Theory of International Trade," in J.H. Dunning, eds., *Economic analysis and the multinational enterprise*. London: Allen & Unwin, 1974, pp. 184–210.

Corsetti, G., Pesenti, P., and Roubini, N. "What Caused the Asian Currency and Financial Crisis?" NBER Working Paper 6833, Cambridge, MA, 1998.

Damijan, J.P. and Rojec, M. "Foreign Direct Investment and the Catching-up Process in New EU Member States: Is There a Flying Geese Pattern?" wiiw Research Reports, 310, Vienna Institute for International Economic Studies, Vienna, 2004.

Detragiache, E. and Spilimbergo, A. "Crises and Liquidity: Evidence and Interpretation." IMF Working Paper 01/2, IMF, Washington, DC, 2001.

Dewald, W.G. and Ulan, M. "The Twin Deficit-Illusion." *Cato Journal*, 1990, *9*, pp. 689–707.

Doisy, M. and Hervé, A. "Les Déficits Courants des PECO: Quelles Implications Pour Leur Entrée Dans l'Union Européenne et la Zone Euro?" *Économie Internationale*, 2003, *93*, pp. 59–88.

Drabek, Z. and Griffith-Jones, S. "Managing Capital Flows in Transition Economies with a Case Study of Central and Eastern Europe." World Trade Organization (WTO), Staff Working Paper ERAD-98-04, Geneva, 1998.

Driver, R.L. and Wren-Lewis, S. *Real exchange rates for the year 2000*. Policy Analyses in International Economics, Vol. 53, Washington, DC: Institute of International Economics, 1998.

Dunning, J.H. Multinational enterprises and the global economy. London: Addison Wesley, 1993.

Dunning, J.H. *Explaining international production*. London: Unwin Hyman, 1988.

Dunning, J.H. "Explaining the International Direct Investment Position of Countries: Towards a Dynamic or Developmental Approach." *Weltwirtschaftliches Archiv*, 1981, *117*, pp. 30–64.

Dunning, J.H. "Trade, Location of Economic Activity and MNE: A Search for an Eclectic Approach," in B. Ohlin et al., eds. *The international allocation of economic activity*. London: Macmillan, 1977, pp. 395–418.

Dunning, J.H. and Narula, R. "The Investment Development Path Revisited: Some Emerging Issues," in J.H. Dunning and R. Narula, eds., *Foreign direct investment and governments*. London: Routledge, 1996, pp. 1–41.

Eichengreen B. and Irwin, D. "Trade Blocs, Currency Blocs and the Reorientation of Trade in the 1930s." *Journal of International Economics*, 1997, *38*, pp. 1–24.

Eichengreen B. and Irwin D. "The Role of History in Bilateral Trade Flows," in J. Frankel, ed., *The regionalization of the world economy*. Chicago: University of Chicago Press, 1995.

Enders, W. and Lee, B.-S. "Current Account and Budget Deficits: Twins or Distant Cousins?" *Review of Economics and Statistics,* 1990, *72*, pp. 373–381.

Erceg, C.J., Guerrieri, L., and Gust, C. "Expansionary Fiscal Shocks and the Trade Deficit, Board of Governors of the Federal Reserve System." International Finance Discussion Paper 825, Washington, DC, 2005.

European Bank for Reconstruction and Development (EBRD). *Transition report 2004: Infrastructure*. London: EBRD, 2004.

European Bank for Reconstruction and Development. *Transition report 2003: Integration and regional cooperation*. London: EBRD, 2003.

European Bank for Reconstruction and Development. *Transition report 2002: Agriculture and rural transition*. London: EBRD, 2002.

European Bank for Reconstruction and Development. *Transition report 2001: Energy in transition*. London: EBRD, 2001.

European Bank for Reconstruction and Development. *Transition report 2000: Employment, skills and transition*. London: EBRD, 2000.

European Bank for Reconstruction and Development. *Transition report 1999: Ten years of transition*. London: EBRD, 1999.

European Bank for Reconstruction and Development. *Transition report 1998: Financial sector in transition*. London: EBRD, 1998.

European Bank for Reconstruction and Development. *Transition report 1997: Enterprise performance and growth*. London: EBRD, 1997.

European Bank for Reconstruction and Development. Transition report 1996: Building an infrastructure for transition and promoting savings. London: EBRD, 1996.

European Bank for Reconstruction and Development. *Transition report 1995: Investment and enterprise development*. London: EBRD, 1995.

European Central Bank (ECB). AMECO data base. Frankfurt, 2005a.

European Central Bank. http://www.ecb.int/stats/money/long/html/index.en.html, downloaded July 2005, Frankfurt, 2005b.

European Commission (EC). "Assessment of the Convergence Programme of the Czech Republic." ECFIN/B/5/2004/REP/50810-EN, Brussels, 2005a.

European Commission. "Assessment of the Convergence Programme of Estonia." ECFIN/B1/2005/REP/50083/EN, Brussels, 2005b.

European Commission. "Assessment of the Convergence Programme of Hungary." ECFIN/50158, Brussels, 2005c.

European Commission. "Assessment of the Convergence Programme of Latvia." ECFIN/B/4/2005/REP/50403/04-EN, Brussels, 2005d.

European Commission. "Assessment of the Convergence Programme of Lithuania." ECFIN/50408/05-EN, Brussels, 2005e.

European Commission. "Assessment of the Convergence Programme of Poland." ECFIN/2005/50368-EN, Brussels, 2005f.

European Commission. "Assessment of the Convergence Programme of Slovakia." ECFIN/50239/05-EN, Brussels, 2005g.

European Commission. "Assessment of the Convergence Programme of Slovenia." ECFIN/50363/05-EN, Brussels, 2005h.

European Commission. "ECFIN Country Focus 13, 2," Brussels, 2005i.

European Commission. "Convergence Report 2004." COM(2004) 690, Brussels, 2004.

European Community. Treaty Establishing the European Community. Brussels, 2002.

European Council. "European Council Resolution on the Establishment of an Exchange-Rate Mechanism in the Third Stage of Economic and Monetary Union." *Amsterdam, Official Journal C*, 1997, *236* of 02.08.1997.

European Council. "Conclusions of the Presidency." Copenhagen, SN 180/1/1993 REV 1, 1993.

European Forecasting Group. "The Euro Area and the Acceding Countries." Spring Report, Bocconi University, Milan, 2004.

Eurostat. "Structural Indicators." http://epp.eurostat.cec.eu.int/portal/, downloaded in July 2005, Luxembourg, 2005.

Fatás, A. and Mihov, I. "The Effects of Fiscal Policy on Consumption and Employment: Theory and Evidence," CEPR Discussion Papers 2760, 2001,

Federal Reserve Bank of San Francisco. "Financial Crises in Emerging Markets." FRBSF Economic Letter 2001-07, San Francisco, 2001.

Feldstein, M. "Economic and Financial Crisis in Emerging Market Economies: Overview of Prevention and Management," NBER Working Paper 8837, Cambridge, MA, 2002.

Forbes, K.J. "Are Trade Linkages Important Determinants of Country Vulnerability to Crises?" NBER Working Paper 8194, Cambridge, MA, 2001.

Forbes, K.J. and Rigobon, R. "Contagion in Latin America: Definitions, Measures, and Policy Implications," NBER Working Paper 7885, Cambridge, MA, 2000.

Frankel, J.A. "The Asian Model, the Miracle, the Crisis and the Fund, in Currency Crises," in P. Krugman, ed., *Currency Crises*. Chicago: University of Chicago Press, 2000, pp. 327–337.

Fratzscher, M. "Why Are Currency Crises Contagious? A Comparison of the Latin American Crisis of 1994-1995 and the Asian Crisis of 1997-1998." *Weltwirtschaftliches Archiv*, 1998, *134*, pp. 664–691.

Frenkel, M., Funke, K., and Stadtmann, G. "Foreign Direct Investment Flows to Emerging Economies - A Panel Analysis of Bilateral FDI Flows." *Economic Systems*, 2004, *28*, pp. 281–300.

Funke, K. and Nickel, C. "Current Account Balance and Capital Flows: Does Fiscal Policy Matter?", Presented at the 59th International Atlantic Economic Conference, London, England, 2005.

Giavazzi, F., Jappelli, T., and Pagano, M. "Searching for Non-Linear Effects of Fiscal Policy: Evidence from Industrial and Developing Countries." *European Economic Review*, 2000, *44*, pp. 1259–1289.

Giavazzi, F. and Pagano, M. "Non-Keynesian Effects of Fiscal Policy Changes: International Evidence and the Swedish Experience." *Swedish Economic Policy Review*, 1996, *3*, pp. 67–103.

Giavazzi, F. and Pagano, M. "Can Severe Fiscal Contractions be Expansionary? Tales of Two Small European Countries." *NBER Macroeconomic Annual*, 1990, *5*, pp. 75–110.

Giovannetti, G. "Aggregate Imports and Expenditure Components in Italy: An Econometric Analysis." *Applied Economics*, 1989, *21*, pp. 957–971.

Goldstein, M., Kaminsky, G., and Reinhart, C. *Assessing financial vulnerability: An early warning system for emerging markets.* Washington, DC: Institute for International Economics, 2000.

Grubaugh, S.G. "Determinants of Direct Foreign Investment." *Review of Economics and Statistics*, 1987, *69*, pp. 149–152.

Hausman, R., Pritchett, L., and Rodrik, D. "Growth Accelerations." NBER Working Paper 10566, Cambridge, MA, 2004.

Heckscher, E.F. "The Effect of Foreign Trade on the Distribution of Income." *Ekonomiks Tidskrift* (special issue), 1919.

Hjelm, G. "Effects of Fiscal Contractions: The Importance of Preceding Exchange Rate Movements." *Scandinavian Journal of Economics*, 2002a, *104*, pp. 423–441.

Hjelm, G. "Is Private Consumption Growth Higher (Lower) During Periods of Fiscal Contractions (Expansions)?" *Journal of Macroeconomics*, 2002b, *24*, pp. 17–39.

Hogan, V. "Expansionary Fiscal Contraction? Evidence from Panel Data." *Scandinavian Journal of Economics*, 2004, *106*, pp. 647–659.

Hood, N. and Young, S. *The economics of multinational enterprise.* London: Longman, 1979.

Hooper, P., Johnson, K., and Marquez, J. "Trade Elasticities for the G7." Princeton Studies in International Economics 87, Princeton, NJ, 2000.

Houthakker, H. and Magee, S. "Income and Price Elasticities in World Trade." *Review of Economics and Statistics,* 1969, *66*, pp. 608–618.

Hull, L. and Tesar, L.L. "The Structure of International Capital Flows," in H. Siebert, eds., *The world's new financial landscape: Challenges for economic policy*. Berlin: Springer, 2001, pp. 87–109.

Hunya, G. "FDI in Small Countries: The Baltic States." WIIW Research Report 307, Vienna Institute for International Economic Studies, Vienna, 2004.

Hunya, G. "Restructuring through FDI in Romanian Manufacturing." *Economic Systems*, 2002, *26*, 387–394.

Hymer, S. "The International Operations of National Firms: A Study of Foreign Direct Investment." Cambridge, MA: MIT Press, 1976.

Im, K.S., Pesaran, M.H., and Shin, Y. "Testing for Unit Roots in Heterogeneous Panels." *Journal of Econometrics,* 2003, *115*, pp. 53–74.

International Monetary Fund (IMF). "Balance of Payments Statistics." Washington, DC: IMF, 2005a.

International Monetary Fund. "Direction of Trade Statistics Data Base." Washington, DC: IMF, 2005b.

International Monetary Fund. International Finance Statistics, Washington, DC: IMF, 2005c.

International Monetary Fund, International Investment Position, Washington, DC: IMF, 2005d.

International Monetary Fund. "Lithuania: 2004 Article IV Consultation—Staff Report." IMF Country Report 05/123, Washington, DC, 2005e.

International Monetary Fund. "Republic of Slovenia: 2005 Article IV Consultation—Staff Report; Public Information Notice on the Executive Board Discussion; and Statement by the Executive Director for the Republic of Slovenia." IMF Country Report No. 05/253, Washington, DC, 2005f.

International Monetary Fund. "Slovakia: 2004 Article IV Consultation." Staff Report, IMF Country Report 05/71, Washington, DC, 2005g.

International Monetary Fund. *World economic outlook.* Washington, DC: IMF, 2005h.

International Monetary Fund. "Czech Republic: 2004 Article IV Consultation—Staff Report." IMF Country Report 04/266, Washington, DC, 2004a.

International Monetary Fund. "Republic of Estonia: 2004 Article IV Consultation—Staff Report." IMF Country Report 04/358, Washington, DC, 2004b.

International Monetary Fund. "Hungary: 2004 Article IV Consultation—Staff Report." IMF Country Report 04/145, Washington, DC, 2004c.

International Monetary Fund. "Latvia: 2004 Article IV Consultation—Staff Report." IMF Country Report 04/260, Washington, DC, 2004d.

International Monetary Fund. "Poland: 2004 Article IV Consultation—Staff Report." IMF Country Report 04/217, Washington, DC, 2004e.

International Monetary Fund. Debt sustainability in low-income countries—Towards a forward-looking strategy. Washington, DC: IMF, 2003.

International Monetary Fund. *Assessing sustainability.* Washington, DC: IMF, 2002a.

International Monetary Fund. *International investment position: A guide to data sources.* Washington, DC: IMF, 2002b.

International Monetary Fund. Debt- and reserve-related indicators of external vulnerability. Washington, DC: IMF, 2000a.

International Monetary Fund. *World economic outlook.* Washington, DC: IMF, 2000b.

International Monetary Fund. *Balance of payments manual.* Washington, DC: IMF, 1993.

International Monetary Fund and International Development Association (IDA). *Debt sustainability in low income countries—Proposal for an operational framework and policy implications.* Washington, DC: IMF, 2004.

Invest Korea. "What Are the Basic Requirements Concerning the Amount and Ratio of Foreign Investment?" http://www.investkorea.org/templet/type4/1/read.jsp, downloaded on June 15, 2005.

Ivers, C. Aspects of the theory of international capital movements. London: Oxford University Press, 1935.

Johansen, S. "Statistical Analysis of Cointegration Vectors." *Journal of Economic Dynamics and Control,* 1988, *12*, pp. 231–254.

Kaminsky, B. "How Accession to the European Union Has Affected External Trade and Foreign Direct Investment in Central European Countries." Policy Research Working Paper 2578, World Bank, Washington, DC, 2001.

Kao, C. "Spurious Regression and Residual-based Tests for Cointegration in Panel Data." *Journal of Econometrics,* 1999, *90*, pp. 1–44.

Karras, G. "Government Spending and Private Consumption: Some International Evidence." *Journal of Money, Credit and Banking*, 1994, *26*, pp. 9–22.

Kenen, P. "The Theory of Optimum Currency Areas: An Eclectic View," in R. Mundell and A. Swoboda, eds., *Monetary problems of the international economy.* Chicago: University of Chicago Press, 1969.

Kim, S. and Roubini, N. "Twin Deficits or Twin Divergence? Fiscal Policy, Current Account, and Real Exchange Rate in the US." Presented at the Econometric Society, North American Winter Meetings, San Diego, CA, 2004.

Kraay, A. and Nehru, V. "When Is External Debt Sustainable?" World Bank Policy Research Working Paper 3200, Washington, DC, 2004.

Krueger, A.O. "Detecting and Preventing Financial Crises—Recent IMF Approaches, International Monetary Fund." Bretton Woods Committee Annual Meeting U.S. State Department, June 12, 2003, Washington DC, 2003.

Krugman, P. "Policy Problems of a Monetary Union," in P. De Grauwe and L. Papademos, eds., *The European Monetary System in the 1990s*. London: Longman, 1990, pp. 48–64.

Lane, P.R. and Perotti, R. "The Trade Balance and Fiscal Policy in the OECD." *European Economic Review*, 1998, *42*, pp. 887–895.

Lansbury, M., Pain, N., and Smidkova, K. "FDI in Central Europe since 1990: An Econometric Study." *National Institute Economic Review*, 1996, *156,* pp. 104–113.

Levin, A. and Lin, C. F. "Unit Root Tests in Panel Data: Asymptotic and Finite Sample Properties." Discussion Paper 92-93, University of California at San Diego, 1992.

Levin, A., Lin, C. F., and Chu, C. "Unit Root Tests in Panel Data: Asymptotic and Finite-Sample Properties." *Journal of Econometrics*, 2002, *108*, pp. 1–24.

Levy-Yeyati, E., Panizza, U., and Stein, E. "The Cyclical Nature of North-South FDI Flows." Interamerican Development Bank, Working Paper 479, Washington, DC, 2003.

Levy-Yeyati, E., and Sturzenegger, F., "Classifying Exchange Rate Regimes: Deeps vs. Words," 2002. http://www.utdt.edu/~ely/papers.html, downloaded on May 2, 2005.

Li, X., Liu, X., and Parker, D. "Foreign Direct Investment and Productivity Spillovers in the Chinese Manufacturing Sector." *Economic Systems*, 2001, *25*, pp. 305–321.

Loser, C.M. "External Debt Sustainability: Guidelines for Low and Middle Income Countries," United Nations Conference on Trade and Development (UNCTAD), G-24 Discussion Paper 26, Geneva, 2004.

Marquez, J. "Estimating Trade Elasticities," in *Advanced studies in theoretical and applied econometrics*, Vol. 39. Berlin: Springer, 2002.

Martellini, L., Priaulet, P., and Priaulet, S. *Fixed-income securities.* New York: Wiley, 2003.

Mátyás, L. "The Gravity Model: Some Econometric Considerations." *World Economy,* 1998, *21*, pp. 397–401.

Mátyás, L. "Proper Econometric Specification of the Gravity Model." *World Economy*, 1997, *20*, pp. 363–368.

McFadden, D., Eckhaus, R., Feder, G., Hajivassiliou, V., and O'Connell, S. "Is There Life after Debt? An Econometric Analysis of the Creditworthiness of Developing Countries," in Gordon Smith and John Cuddington, eds., *International debt and the developing countries*. Washington, DC: World Bank, 1985.

McKinnon, R. "Optimum Currency Areas." *American Economic Review*, 1963, *53*, pp. 717–725.

Metzger, M. "Of Magic Dragons and Other Strange Beasts: A Reassessment of the Latin American and Asian Crises." *South African Journal of Economics, 69*, 2001, pp. 191–217.

Moser, T. What Is International Financial Contagion?" *International Finance, 6*, 2003, pp. 157–178.

Mundell, R. "A Theory of Optimum Currency Areas." *American Economic Review*, 1961, *51*, pp. 657–665.

Niedernhauser, E. *A history of eastern Europe since the Middle Ages*. New York: Columbia University Press, 2003.

Normandin, M. "Budget Deficit Persistence and the Twin Deficits Hypothesis." *Journal of International Economics*, 1999, *49*, pp. 171–193.

Nurske, R. "Causes and Effects of Capital Movements," reprinted in J. H. Dunning, ed., *International investment*. Harmondsworth: Penguin Books, 1972.

Ohlin, B. *Interregional and international trade*. Cambridge: Harvard University Press, 1933.

Organisation for Economic Co-operation and Development (OECD). *International direct investment statistics yearbook*, electronic ed. Paris: OECD, 2005a.

Organisation for Economic Co-operation and Development. Main Economic Indicators, electronic database. Paris: OECD, 2005b.

Organisation for Economic Co-operation and Development. "Regulatory Environment for Foreign Direct Investment." Presented at Investment for African Development: Making It Happen conference, Entebbe, Uganda, 2005c.

Organisation for Economic Co-operation and Development. *Foreign direct investment for development*. Paris: OECD, 2002.

Organisation for Economic Co-operation and Development. "Recent Trends in Foreign Investment." *Financial Market Trends*, 2000, *76*, pp. 23–41.

Organisation for Economic Co-operation and Development. *OECD Benchmark Definition of Foreign Direct Investment*, 3rd ed., Paris: OECD, 1996.

Pedroni, P. "Critical Values for Cointegration Tests in Heterogenous Panels With Multiple Regressors." *Oxford Bulletin of Economics and Statistics*, 1999, *61*, pp. 653–678.

Pedroni, P. "Panel Cointegration: Asymptotic and Finite Sample Properties of Pooled Time Series Tests With an Application to the PPP Hypothesis." Working Paper in Economics, Indiana University, 1995.

Perotti, R. "Fiscal Policy in Good Times and Bad." *Quarterly Journal of Economics*, 1999, *114*, pp. 1399–1436.

Pesaran, M. H., Shin, Y., and Smith, R. "Pooled Mean Group Estimation of Dynamic Heterogeneous Panels." *Journal of the American Statistical Society*, 1999, *94*, pp. 621–634.

Piersanti, G. "Current Account Dynamics and Expected Future Budget Deficits: Some International Evidence." *Journal of International Money and Finance*, 2000, *19*, pp. 255–271.

Questa, G.S. "Fixed-Income Analysis for the Global Financial Market." New York: Wiley, 1999.

Radelet, S. and Sachs, J. "The Onset of the East Asian Financial Crisis." NBER Working Paper 6680, Cambridge, MA, 1998.

Reinhart, C.M., Rogoff, K., and Savastano, M.A. "Debt Intolerance." NBER Working Paper 9908, Cambridge, MA, 2003.

Reisen, H. "Sustainable and Excessive Current Account Deficits." *Econometrica*, 1998, *25*, pp. 111–113.

Republic of Poland, Ministry of Economic Affairs & Labour. Document on the Investment Increasing Strategy, 2001. http://baltic.mg.gov.pl/Investments/invest_strat/, downloaded on May 2, 2005.

Resmini, L. "The Determinants of Foreign Direct Investment in the CEECs." *Economics of Transition*, 2000, *8*, pp. 665–689.

Rogoff, K. "International Institutions for Reducing Global Financial Instability." *Journal of Economic Perspectives*, 1999, *13*, 21–42.

Roubini, N. "Debt Sustainability: How to Assess Whether a Country Is Insolvent." Working Paper, Stern School of Business, New York, 2001.

Rugman, A.M. International diversification and the multinational enterprise. Lexington, MA: DC Heath, 1979.

Schclarek, A. "Fiscal Policy and Private Consumption in Industrial and Developing Countries." Working Papers 20, Department of Economics, Lund University, 2003.

Seater, J.J. "Ricardian Equivalence." *Journal of Economic Literature*, 1993, *31*, pp. 142–190.

Singh, A. "Capital Account Liberalization, Free Long-Term Capital Flows, Financial Crises and Economic Development." ESRC Centre for Business Research Working Paper 245, University of Cambridge, 2002.

Tang, T.C. "Determinants of Import Demand in Thailand: A View from Expenditure Components and Bounds Testing Approach." Presented at the Seventh International Conference on Global Business and Economic Development, Bangkok, 2003.

Tinbergen, J. Shaping the world economy: Suggestions for an international economic policy. New York: Twentieth Century Fund, 1962.

Tower, E. and Willett, T.D. "The Theory of Optimum Currency Areas and Exchange Rate Flexibility." Special Papers in International Economics 11, Princeton University Press, Princeton, 1970.

United Nations Conference on Trade and Development (UNCTAD). http://stats.unctad.org/fdi, Geneva, downloaded on June 2005.

United Nations Conference on Trade and Development. *Debt sustainability: Oasis or mirage?* New York: UNCTAD, 2004a.

United Nations Conference on Trade and Development. *World investment report 2004.* Geneva: United Nations, Geneva, 2004b.

United Nations Conference on Trade and Development. *World investment report 2003.* Geneva: United Nations, 2003.

United Nations Economic Commission for Africa (UNECA). *A critical assessment of existing debt proposals.* New York: UNECA, 2003.

Vernon, R. "International Investment and International Trade in the Product Life Cycle." *Quarterly Journal of Economics*, 1966, *80*, pp. 190–207.

Vienna Institute for International Economic Studies. "Back from the Peak, Growth in Transition Countries Returns to Standard Rate of Catching-up." Research Report 320, Vienna, 2005.

Von Hagen, J., Hallett, A.H., and Strauch, R. "Budgetary Consolidation in EMU." CEPR Economic Papers 148, 2001.

Webb, A. Central and Eastern Europe since 1919. London: Longman, 2002.

Wei, S.-J. "How Taxing Is Corruption on International Investors? *Review of Economics and Statistics*, 2000, *82*, pp. 1–11.

Williamson, J. "Estimates of FEERS," in J. Williamson, ed., *Estimating equilibrium exchange rates*. Washington, DC: Institute for International Economics, 1994.

Williamson, O.E. Markets and hierarchies: Analysis and antitrust implications, a study in the economics of international organization. New York: Free Press, 1975.

World Bank. *Global development finance.* Washington, DC: World Bank, 2005a.

World Bank. Some Commonly Used Terms. http://web.worldbank.org/WBSITE/EXTERNAL/TOPICS/EXTDEBTDEPT/0,,contentMDK:20268582~menuPK:576555~pagePK:64166689~piPK:64166646~theSitePK:469043,00.html#i9, downloaded June 2005, 2005b.

World Bank. "Special Topic: Baltic Growth Acceleration—Is It Sustainable?" World Bank EU-8 Quarterly Economic Report, Washington, DC, 2005c.

World Bank. "World Development Indicators." Washington, DC, 2005d.

World Bank. http://www.worldbank.org/data/countryclass/classgroups.htm, downloaded July 2005, 2005e.

World Bank. *Global development finance*. Washington, DC: World Bank, 2004a.

World Bank. *World development indicators*. Washington, DC: World Bank, 2004b.

World Bank. *Global development finance*. Washington, DC: World Bank, 2002.

World Bank. *World development indicators*. Washington, DC: World Bank, 2000.

World Bank. *Global development finance*. Washington, DC: World Bank, 1999.

World Bank, International Monetary Fund, Bank for International Settlements (BIS), and Organisation for Economic Co-operation and Development. *External debt: Definition, statistical coverage and methodology*, Washington, DC: World Bank, IMF, BIS, and OECD, 1988.

World Trade Organization (WTO). "Managing Capital Flows in Transition Economies with a Case-Study of Central and Eastern Europe." Staff Working Paper ERAD-98-04, Geneva, Switzerland, 1998.

Zanghieri, P. "Current Accounts Dynamics in new EU members: Sustainability and Policy Issues." Centre d'Etudes Prospectives et d'Informations Internationales, Working Paper 7, 2004.

Studien zu Internationalen Wirtschaftsbeziehungen

Herausgegeben von Prof. Dr. Michael Frenkel

Band 1 Christiane Nickel: Insider und Outsider bei der Osterweiterung der Europäischen Währungsunion. 2002.

Band 2 Georg Stadtmann: Noise-Trader auf Devisenmärkten. Viel Lärm um Nichts? 2002.

Band 3 Wolf-Heimo Grieben: Trade and Technology as Competing Explanations for Rising Inequality. An Endogenous Growth Perspective. 2003.

Band 4 Alexander Mende: Order Flow Analyses and Foreign Exchange Dealing. 2005.

Band 5 Torsten Wezel: Determinants of Foreign Direct Investment in Emerging Markets. An Empirical Study of FDI Flows from Germany and its Banking Sector. 2005.

Band 6 Steffen Kern: The Behaviour of Interest Groups in Trade and Industry Towards Monetary Policy and Central Banks. Theory and Evidence on Germany and the Euro Area. 2006.

Band 7 Holger Michaelis: Kapitalbilanzliberalisierung in der Volksrepublik China und ihre Einbettung in den volkswirtschaftlichen Reformprozess. 2006.

Band 8 Ralf Fendel: Monetary Policy, Interest Rate Rules, and the Term Structure of Interest Rates. Theoretical Considerations and Empirical Implications. 2007.

Band 9 Katja Funke: Balance of Payments Issues in Central and Eastern European Countries' Run-Up to Euro Area Accession. 2007.

www.peterlang.de

Peter Lang · Europäischer Verlag der Wissenschaften

Ralf Fendel

Monetary Policy, Interest Rate Rules, and the Term Structure of Interest Rates

Theoretical Considerations and Empirical Implications

Frankfurt am Main, Berlin, Bern, Bruxelles, New York, Oxford, Wien, 2007.
XIII, 187 pp., num. tab. and graphs
Studien zu internationalen Wirtschaftsbeziehungen. Edited by Michael Frenkel.
Vol. 8
ISBN 978-3-631-55894-2 · pb. € 39.–*

Interest rate rules play an important role in the empirical analysis of monetary policy as well as in modern monetary theory. Besides giving a comprehensive insight into this line of research the study incorporates the term structure of interest rates into interest rate rules. This is performed analytically as well as empirically. In doing so, state of the art techniques of modern finance for the analysis of the term structure of interest rates are introduced into the macroeconomic concept of interest rate rules. The study implies that from the theoretical perspective term structure effects are an important extension of interest rate rules. From an empirical perspective it shows that including term structure effects in interest rate reaction functions improves our understanding of the interest rate setting of the Deutsche Bundesbank and the European Central Bank.

Contents: Analysis of the monetary policy of the ECB and the Bundesbank · Derivation and estimation of interest rate rules · Special focus on the term structure of interest rates · Combination of the concept of interest rate rules with affine no-arbitrage term structure models

Frankfurt am Main · Berlin · Bern · Bruxelles · New York · Oxford · Wien
Distribution: Verlag Peter Lang AG
Moosstr. 1, CH-2542 Pieterlen
Telefax 00 41 (0) 32 / 376 17 27

*The €-price includes German tax rate
Prices are subject to change without notice

Homepage http://www.peterlang.de